Memories of Philippine Kitchens

Stories and Recipes from Far and Near

Amy Besa and Romy Dorotan   Photographs by Neal Oshima

Stewart, Tabori & Chang • New York

Previous spread: Bicol (left), sago (right); Sorsogon, Bicol (above left), making piaya in Silay. Bitter melon (right).

Memories of Philippine Kitchens

Stories and Recipes from Far and Near

Amy Besa and Romy Dorotan Photographs by Neal Oshima

Stewart, Tabori & Chang • New York

Previous spread: Bicol (left), sago (right); Sorsogon, Bicol (above left), making piaya in Silay. Bitter melon (right).

CONTENTS

Foreword

PETER KAMINSKY

Some people feel at home in the corner bar where just as soon as they walk in the bartender knows to pour "the usual." Others have a local breakfast joint where the comforting clatter of coffee cups and the smell of sizzling bacon is as familiar as their favorite easy chair.

I have Cendrillon.

I discovered it in the mid-nineties, shortly after it opened. *New York Magazine* had made me their Underground Gourmet, which meant I sought out ethnic food and entry level fine dining. I much preferred the ethnic stuff. In Cendrillon I found both. I remember crisp soft-shell crab perched atop a salad of bean thread noodles. It was clean tasting, the mark of a chef who could assemble a panoply of tastes without confusing them in a saucy jumble. Also, a red snapper in a slightly sweet slightly sour broth with greens that were unfamiliar but struck just the right balance with the delicate white-fleshed fish. Barbecued pork chops with plum glaze (I am a porkophile and Cendrillon never disappoints) were served alongside suman, rice cakes steamed in banana leaves topped with a pat of butter and sugar.

And then, the ultimate test — my kids. We went for Sunday brunch and filled up on bibingka — a puddingish cake of eggs with coconut milk, sugar, and feta cheese. If no one had used the phrase "comfort food" before, it would surely have been invented right there and then.

I was sold. But I was new on the job, so I called for a second opinion from my friend Bryan Miller, who had been the restaurant critic at the *New York Times*. Miller gave an enthusiastic thumbs up. I think his exact words were "This is the real deal."

Equally pleasing to both of us — here was a chef making Asian food and actually pairing it with wine! Who knew? Prior to that I was of the opinion that in matters Asian, beer was the only way to go, but if you really insisted and just had to drink wine, well then it had to be a Rhône or Riesling. But the chef, Romy Dorotan, was pouring light burgundies and grassy Basque whites, sharp-edged Syrahs, and velvety tempranillos, and they all worked.

Romy is one half of the reason that Cendrillon became my go-to restaurant whenever I wanted something unusual and guaranteed delicious. The other half is his wife and partner, Amy Besa. She fills the front of the house with the bonhomie of a great restaurateur. Like her husband, she's an intellectual who went from Manila to Manhattan when things got a little hot for thinking people with a political opinion. New York's SoHo — hip, Downtown, where everyone dressed in black — was a perfect fit.

When asked to describe Romy's cooking, I often say "it's fusion but coming from the other direction." By that I mean he's not a Western chef who went to Thailand on a cruise and discovered lemongrass. For starters, Filipino food is, by its very nature, fusion — a mix of a number of Asian cuisines and, reflecting its colonial past, Spanish with some Mexican thrown in (for nearly three hundred years the Spaniards ran their colony through the viceroyalty of Acapulco). Add to that Romy's experience at one of Manhattan's first modern fine dining restaurants — the pioneering Hubert's. He picked up precise French-inspired technique and a willingness to experiment that has kept him in the vanguard of Manhattan — make that American — dining ever since.

Then there's Amy's unflagging and infectious good cheer that keeps you smiling through dinner. She is also the self-appointed, and universally acknowledged, den mother of Asian chefs in America. Thai, Cambodian, Filipino, Vietnamese, Indonesian, Keralan, Malaysian — whenever there is an Asian chef doing something new and interesting, Amy is sure to invite him or her to prepare a meal for adventurous diners.

Perhaps the best recommendation I can share with you — least clouded by my obvious love for the place and its proprietors — is the fact that all the food journalists, cookbook writers, chefs, and gourmets I have sent there over the years have reported that they had a great meal . . . and, most convincingly, they all came back.

Peter Kaminsky is the author of numerous books on cooking. Currently his food writing appears in Food & Wine, HG, *and* Condé Nast Traveler. *His Outdoors column has run in the* New York Times *for eighteen years, and he is also the author of a number of books on angling.*

You Can Go Home Again

AMY BESA

In September 2003, I finally found my way home again. I had left Manila thirty years before, a few weeks before martial law was declared on September 21, 1972. Shortly before my departure a fire destroyed the Manila International Airport, and I had to ride a bus to a makeshift terminal to catch my flight. My parents could not ride with me, so I waved at them from the back of the bus, their heads bobbing up and down and finally disappearing from view as the bus navigated the potholes of Manila's streets. The future looked bleak for this forsaken land. I looked hard at the palm trees, shacks, and people and said my farewell to a country that shaped my soul and to a people that wounded my heart. I was twenty-one years old and felt that my life was ahead of me, but I knew, too, that a part of my life was ending.

I arrived in Germany and spent a year there as an exchange student, then several years in Philadelphia completing a master's degree in mass communications at Temple University. There I met my future husband, Romy Dorotan, another unsettled student, who was working on his PhD in economics while navigating a never-ending love affair with cooking. It started at the Frog Restaurant, where Romy was promoted from dishwashing to cooking staff meals when the Thai chef walked out.

In 1979 we moved to New York City, and food became more central in our lives. Romy became a lunch chef at the legendary Hubert's on Park Avenue South. I vividly remember the moment when he burst into our home with the wonderful news that he had at last found a job that he was excited about. "They're all crazy," he exulted, "especially the dinner chef, Jim. Everything is cooked to order. If you order a chocolate soufflé, then that is when he melts the chocolate, whips the egg whites . . . You have to wait about forty minutes for your dessert! They are all fanatics!"

It was a heady time in the food world. Alice Waters, in Berkeley, California, was changing the rules, and Hubert's was heeding her call for cooking honest food without shortcuts based on organic produce and fresh ingredients. Hubert's was all passion, all philosophy and commitment. Uncompromised Food was the muse, and many movers and shakers in the New York food world emerged from its fold. Romy defined his palate and chef's touch in that environment. Freed to go wherever his imagination led him, he started steaming fish with gingko nuts wrapped in banana leaves. For brunch, he made his own bacon, curing pork belly in his specially-made brine. At one point he told me the restaurant owner had yelled at him for using a $100 bottle of cognac for an ice cream he created. "The ice cream tasted good, though," he said, his satisfaction unfazed.

The 1990s were a time of change, and Romy and I decided it was time to open our own restaurant. We wanted the food of our youth and our culture to be the foundation for our restaurant's concept but would also embrace the other cuisines of Southeast Asia.

Cendrillon (Cinderella in French, named for a ballet) opened its doors on August 8, 1995, in Manhattan's SoHo. Our first decade has been an interesting time. We've learned a great deal about our culture and its food—and about human nature. The most pleasant surprise has been the former grade school, high school, and college friends and acquaintances we had not seen in twenty or thirty years who found their way to our door. This renewal of friendships has proved to be a valuable source of emotional and intellectual support for us.

In 2003 we were asked to write a cookbook on Filipino food. We immediately felt that it had to be more than a standard cookbook of measurements and cooking steps. Filipino food, in order to be better understood and fully appreciated, had to be seen in the context of culture and history. We decided to anchor our research on the food of our generation—those born in the late 1940s and the early 1950s. We began this project by asking questions of our friends, customers, and acquaintances: What are your early childhood food memories? What are your comfort foods? Are these foods still being made? Do you have recipes? Do you know anyone who could show us how to make them so that we can preserve them? The response was tremendous. People would talk for hours about their food memories—and refer us on to other friends and relatives, both in the States and in the Philippines. And as these friends led us on a personal journey searching for the foods of our youth, we began to ask more questions. Why did we eat these foods? Where did we get these ingredients and cooking methods that shape our food preferences today? What is authentic and what is borrowed?

We tried to find those answers not only in Philippine history and food books, but in the local histories of the towns, provinces, and regions where these families are rooted. And although these families represent several regions of the Philippines, this is by no means a regional cookbook of the Philippines. To do justice to all the regions would mean more years of research and, hopefully, more books on the subject.

Romy and I also share our personal recipes, which took us years to develop and refine. Each and every one was hard fought, sometimes bitterly dividing us, simply because our memories of how some food tasted and what its texture should be were devastatingly different. I lean more toward what I remember; Romy is usually guided by what he thinks is the right texture and balance of flavors. It is in this nuance of compromises and elaborations that the future of Philippine food should be brought forth.

My desire to document traditions, to bring Philippine food into the twenty-first century while preserving the strong foundation of our past, led me back home in 2003. It was only my fourth trip back since I had broken my self-imposed exile in 1991. I went with open eyes and heart—and my purpose was generously rewarded. Wherever I traveled, only the most sincere hospitality and generosity filled my empty cup. I found my balm. I had come home.

Introduction

The other day, I was prowling the aisles of a fancy market near my home in Greenwich Village when a man came up and thrust his hand at me. "I'm Ilocano, too," he said warmly. I had forgotten I was wearing a souvenir T-shirt from the Philippine province of Ilocos Norte. My newly found countryman looked a little disappointed when I explained I'd just been a tourist on his native turf.

Still, we had a bond stretching thousands of miles to a tropical place with its own Wild-West past (Ferdinand Marcos started out in Ilocos Norte and his son Bong Bong is the current governor), colonial mansions and churches, and its own cuisine.

I'm not here to give you a rundown on pinakbet and all the other Ilocano specialties. That's what Amy and Romy do in this encyclopedic but also intimate collection of recipes and anecdotes about visits they made to see cooks all over the Philippines. These were really voyages of exploration, forays into a nation so diverse it can seem exotic even to a native.

Start with several major indigenous languages, two lingua francas—Tagalog and English—and the ghostly omnipresence of Spanish. Add some 7,000 islands, with the only Roman Catholic majority in Asia and a restless Muslim minority that dominates the South.

And then try to imagine how this translates into a multiplicity of food cultures. Did I mention the pre-Hispanic and continuing influence of Chinese "settlers" who began arriving in what we know as the Middle Ages?

From them came the noodle dishes and egg rolls that now bear both Tagalog names and other traces of the fundamentally Malay population that runs the place. Spanish invaders brought foods from home and Mexico. American latecomers in the colonial game introduced the concept of pie, which was quickly assimilated as a new way of exploiting the coconut.

The late Doreen Fernandez, an inspiration to Amy, Romy, and me, among legions of other gastronomes and students of food history (not to mention her official students in the English Department of the Ateneo de Manila), plunged into this chaos of dishes that had emerged from 400 years of colonization and the even more denaturing decades of modernization, and made giant strides in recording the whole delicious mess. I read her seminal book *Sarap* (delicious) in preparation for my first trip to the Philippines in 1991. Thus oriented, I could immerse myself with some confidence in a world dominated by sour tastes and the heritage of cooks operating in the socially intense and creatively isolated ecologies of Filipino village life. Doreen prepared me for that and for the vivid, ironic world of Manila street food, the duck eggs with embryos in them, the chicken feet sold as "Adidas," green mango with a salty, sour sauce.

Amy and Romy brought their own ideas to this huge repertoire of dishes at Cendrillon in New York. Now they have brought us (not to mention millions of cooks in the Philippines) this dazzling compendium of traditional food and food knowledge.

There is a Tagalog word for gifts carried from a distant place—*pasalubong*. It's something precious you bring back to friends from a trip abroad. Thank you, Amy and Romy, for this *pasalubong. Masarap!*

Raymond Sokolov is the author of many books about food (The Cook's Canon, Why We Eat What We Eat), *as well as a novel* (Native Intelligence) *and a biography* (Wayward Reporter, the Life of A.J. Liebling). *He recently completed his PhD in classical philology at Harvard after an interruption of thirty-five years. At various points, he worked for* Newsweek, *the* New York Times, Time, Natural History, *and the* Wall Street Journal, *in various capacities. He has a wife, two sons, three granddaughters, and three motor vehicles, whose mileage totals 300,000.*

PHILIPPINES

Taiwan

BATAN ISLANDS

BABUYAN ISLANDS

South China Sea

ILOCOS

LUZON

Philippine Sea

MANILA

BICOL PEN.

N

MINDORO

VISAYAS

SAMAR

PANAY

LEYTE

CEBU

NEGROS   BOHOL

PALAWAN

ZAMBOANGA PEN.

Sulu Sea

MINDANAO

Malaysia

SULU ARCHIPELAGO

Celebes Sea

Indonesia

A Living History

Water was a determining theme in the early life of the Philippine islands. Surrounded by oceans and lined with rivers and streams inland, its watery lanes defined the character of the lives of people who settled on its coasts. Water yielded the pristine fruits of the sea that formed the basis for much of the early Philippine diet. Water brought the boats of Arab traders from the Middle East, opened the gates to Chinese traders, and finally brought in two colonial powers, Spain and the United States, which would throw the Philippines into the vortex of European intra-colonial fighting and introduce the concepts of nationhood and democracy.

As we researched Filipino food, cooking methods, ingredients, and their origins to discover why and how we came to eat the things we do, we became increasingly interested in Filipino history. But the historical events tell only part of the story of the influences that shape Filipino culture. The family stories and personal memories we heard as we traveled and interviewed for this cookbook proved even more rich and interesting. We set out to record these living histories through the recipes and memories in this book.

What Is Filipino Food?

From top to bottom: puto, kakanin, baby swordfish on the line, rabbit morocon at Cendrillon. Opposite: kalamansi limes.

Filipinos often describe the food of the Philippines in terms of its most popular dishes: adobo [a vinegar-tart stew], lumpia [a fresh pancake wrapped around vegetables and/or meat], and pancit [a noodle dish]. These reliable favorites represent the cuisine at its most accessible to the non-Filipino palate, and are among the easiest recipes for Filipino ex-pats to re-create on foreign soil. They're a simple and delicious introduction to a rich, nuanced cuisine.

In his book *Why We Eat What We Eat*, Raymond Sokolov writes that the Philippines, in contrast to other cultures whose foodways were profoundly altered by Spanish colonial rule, was able to maintain its indigenous foods. These foods today exist alongside the foods that we borrowed from the West. Local fermented brews such as the tuba [coconut toddy] and native rice cakes such as the suman [steamed cakes] date back to pre-Hispanic times, and their methods of preparation have remained virtually unchanged.

So which are the foods that we can truly call our own, and which ones were borrowed before we made them our own?

We found that adobo, sinigang, kinilaw, kare kare, and kakanin (native desserts, the majority of which are based on rice) are universal to all the regions of the Philippines. They are eaten on a daily basis by all classes of society and made with ingredients that occur naturally in our environment. Adobo, sinigang, and kinilaw, which use native sour fruits and vinegars as a main ingredient, signify more than a particular dish—they also describe methods of preparing all manner of seafood, poultry, meat, and vegetables. We also embraced the foods, cooking methods, and condiments of other cultures in Southeast Asia as our own, as early inhabitants of the Philippines came from islands that are now called Indonesia and Malaysia. The kare kare is a distinctly Malay dish whose name is derived from the Tamil word *kari*, meaning a sauce for a stew. The kare kare is cooked without any salt or spices and is eaten with the salty bagoong [fermented shrimp paste], a condiment that we share with our Southeast Asian neighbors. The art of making kakanin is alive and well in the Philippines. It is impossible to document and list all these local delicacies because they vary greatly among the regions, localities, and even households. In Barrio Maronquillo, Bulacan (north of Manila) alone, we could have spent a whole week just sampling the different kakanin that this tiny community produces and sells in the local markets.

The kalamansi lime is indigenous to the Philippines and plays a large role in Philippine cuisine. This little deep-green-colored lime provides a tiny amount of juice, but it goes a long way. The juice is so flavorful that Filipinos use it for everything from lemonade to marinades and dips. It is squeezed over pancit, kinilaw, and grilled fish. The kalamansi should not be confused with another Philippine lime called dayap, which is similar to the limes available here in the United States.

Outside culinary influences primarily came from China, Spain, Mexico, and the United States through trade and conquests. From China came the pancit and lumpia. Early Chinese traders brought cooking implements (woks), condiments (soy sauce, fermented beans), spices (Szechuan peppercorns), and livestock such as ducks and pigs. They married Filipino women and settled in communities all over the Philippines. The Chinese became the local bakers, storekeepers, and restaurant owners, popularizing Chinese food and ingredients.

The Spanish came in 1521 as colonizers, bringing in Spanish food products such as ham and chorizo, while the galleon trade brought in fruits, vegetables, and rootcrops from Mexico. Today most Spanish dishes served on Philippine tables, such as morcons [filled rolled meats], rellenos [stuffed dishes], and afritada [dishes fried and simmered in tomato sauce] exist as fiesta fare served during special occasions, as these dishes are made with expensive ingredients that the majority of the native populace could not afford.

The major culinary influences of China, Spain, and Mexico are so fused in the culture that sometimes it is impossible to tell whether a dish is Chinese or Spanish. The best example is the fish escabeche [fish in sweet and sour sauce]. Historical Filipino cookbooks show escabeche prepared like a ceviche, steeping the fish in hot oil and then later flavoring it in vinegar and spices. Now it is essentially the Chinese deep-fried fish with sweet and sour sauce.

During the first half of the twentieth century, the Philippines became a colony of the United States. Filipinos (along with the rest of the world) began to incorporate American food into their diet. Hamburgers, hot dogs, pizza, soda, and fries gained popularity among the post-war generation, and the U.S. influence continues to spread today. Canned goods such as Spam, Vienna sausage, fruit cocktail, and evaporated milk were in most family cupboards by the 1950s. Today chiffon cake is the most popular cake in the Philippines.

The Philippines celebrates Christmas by bringing out all these foods and putting them on the *Noche Buena* [Christmas Eve meal] table and giving them out as Christmas gifts. A traditional Christmas meal includes ham, stuffed poultry (chicken or turkey), fresh lumpia and noodles, ensaimadas [coiled brioches], and hot chocolate, along with native kakanin such the puto, suman, and bibingka.

What does Filipino food look like today? What are families eating? Are they preserving traditional dishes that were eaten a previous generation ago? Does regional cooking still exist amid the malls and fast food courts that have spread throughout the major cities of the islands?

The good news is that we find that Filipino food is alive and well. The recipes we've collected and share with you in this book provide a glimpse into how families have

been savoring their food for generations and providing some good examples of what may still be regional.

For Filipinos who now live outside the Philippines, the desire to eat Filipino food becomes greater. These are the Filipinos who are the most nostalgic for the foods of home. However, wherever they are they have new foods to savor and new ingredients to experiment with and to add to their Philippine repertoire. It will be exciting to see how the adobo, sinigang, and kinilaw can be transformed in the United States, where all types of cuisines are flourishing and new fusions of ideas and flavors are happening every day.

The Cultural Roots of Filipino Food Run Deep

It takes more than a superficial exposure to Filipino cooking to get an overall sense of the cuisine. This may explain why, as Filipinos observe to each other whenever the subject of Filipino food comes up (which it does constantly among people from such a food-loving culture), the cuisine isn't as well-recognized in the West as that of neighboring countries.

To fully understand and appreciate Filipino food in context, one must consider the importance of hospitality and generosity—two of the most universal aspects of Filipino culture. Filipinos are truly the most giving, open, embracing, sentimental, and maddeningly hospitable people I've ever known. Never make the mistake of going to the Philippines without first shedding a few pounds in preparation. Once there, you'll be fed as many as six or seven times a day.

I'm still not sure how I survived the visit to my cousin Lyn Besa-Gamboa near Bacolod in Silay, Negros Occidental, during my first trip home as an adult. I'll never forget the bright twinkle in my cousin's eye as, within minutes of a huge lunch (which had followed a heavy breakfast), she said, "And now, would you like to try the Bacolod version of batchoy [pork and noodle soup]?"

Filipino food is also an expression of cultural passion and pride. During my research for this book, I became used to the sumptuous spreads of festive food served in grand, opulent homes in the Visayas and Luzon. But nothing prepared me for the deep love for our culture that I found in the most humble barrios of the provinces. We trudged through muddy lanes too narrow for cars and knocked on the doors of strangers famous for a particular delicacy sold in the market or in roadside carinderias [restaurants selling prepared food]. We were interrupting their work, yet they invariably seemed more delighted than inconvenienced by our desire to know about their cooking.

Making puto in Laguna. Opposite: alamang [shrimp fry].

In Candon, Ilocos Sur, we were shown, with great pleasure, to the back of a house where caramel bubbled in huge vats, to be turned into kalamay [sticky rice treats]. In Sorsogon, Bicol, we were taken to see the covered shed where pots of taro leaves were braising in coconut milk. At the table in one tiny Sorsogon home, we were educated about the various dried fish that are good to cook with taro leaves. There was an in-depth discussion of how to avoid taro leaves that would cause unwanted itchiness in the mouth and throat.

Everywhere I went, I got caught up in the refinements of bananas, which species to use for which dish, and what to do with them when they're ripe, unripe, or overripe. In rural areas, I learned the terms for every stage of coconut maturity (see page 144) and its corresponding uses. To write this book, I set out to investigate the endless nuances of the Filipino kitchen. After years of traveling, cooking, tasting, and interviewing, I have much to tell, and more to find out

Filipino Food as Part of Southeast Asian Cuisine

From fish sauce to shrimp paste, noodles to rice, Filipino food shares flavors, ingredients, and techniques with its Southeast Asian neighbors. Yet through the course of its unique history, the Philippines has developed distinct culinary preferences of its own.

Southeast Asian cooking is profoundly influenced by the two ancient cultures of India and China. These cuisines (Thai, Laotian, Burmese, Cambodian, and Vietnamese) were developed and preserved in lavish imperial courts, and their complexity and extravagance was used to set the royals apart from their subjects.

In the Philippines, by contrast, where there were no royal households, many culinary traditions originated in the homes of elite, landed families. Each household developed its own specialties and passed them down to the next generation. This is why, to this day, the best Filipino food is usually found in homes with a tradition of excellent home cooking, rather than in restaurants.

The water that surrounds the Philippine archipelago yields its historically most important food source: fresh seafood. Combined with fresh vegetation and coconuts, these ingredients form the heart of the cuisine. While much of the cooking of the Southeast Asian mainland demonstrates the Indian influence in bright, aromatic curries, chiles, and herbs, these are far less important in Philippine cooking, in which heavy spicing seems almost extraneous to the wealth of pristine seafood, vegetables, and fruits.

ACHARA

This pickled condiment, made of shredded green papaya, is usually quite sweet as well as tart. We tone down the sweetness, and we like to add green or red chiles (siling haba, which are not too hot).

Note that the pickling solution and the salted papaya and vegetable mixture must rest (separately) overnight in the refrigerator before they are combined. Once the pickle is made, refrigerate at least 1 day before serving.

MAKES ABOUT 2 QUARTS

4   cups rice vinegar
1½ cups sugar
3   tablespoons salt
4   garlic cloves, thinly sliced
One 2-inch piece fresh ginger, peeled and cut
    into matchsticks
1   teaspoon freshly ground black pepper, or to taste
1   green papaya, about 2 pounds, peeled, seeded,
    and grated (see Note)
3   large carrots, grated
3   red or green long chile peppers, cored, seeded
    and thinly sliced
2   large onions, cut in half and thinly sliced

1. In a large nonreactive saucepan over high heat, combine the vinegar, sugar, 1 tablespoon of the salt, the garlic, and ginger. Bring to a boil, stirring to dissolve the sugar and salt. Reduce the heat to medium-low and simmer until the flavors are well combined, 15 to 20 minutes. Add the ground black pepper. Cool to room temperature, cover, and refrigerate overnight.

2. In a large nonreactive bowl, toss together the papaya, carrots, peppers, and onion with the remaining 2 tablespoons salt. Cover and refrigerate overnight.

3. Line a colander with a double layer of rinsed cheesecloth. Place the papaya mixture in the colander and rinse well under running water. Pull up the ends of the cloth and squeeze to remove excess moisture (you may need to do this in two batches).

4. Transfer the papaya mixture to a bowl and pour enough of the pickling solution over to cover it. (Reserve any excess solution for marinades, dipping sauces, or similar uses.) Achara keeps for up to 6 months stored in an airtight container in the refrigerator.

Note: Look for green (completely firm and unripe) papaya in Southeast Asian markets.

ACHUETE OIL

Mild, with a hint of heat from the chiles, this bright red oil is used for basting Chicken Inasal (page 175), sautéing oxtail for Kare Kare (page 55), or any dish that needs that trademark reddish hue from the achuete (or annatto) seeds. You can use the oil as you would any other oil, so cook with it in any of your favorite dishes.

Achuete seeds are sold in packages in Asian and Latin groceries. This recipe yields 2 cups —enough to tide you over several meals. Keep the remaining oil in an airtight jar and refrigerate for up to 2 weeks.

MAKES 2 CUPS

2   cups vegetable oil
½ cup achuete (annatto) seeds
6   whole garlic cloves
2   bay leaves
2   ancho chiles, crushed, stemmed, and seeded

In a medium saucepan over medium heat, warm the oil with the remaining ingredients. When it begins to bubble, turn off the heat and allow the mixture to steep for at least 1 hour or up to 2 hours. Strain the oil through a fine-mesh strainer and let cool. Store in an airtight container and refrigerate.

Opposite (clockwise from top left): achara, green mango and tomato salsa, shredded cucumber and jicama, bagoong na alamang, bagoong na padas.
Overleaf, clockwise from top left: durian, chiles, saba, bangus [milkfish], coconut bud, garlic, saba, sugar palm seeds.

Heritage homes, Luzon.

I was eight or nine years old. We were in Nanay's kitchen in Iba, Zambales. It was the summer I told my parents not to come fetch me yet—I'd decided I wanted to spend the entire two months of summer vacation with Nanay, savoring the life of a grandchild. That particular morning, I was up as the gray heavens were being roused by the crowing of the roosters. One of the kitchen help brought in the first rolls of pan de sal [traditional Filipino breakfast rolls] from the local bakery, neatly packaged in the crisp brown envelopes that the Chinese use for newly baked bread. The local baker's old ovens produced a pan de sal that is elusive today. Within the crunchy crust was a moist chewy bread, best eaten hot with melting fresh butter. That was my first inkling of the power of food, and that particular pan de sal is my Holy Grail. I constantly search for the perfect pan de sal. Never finding it, I discover other good things along the way.

Carmen Oliva Camara, my maternal grandmother, was called Nanay by her children, grandchildren, and people who were not related to her. Nanay means mother in Tagalog. Nanay was the earthly soul of the kitchen, hearth, home, and the heart, and for a woman born in her time she was quite modern. Beyond filling up the larder with sweets and local delicacies, she saw to it that my brothers could catch the American B-movies when they came to the local makeshift theater. My older brother, Tristan, said he must have seen every Ronald Reagan movie ever made. Nanay made sure that our time was filled with books, adventures, and little luxuries. No one ever got bored if she could help it.

Thanks to her sharp eye and imagination, Nanay's food was simply unforgettable.

In her memoir, *Up Close with Me*, my mother, Dr. Solita Camara-Besa, remembered that Nanay "was never idle. At home, we used only homemade bagoong, patis, beef tapa, venison tapa, and longaniza. She would make bagoong from tamban [local fish]. She cleaned them well, layered them in earthen tapayans [jars] alternately with salt, and aged them in a concrete-walled room beneath our batalan [open veranda]."

Graduation Day, March 1938

My grandparents stayed with us in Manila for extended periods of time when they were not in Iba. Nanay would always bring goodies from Iba: suman sa ibus, tapa, bagoong, Zambales mangoes, yemas [egg yolk–based candies], and homemade mango jam. When Nanay was there, I looked forward to getting sick because she would make me meringue as a special treat. The soft, foamy, delicate treat was baked in a loaf pan and flavored with kalamansi lime. It was brown and a bit chewy on top, and so soft at the bottom that after a few days it would start to melt into a lemony curd, which I loved to scoop up.

In 1991, when I returned home for the first time in almost nineteen years, I went back to Iba. A sense of scale distortion immediately hit me. Decades earlier, the Manila house would feel so much smaller after a whole summer in Iba. Returning this time to Iba, in place of the huge spaces of my imagination, I was surprised to find a house of normal proportions.

Looking toward the back of the kitchen where I would sit on a swing and play, I thought of that wonderful morning filled with the aroma of freshly baked pan de sal. I remembered a time when Nanay brought me underneath the house with all its chickens clucking about and handed me a soft egg without a shell. I held on and played with that little oval pillow until it finally burst. The summer I spent with Nanay was my summer of independence, without any siblings, cousins, or parents around. It turned out to be the last summer I would spend in Iba. The next year, Nanay suffered a stroke. She died when I was ten, leaving an empty space in our lives.

UBE PAN DE SAL

For an early meeting with our book editor, Marisa Bulzone, Romy came up with a whimsical version of the adobo sandwich by layering crispy adobo flakes (page 38), homemade mayonnaise, and sliced tomatoes on his ube pan de sal. It immediately became Marisa's favorite recipe in the book.

Romy's creation is a riff on a classic sandwich that was popular back in our college days at the University of the Philippines. Down in one small, claustrophobic eatery called the Basement, the specialty was the pork adobo in pan de sal, which made for a hip merienda.

Romy can't resist using purple yam flour in all baked things, such as ube crostini and pizza crust with ube, for the unusual color and nice texture it imparts.

MAKES ABOUT 18 ROLLS

3   cups bread flour, plus additional as needed
½   cup ube (purple yam) flour
2   envelopes active dry yeast
2   teaspoons salt
¼   cup sugar
4   tablespoons (½ stick) unsalted butter,
    at room temperature, plus additional for the bowl
½   cup fine dry bread crumbs

1. In the bowl of a standing electric mixer fitted with the paddle attachment, combine half of the bread flour and all of the ube flour. Add the yeast, salt, and sugar. Pour in 1½ cups warm water (it should be between 90° F and 100° F) and mix to form a smooth batter. Blend in the butter.

2. Change the mixer attachment to the dough hook. With the hook in motion, add the remaining bread flour, ½ cup at a time, until the dough has worked into a rough mass that easily pulls away from the sides of the bowl.

3. Transfer the dough to a large buttered bowl and cover with plastic wrap. Place in a warm, draft-free spot and let rise until doubled in bulk, about 1 hour.

4. Punch down to deflate, cover with plastic wrap, and let rise a second time until doubled in bulk, about 30 minutes.

5. Punch down once more and cut the dough in half. Working with one half at a time, form about 18 equal rolls (they should weigh 2 ounces each). Roll the balls in bread crumbs to coat and place on a baking sheet. Cover loosely with a damp kitchen towel and let rise for 30 minutes.

6. During the final rise, preheat the oven to 400° F. Sprinkle the rolls with more bread crumbs and transfer to the oven. Bake until lightly browned and hard on the bottom, 20 to 25 minutes. Cool on wire racks.

LONGANIZA

This is Romy's recipe, and it astonishes me how closely it approximates the taste of my grandmother's longaniza. Since grinders weren't available in my grandmother's time, she had to cut the meat and the fatback by hand, and this texture is what gives it its authenticity.

You can serve this sausage either in the casing or loose, which we call hubad (which literally means naked). My grandmother served her longaniza hubad when I was growing up as part of the classic Filipino breakfast, eaten with scrambled eggs, fried rice, tomatoes, and vinegar.

MAKES ABOUT TWENTY 3-INCH LINKS

2   pounds finely chopped wild boar
½   pound finely chopped pork fatback
2   tablespoons achuete oil (see page 17)
2   tablespoons rice wine
1   tablespoon rice vinegar
1   teaspoon minced garlic
1   teaspoon finely grated lime zest
1   tablespoon salt
1   teaspoon freshly ground black pepper
Pork casing (optional)
Canola oil, for pan-frying

1. Combine all the ingredients except the pork casing and canola oil in a large bowl. Mix very well, using your clean hands to incorporate all the ingredients. Cover and refrigerate for at least 2 hours, or overnight.

2. If stuffing the sausages, soak the sausage casing in a bowl filled with warm water for 30 minutes, then put one end of the casing over the end of your kitchen faucet and wash the inside with warm water. Change the water in the bowl and soak for another 30 minutes.

(continued)

3. To stuff the sausage, fit the sausage horn over a sausage grinder. Pull the entire length of casing over the tip of the horn and tie a knot at the end. Fill the feed tube with the meat mixture and crank the meat through the grinder to fill the casing until you have used all the meat. Remove the casing from the horn and tie the sausage twice every 3 inches with kitchen twine. Prick with a pin to remove any air bubbles and cut into individual links.

4. Place half the sausage links in a large skillet and add water to come halfway up the sides of the links. Place over medium-high heat and cook, turning the sausages, until the water is evaporated, about 5 minutes. Add about 2 tablespoons oil and continue frying until nicely browned, about 3 minutes on each side. Repeat with the remaining links.

POCHERO

Pochero was the classic Sunday lunch or dinner for many Filipino families of my generation. It is a simple one-pot meal with boiled meats (either beef, chicken, and/or pork), flavored with chorizo de Bilbao (sausages packed in lard in tin cans, which do not come from Bilbao). Potatoes, plantains, cabbage, carrots, and string beans are cooked separately in the broth and served on a platter. The classic condiments (shown opposite) are chopped tomatoes and eggplant caviar.

SERVES 10 TO 12

Eggplant Caviar:
6 medium Chinese eggplants
1 garlic clove, finely chopped
3 tablespoons rice vinegar or paombong [palm vinegar], or to taste
½ teaspoon salt, or to taste
¼ teaspoon freshly ground black pepper, or to taste

Pochero:
5 pounds beef shanks, cut into 3-inch-thick pieces
4 large onions, peeled and halved through the root end
4 pieces Spanish chorizo (about 1 pound)
Salt, if necessary
1 tablespoon whole black peppercorns
½ pound string beans, trimmed
3 medium carrots, peeled, trimmed, halved lengthwise, and quartered crosswise
1 small green cabbage, trimmed, outer layers removed, and cut lengthwise into 6 wedges
3 whole, ripe saba or plantains, peeled
4 medium russet potatoes, peeled and quartered

Dipping Sauce:
½ cup fish sauce
¼ cup freshly squeezed lime juice

5 firm, ripe tomatoes, chopped for serving

1. For the eggplant caviar, preheat the broiler. Place the eggplants on a broiler pan and broil 6 inches from the heat source, turning once with tongs, until blackened on all sides, 6 to 8 minutes, depending on the size of the eggplants. Remove the eggplants from the broiler and cool until just cool enough to handle (it's easier to remove the skins when the eggplants are still steamy). Peel the skin from the eggplants using your hands. Transfer the eggplants to a medium bowl and mash with the garlic. Add the vinegar, salt, and pepper. Taste and adjust the seasoning if needed. Refrigerate until ready to serve.

2. For the pochero, place the beef in a large pot and add water to cover the beef by 3 to 4 inches. Add 2 of the onions. Place the pot over high heat and bring to a boil. Lower the heat, cover, and simmer for 1 hour, skimming off any foam or fat that rises to the top. Add the chorizo and continue cooking until the beef is tender and falling off the bone, about 30 minutes more. Using a slotted spoon, transfer the beef and chorizo to a bowl and tent with foil to keep warm. Taste the broth and add water if it's too strong and salt, if necessary. Strain the broth through a fine-mesh strainer and keep warm.

3. While the beef is cooking, blanch the vegetables: Fill a large pot with water and add the remaining 2 onions and the black peppercorns. Bring to a boil over high heat.

4. Add the string beans to the broth and cook until tender but al dente, 3 to 5 minutes. Using a slotted spoon, transfer the beans to a serving platter. Repeat with the remaining vegetables, blanching each type of vegetable separately, and allowing the water to return to a boil each time: Cook the carrots until tender, 3 to 5 minutes; cook the cabbage until softened, about 5 minutes; cook the plantains until softened, about 10 minutes; lastly, blanch the potatoes until softened, about 15 minutes.

5. To make the dipping sauce, combine the fish sauce and lime juice in a small serving bowl.

6. Place the eggplant caviar and chopped tomatoes in separate serving bowls. Arrange the beef, chorizo, string beans, carrots, cabbage, plantains, and potatoes on a serving platter, and serve.

Family Rituals and Traditions

In our home in Manila, my grandmother, Nanay, introduced us to the Sunday ritual of pochero. One culinary quirk that my grandmother added to this experience was dislodging the bone marrow from the beef shank onto a plate of hot, steaming rice and mixing it with mashed bananas (latundan) and rock salt. This had to be consumed quickly before the marrow grew cold and congealed. It was the best part of the meal.

Reggie Aguinaldo, a dear friend and wonderful cook, tells me that her family tradition was to use whatever fresh ingredients were available in the markets. "The broth would incorporate all the flavors and nutrition of the ingredients, which would be boiled separately with fideos [thin egg noodles] and served before the main dish. Tomato sofrito and eggplant-garlic sauce were served with the dish. As we gathered around the dining table, each of us was assigned to cut up the meats and vegetables into bite-size pieces on our plates. We would then transfer these to a large serving bowl wherein my father would add measured amounts of the tomato sofrito and the eggplant-garlic sauces along with olive oil and balsamic vinegar. He would mix everything together and spoon portions into bowls for each of us."

Some versions of pochero incorporate the tomato sauce into the pot while boiling the meats. I prefer a "white pochero" with a simple plain broth from the meat and the vegetables to start the meal. And I am not fond of recipes that include ham or bacon because I prefer to keep the flavor of the beef unadulterated. In fact, in my re-creation of Nanay's recipe, I prefer a milder authentic Spanish chorizo to the classic chorizo de Bilbao, which tends to overpower the wonderful delicate flavors of the dish.

Summer Vacations in Iba

This is what my brother, Dr. Emmanuel Besa, who is now a hematologist-oncologist in Philadelphia, recalls of the vacations he and my other brothers, Tristan and Vicente, spent with Nanay in Iba.

Summer vacations in Iba were unforgettable. Nanay didn't want any of us to get bored, so she planned activities and prepared special foods. Most mornings were spent at the library. There was a makeshift movie theater under a house along the town square, with canvas walls and folding chairs. If there was a nice movie, she would make sure that we would go see it. In the middle of the show, Nanay would send us a snack through the maid, who would sneak in and find us.

Then there were picnics. We floated on the Bangkal River in Botolan on rafts with a roof made of coconut leaves. Two rafts were tied together with bamboo poles, which allowed us to jump into the water and swim safely. During the mango harvest, we would ride a carabao-drawn cart to the mango grove. While the workers went to work to harvest fruits for us, we ate our picnic. After the meal, people napped in a small nipa hut while we boys went exploring and hiking. I remember coming back with a dead owl I found on the trail.

The foods I associate with Nanay were her lumpia with shrimp juice, her bagoong, known all over for its quality, the nata de coco and pina, which she grew in jars, her yemas during Christmas, her fried frogs (which looked to me like small humans), and the wild boar or deer she dried in the sun for tapa. The tapa was fried and crushed so that the crispy fibers separated, and we ate it with tomatoes, onions, vinegar or suka, and patis manteca sauce.

One day we woke up to find small turtle eggs with soft shells for breakfast. Nanay showed us how to tear a portion of the soft skin and suck the inside of the eggs. We would also have halabos—steamed fresh shrimp—still jumping before they hit the hot water. One of the boys would climb a coconut tree in the backyard for buko [young coconut] and chop a hole in the husk for the fresh juice.

In the backyard, jackfruit, kamias, star apple, coconut, guava, santol, macopa, aratiles, and cashews grew. The cashew has a bright yellow cuplike fruit with a nut sitting on top likened by local legends to a princess sitting on a yellow cushion. The fruit pulp has an acrid aftertaste, so Nanay would cut it up and cook it in a lot of syrup for dessert. The accumulated nuts were then cooked by burning off their tough shells directly in a bonfire. We salvaged them from the ashes when the fire died down and cleaned them. Duhat [Java plum] was a berry with one big seed and purple flesh, which stained our tongues, teeth, lips, and shirts.

BEEF (OR VENISON) TAPA

Traditionally raw, marinated strips of beef or venison are allowed to air-dry in the sun until they are tough and resemble beef jerky. Then they are fried and served with garlic-fried rice and eggs. At the restaurant, we use an electric fan to speed up the time needed to dry the meat – just enough to give it a chewy texture.

Eating venison tapa was one of the fondest memories my brothers and I have of Nanay's cooking in Iba. The venison meat was marinated with kalamansi lime juice, salt, and a little bit of sugar and then hung to dry in the kitchen. Once dry, it was pounded with a mallet until thin, then grilled and fried until crisp. These crisp venison flakes were crumbled on freshly steamed rice and eaten with scrambled eggs and tomatoes with a vinegar dip.

SERVES 4 TO 6

2 pounds flank steak (or venison)

Marinade:

½   cup soy sauce
1½   cups Shaoxing [Chinese rice wine]
⅓   cup kalamansi or regular lime juice
1   cup rice vinegar
2   tablespoons minced garlic
¼   cup sugar

Canola oil, for pan-frying

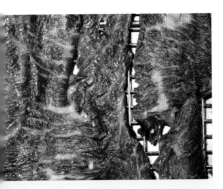

1. Place the steak in the freezer for about an hour to firm it up and make slicing easier. Slice with a sharp knife ¼-inch thick along the grain.

2. In a large nonreactive bowl, combine all the marinade ingredients. Add the meat and marinate in the refrigerator for at least 1 hour or overnight, turning the meat occasionally.

3. Remove the beef from the marinade and lay the slices across a wire rack placed over a rimmed baking sheet to catch the drips. Place under an electric fan for 1 hour to air dry.

4. In a large skillet over medium-high heat, warm 2 tablespoons canola oil. Add some of the steak strips and pan-fry until nicely browned, about 3 minutes on each side. Add more oil to the pan as needed to fry the remaining steak.

The Mangoes of Zambales

as recounted by Solita Camara-Besa

The best mangoes came from Candelaria and Santa Cruz, the north of Zambales, near the Pangasinan border. The variety is called kalabaw, which is not fibrous. The people transporting the mangoes down to Manila would put them on the pontins—sailboats—and when the wind wasn't favorable the mangoes would already be ripened by the time they had reached Iba. At the beach they would announce that there were mangoes on sale, and we kids would go there in a kalesa [a horse-drawn carriage for passengers] and a karitela [a carriage for hauling passengers and freight]. The nice mangoes would be sold for 20 centavos a hundred; the ripe ones—with black spots—would go for 10 centavos a hundred. We would fill up the karitela with these mangoes, going back and forth to get more.

In our house in Iba, Zambales, the mangoes that weren't ripe would go on the ledge around the house. The mangoes would be placed with the stems of the fruit facing out. When the mango starts to ripen, you see it in that spot, and that's how we chose which ones to eat.

Nanay made the ripe or overripe mangoes into a jam. We would start with a whole tacho [copper pot] of sweet pulp and cook it over several hours, ending up with just a small amount of mango jam so sweet that we didn't need to add any sugar.

MANGO TART WITH QUICK PUFF PASTRY

The mango tart is one of the most popular desserts we have at Cendrillon. It was even featured on the *Martha Stewart Living* show in 1997. Filipinos love it because it reminds them that the best mangoes in the world come from the Philippines. Naturally, the Visayans will claim that the Guimaras mangoes are the best, but in Luzon, Zambales mangoes, especially the variety called kalabaw (translated as water buffalo) are the best because they are full of sweet, juicy pulp.

SERVES 6

Quick Puff Pastry:

1 ½   cups all-purpose flour, plus additional for rolling

½   teaspoon salt

½   pound (2 sticks) unsalted butter, chilled
       and cut into pieces

Up to ½ cup ice water

Mangoes:

6   firm but ripe mangoes

Melted unsalted butter, for brushing the tarts

Sugar, sprinkled on the mangoes before baking and
       for caramelizing the pastry

Mango Ice Cream (page 214), for serving

Mango Caramel Sauce (page 30), for serving

1. In the bowl of an electric mixer fitted with the paddle attachment, sift together the flour and salt. Add the butter and beat until very coarse crumbs form (coarser than a typical pie pastry).

2. Drizzle 4 tablespoons of the ice water over the mixture and beat until the mixture comes together loosely. Squeeze a small handful of dough, and if it doesn't hold together add more ice water ½ tablespoon at a time, beating until just incorporated. Don't overwork the dough or the pastry

will be tough. Gather the dough into a ball, then flatten it into a disk. Wrap in plastic and refrigerate for 30 minutes to 1 hour.

3. Turn the dough out onto a lightly floured work surface and, using a lightly floured rolling pin, roll out into a ½-inch-thick rectangle that measures about 12 by 6 inches. The dough will be fairly crumbly. Position the dough with the shorter side nearest you. Fold the top and bottom thirds in toward the center, then fold the dough in half. Turn the dough a quarter turn so the longer end is facing you. Roll out the dough again to about the same size you began with. Brush off the excess flour. Repeat the folding process twice more for a total of three times, then cover with plastic and refrigerate at least 1 hour or overnight.

4. On a lightly floured work surface, roll out the dough ¼-inch thick. Using a plate or bowl as a guide, cut out six 5-inch circles. Using a large spatula, transfer the rounds

to one or two parchment-lined baking sheets, and cover with plastic wrap. Chill until firm, at least 30 minutes.

5. Preheat the oven to 450° F. Peel the mangoes and position them flat side down. Thinly slice the fruit away from the pit on the diagonal. Remove the puff pastry rounds from the refrigerator. Working quickly, arrange the mango slices, starting with the larger slices and adding increasingly smaller slices, over the pastry rounds, fanning the slices in an overlapping circular fashion almost to the edges.

6. Brush the tarts with melted butter and sprinkle each tart evenly with about ½ teaspoon sugar. Bake for 8 to 10 minutes, until the pastry is lightly browned and firm enough to flip. Remove from the oven and carefully flip the tarts with a spatula. Return to the oven and bake for another 8 to 10 minutes, until lightly browned and slightly puffed. Let cool a little, then prepare to caramelize the tops.

7. Cut the parchment out around each tart and slowly pull the surrounding parchment away from the tarts, then pull the rounds of parchment gently out from under each tart without lifting the tarts. Sprinkle each tart (keeping them pastry-side up) with about 1 teaspoon sugar. Using a handheld kitchen torch, caramelize the sugar on the top of each tart (alternately, broil about 6 inches from the heat source, watching carefully, until the sugar is caramelized, 1 to 2 minutes). Serve each tart, still mango-side down, topped with Mango Ice Cream and Mango Caramel Sauce.

MANGO CARAMEL SAUCE

This sauce is also delicious on ice cream, pancakes, or waffles.

MAKES ABOUT 1 ¼ CUPS

¾ cup sugar
½ cup mango juice
½ vanilla bean, split length-wise, pulp scraped
2 teaspoons freshly squeezed lemon juice, or to taste

In a small saucepan over medium heat, combine the sugar with ¾ cup water. Bring to a simmer and cook until the sugar is dissolved, about 5 minutes. Add the mango juice and stir until incorporated. Add the vanilla bean and pulp and simmer for 2 minutes to bring out the flavor. Add the lemon juice, taste, and add more lemon juice if needed. The sauce should be a pourable consistency; if it's too thick, add a little water. Remove the vanilla bean before using.

The Wedding of the Century

This is the story of my grandparents' courtship and their memorable wedding on November 11, 1911 (11/11/11). The number 11 has always been considered a number with an ominous shadow on it, as some unfortunate incidents in my mother's family life happened involving the number 11. My mother's brother Dody died at the age of eleven from a football accident, and her brother Toto developed a serious illness, also at the age of eleven, which luckily he survived.

This account is based on an interview with my mother, Dr. Solita Camara-Besa, in late 2003 from her own recollections and stories from her brother, Dr. Augusto Camara. Uncle Toto, a renowned cardiologist in the Philippines, amazingly has compiled little bits and pieces of history from his patients, some of whom attended the wedding in Nasugbu, Batangas, as little children.

My grandfather, Lolo Vicente Camara, father of Alejandro, went to a party in Manila and met a girl who came from Nasugbu, Batangas. He was impressed by her and he thought that she would make a good wife for his son, Alejandro (my father). So when he went home to Iba, Zambales, he told his son, "I have met the girl that you should marry. So we will go to Nasugbu, Batangas." During that time, it took two weeks to travel from Iba to Nasugbu by horseback and karitela.

When they reached Nasugbu, they went to a relative of my father, Gaudencio Medina, known as Manong Uding, and explained why they'd come. Manong Uding knew the family and said he knew of a more appropriate lady for him. So Manong Uding took the two of them to the home of the Olivas to meet Carmen.

So Tatay met Nanay. I think they really clicked. It was not just an arranged marriage. When my father went back home to Iba, he started a correspondence with her, which began the relationship. Once he had settled for himself that he wanted to marry Nanay, Tatay went back by himself to Nasugbu to set the date and make the arrangements for the wedding.

For the wedding, Tatay was offered the use of the Coast Guard cutter to ferry the guests and food from Zambales and Manila to Batangas. It was called the Wedding of the Century in Nasugbu. Nanay walked with her father from her house to the church on a white cloth that led to the altar. She was not allowed to step on the ground.

The ceremony was followed by a week-long celebration. New guests came every day. Ramon Mitra, Sr. (a patient of Toto's) was a nine-year-old boy at the time, taken to the festivities by his father. During the week, he remembers that Lola Enchang, Nanay's mother, complained that the plates were not being properly washed. So Lolo Vicente ordered that the plates be used only once, then thrown away and new sets brought in.

The food was prepared by a catering company in Manila. Gifts for the guests were ivory-rimmed fans for the ladies and silver-backed hairbrushes for the gentlemen.

Overleaf, clockwise from top left: I Sol Bakery, San Nicolas cookie mold, tapayan [clay urns for storing water], suha [pomelo], cookstove, rambutan, cooked rice wrapped in Anahaw [palm] leaf, rice being washed, lima beans in two colors and sitao [longbeans].

From left: coconuts, alamang, winnowing rice, squeezing green papaya.

chapter 2

Adobo, lumpia, and pancit are the dishes Filipino cooks present to non-Filipinos, but adobo, sinigang, and kinilaw are the three most common dishes I saw prepared in homes throughout the Philippines. Adobo, essentially a vinegar-laced stew, is always ripe for comparison: at the restaurant, Filipinos often ask, "Is your adobo better than my mother's?" And we never take the bait. Of course, your mother's adobo is infinitely better—everyone's is! Sinigang, a soupy mix of seafood or meat and vegetables soured with tropical fruits, is humble Filipino comfort food, considered too plebeian to serve special guests, and, in my opinion, too reliant upon fresh, carefully balanced ingredients to order in most restaurants. Kinilaw, an age-old Filipino use of seafood similar to ceviche, preserves memories of the days when sweet, utterly fresh fruits of the sea were the most basic, readily available of foods.

These native dishes share a strong acid component, derived from either vinegar or sour fruits, a basic element of Filipino taste. All three recipes are easily prepared and are eaten at home on a daily basis, and their accessibility has given rise to countless personal variations. The more versions of adobo, sinigang, and kinilaw you try, the more you'll understand the flavors and techniques of the Philippine kitchen.

Kare kare is another dish that Filipinos will call their own. Its name is derived from *kari,* a Tamil word meaning sauce. It is a stew made with oxtail or calf's feet with a sauce thickened with ground rice or peanuts. It is always eaten with bagoong na alamang [fermented shrimp paste], a condiment that we share with other Southeast Asian cultures.

If these dishes are found in most kitchens throughout the country, one staple is found in *every* kitchen. Rice. Philippine food scholar Doreen Fernandez notes in her book *Palayok* that a seventeenth-century Tagalog-Spanish dictionary lists more than 200 words related to rice, which indicates the significant role this grain played in people's lives even during pre-Hispanic times. Just as today, different rice varieties were grown for different purposes: regular white for daily meals, glutinous and violet rice for kakanin [native desserts], red for making tapuy [rice wine], and fancy grains for feasts and celebrations.

Making sukang Iloko [sugarcane vinegar]; burnay [clay urns] for fermentation.

Adobo

If you only master one Filipino recipe, make it adobo. Filipinos are as likely to agree that adobo should be considered the national dish of the Philippines as they're liable to disagree on every other point about its preparation and enjoyment. The recipe has endless variations, each accompanied by a different set of pamahiin [superstitions]. When I would prepare my evening meal after long workdays, adobo was my best friend. A braise flavored with vinegar, salt, and garlic, it's easy to make and gets better the longer you keep it. These piquant seasonings, which preserved the dish prerefrigeration, permeate, lending the main ingredients a greater depth of flavor.

Chicken, pork, goat, lamb, vegetables, or seafood can all be cooked adobo. According to Doreen Fernandez, traditionalists insist that adobo be seasoned with salt, as soy sauce is a later modification attributed to the pervasive Chinese influence on Philippine food (see The Chinese Influence, page 75).

In Spain, the word *adobo* refers to a condiment of oil, garlic, and marjoram. In Mexico, specifically in Oaxaca, adobo is a marinade of guajillo chiles, garlic, cider vinegar, thyme, bay leaves, avocado leaves, oregano, black peppercorns, and canela [Oaxacan soft cinnamon], used for grilled meat. Nonetheless, Ray Sokolov, in his book *Why We Eat What We Eat,* asserts that adobo is truly our own. When the Spaniards came to the Philippines, he suggests, they ascribed the Spanish name to this native dish because of its mild resemblance to their adobo.

CHICKEN ADOBO

This is the recipe we use at the restaurant. The coconut milk helps keep the chicken moist and it makes a rich sauce. We serve this with Mushroom and Bamboo Shoot Rice (recipe follows) and sauteed mustard greens or bok choy. There are countless variations of chicken adobo; Mary "Inday" Gancayco serves a memorable mixture of chicken and pork adobo coated with mashed chicken livers and topped with fried garlic.

SERVES 4 TO 6

Marinade:

1½ cups rice vinegar
1   cup coconut milk
¼   cup soy sauce
12 garlic cloves, peeled
3   bay leaves
3   whole birdseye chiles
1½ teaspoons freshly ground black pepper

One 3½-pound whole chicken, quartered and cut into pieces

1. In a large nonreactive bowl or heavy-duty, resealable plastic bag, combine all of the marinade ingredients. Add the chicken pieces and turn to coat in the marinade. Refrigerate for at least 2 hours or overnight.

2. In a large casserole or Dutch oven, heat the chicken and marinade over high heat. Bring to a boil, then reduce the heat and simmer, stirring occasionally to make sure the chicken is covered in the marinade, until the chicken is cooked through and tender, 20 to 25 minutes.

3. Transfer the chicken pieces to a large bowl, raise the heat to medium-high, and reduce the sauce until it is the consistency of heavy cream, about 5 minutes. Remove the bay leaves and chiles. Return the chicken to the sauce and cook until just warmed through.

ADOBO FLAKES

Recently my brother Tris mentioned that he goes to Glenda Barretto's restaurant, Via Mare, regularly to order the adobo flakes, because they remind him of Nanay's angel hair, which was made from leftover boiled chicken, finely shredded, marinated in vinegar, salt or soy sauce, and garlic and then deep-fried until crisp. I use leftover chicken adobo for my version.

1. Shred leftover chicken breast from the adobo and marinate in the adobo sauce for 30 minutes. Then squeeze most of the marinade from the chicken and pat dry with paper towels.

2. Fill a medium saucepan with canola oil to come ½-inch up the sides of the pan. Warm over medium-high heat. Add the shredded chicken and fry, stirring, until crisp and golden brown, about 5 minutes. Use a slotted spoon to transfer the chicken to paper towels to drain. Serve hot, on Ube Pan de Sal (page 22), if desired.

MUSHROOM AND BAMBOO SHOOT RICE

Other wild mushrooms, alone or in combination, can be used in place of the shiitakes. I serve this with Chicken Adobo.

SERVES 6

3   cups jasmine rice
3   tablespoons vegetable oil
1   small onion, finely chopped
1   small carrot, trimmed and cut into ¼-inch dice
2   garlic cloves, minced
½   pound shiitake mushrooms, stemmed, cleaned, and thinly sliced
½   cup canned bamboo shoots, rinsed and cut into ½-inch pieces
½   teaspoon ground turmeric
4½ cups chicken stock or water
1½ teaspoons salt
¼   teaspoon freshly ground black pepper

1. Rinse the rice well and drain. Pour the oil into a large saucepan and add the onion and carrot. Cook over medium-high heat, stirring often, until softened, 3 to 5 minutes. Add the garlic and cook 1 minute longer. Stir in the mushrooms, bamboo shoots, and turmeric. Cook, stirring often, until the mushrooms start to give off liquid, about 5 minutes.

2. Stir in the rice and chicken stock or water. Add the salt and pepper and bring to a boil over high heat. Reduce the heat to medium-low, cover, and simmer until the liquid has been absorbed, about 15 minutes.

3. Take the pan off the heat and stir lightly with a fork to fluff. Cover again and let stand for 5 minutes. Taste and adjust the seasoning if needed before serving.

BABY-BACK RIBS ADOBO

This adobo is great served with steamed yellow wax beans sprinkled lightly with rice vinegar. I like to put steaming, freshly cooked rice right into the pan to catch the adobo sauce. If you have an abundance of apples, chop some up and add them to the cooking liquid for a wonderful flavor. This is even better the next day, so you might want to double the recipe to have some left over.

SERVES 4

1   cup organic apple cider vinegar
      (preferably aged in wood)
1   tablespoon soy sauce
3   small bay leaves
1–2   large jalapeño chiles, to taste
1   side of baby-back ribs (about 2 pounds),
      cut up into individual or 2-rib portions
2   teaspoons rock salt
6   garlic cloves, peeled
2   teaspoons tellicherry peppercorns

Steamed rice, for serving

1. In a small bowl, combine the vinegar, soy sauce, bay leaves, and jalapeño.

2. Arrange the ribs in a baking pan and season them with the salt. Using a mortar and pestle, gently pound the garlic cloves and peppercorns until they are combined and coarsely ground. Rub the spices into the pork. Pour the vinegar mixture over the ribs, turning the meat to coat evenly with the liquid. Cover the pan tightly with plastic wrap and refrigerate for at least 1 hour or overnight.

3. When you're ready to cook the ribs, transfer the ribs and marinade to a large, heavy saucepan. Bring the mixture to a boil, then reduce the heat, cover, and cook until the meat is tender and falling off the bone, about 1 hour. Transfer the ribs to a plate.

4. Increase the heat to high and cook the marinade, uncovered, until it is reduced to a medium-thick sauce, 5 to 10 minutes more. If the sauce is still thin, simmer for a few more minutes until thickened. Discard the bay leaves and jalapeño.

5. While you're reducing the sauce, preheat the broiler. Transfer the ribs to a broiler pan lined with foil. Pour the sauce over the ribs.

6. Broil the ribs until nicely browned, 3 to 5 minutes on each side.

My Most Perfect Adobo

While compiling adobo recipes for this book, I decided to cook one, to see if I still had what it took to make a good adobo. I hadn't made one at home since we opened the restaurant ten years ago. Whenever customers in the restaurant ask for Cendrillon's chicken adobo recipe, I challenge them to make their own version without giving specific measurements. I give people the basic concepts, emphasizing the use of the best ingredients. My theory is that if you free people from the tyranny of exact measurements, they can create their own perfect adobo. Achieving the ultimate nuances of flavors in an adobo is a very personal and subjective experience. It is a search for the balance of vinegar to salt that will complement the rest of the dish.

Labor Day 2004, one of our rare days off, I made baby-back ribs adobo. Romy and I shopped for the ribs and natural, organic, unpasteurized apple cider vinegar. Born and bred in Manila, a city filled with supermarkets, I grew up eating adobo cooked with imported Heinz apple cider vinegar and I was craving that particular apple flavor to counter the pork. We had also gone to get rock salt from the Bay of Bengal, tellicherry black peppercorns, and bay leaves. As a child I never liked to eat the black peppercorn pieces and used to spend a lot of time fishing them out of the sauce. However, ever since I discovered tellicherry pepper, I love the sensation of biting into these coarsely ground pieces. The rest of the adobo ingredients came from our regular Saturday morning forays to the Brooklyn farmers' market.

The recipe given here is what I came up with. I did not use precise measurements and just poured whatever amount I felt would be good for the pot. But this is a close approximation of what I put in. Feel free to improvise and experiment with the complexities of adobo.

BEEF SHORTRIBS ADOBO

This thick, rich, dark brown, almost chocolaty sauce becomes even richer if you replace half the stock with coconut milk.

SERVES 4

3 tablespoons canola oil
3 pounds beef short ribs, cut into 4 equal pieces
½ teaspoon sea salt or kosher salt
1½ teaspoons freshly ground black pepper
2 cups chicken stock or 1 cup chicken stock plus 1 cup coconut milk
1 cup sherry vinegar or apple cider vinegar
½ cup soy sauce
1 head garlic, cloves separated and peeled
3 bay leaves
3 whole birdseye chiles (optional)

1. In a large saucepan over medium-high heat, warm the oil until very hot but not smoking. Season the ribs with the salt and ½ teaspoon pepper. Add the ribs to the pan, in batches if necessary, and brown well on all sides, about 3 minutes total.

2. Transfer the ribs to a plate, pour off the oil, and return the ribs to the pan.

3. Add the chicken stock (and coconut milk, if using), vinegar, soy sauce, garlic, bay leaves, remaining 1 teaspoon black pepper, and whole chiles, if using.

4. Bring the mixture to a boil, then reduce the heat and simmer, partially covered, until the meat is tender and falling off the bone, about 1 hour and 20 minutes, skimming off excess fat as you cook.

5. Transfer the ribs to a plate, increase the heat, and reduce the sauce until thickened, 10 to 15 minutes. Discard the bay leaves and chiles. Return the ribs to the sauce or arrange the ribs on a platter and pour the sauce on top.

SQUID ADOBO

We encountered squid adobo in the kitchen of Mama Auyan in Polangui, Albay. This is a simple, fresh, and flavorful dish that cooks quickly—a great way to prepare squid.

SERVES 4 TO 6

3 tablespoons olive oil
5 garlic cloves, sliced
1 medium onion, chopped
3 tomatoes, seeded and chopped
1 cup red wine vinegar
1 tablespoon squid ink (optional)
1½ teaspoons salt
½ teaspoon freshly ground black pepper
3 bay leaves
2 jalapeño or green chiles, seeded and diced
3 pounds whole fresh baby squid, cleaned

1. In a large saucepan over medium heat, warm the oil. Add the garlic and onions and sauté until softened, about 5 minutes. Add the tomatoes and cook for 1 minute.

2. Add the vinegar, squid ink, if using, salt, pepper, bay leaves, and jalapeños. Bring to a boil, then reduce the heat and simmer for 5 minutes. Add the squid, including the tentacles, and bring back to a simmer. Cover and simmer until the squid is tender, about 5 minutes, taking care not to overcook the squid. Discard the bay leaves before serving.

DINAING NA TROUT/BANGUS

This is a flavorful, moist, lightly fried fish dish that is quick and easy enough to make anytime—just allow an hour for marinating and 10 minutes for air-drying.

We use fresh trout as a substitute for the classic Filipino Dinaing Na Bangus, butterflied milkfish. Frozen bangus is sold in some Chinatowns, and can be substituted here if you prefer the authentic fish.

SERVES 4

Marinade:

1   cup rice vinegar
½   cup soy sauce
1   tablespoon sugar
1   tablespoon minced garlic
1   teaspoon freshly ground black pepper

Four 8- to 12-ounce whole trout, cleaned and butterflied
Canola oil, for frying

1. In a large bowl, combine all the marinade ingredients. Transfer the trout to a large nonreactive baking dish or other container large enough to fit the trout lying down. Add the marinade, turning the trout to coat evenly. Cover tightly with plastic wrap, and refrigerate for 1 hour (you can also use a heavy-duty resealable plastic bag).

2. Remove the trout from the marinade and place the fish on a wire rack to air dry for 10 minutes. Discard the marinade.

3. While the trout is air-drying, place two large skillets over medium-high heat. Pour in enough oil to come about 1 inch up the sides of the pans. When the oil is very hot but not smoking, add the trout and fry until the skin is crisp and the flesh is cooked through and tender, about 5 minutes per side.

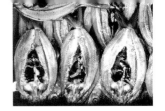

Give Us This Day Our Daily Bangus

Bangus is the most popular fish among Filipinos. While I was growing up, my mother coined the prayer "Give us this day our daily bangus" because we refused to eat our meals unless we had our pan-fried milkfish.

The term *dinaing* refers to the way the fish is cut from the back, keeping the belly together. In the Philippines, bangus is plentiful in areas where there are palaisdaan, or fish farms. Dagupan in Central Luzon is famous for its bangus farms. One can get bangus in different sizes. I remember that the baby bangus that were too small for making dinaing were stuffed with diced tomatoes, onions, and sliced ginger, wrapped in banana leaves, grilled, then eaten with green mangoes, fresh tomatoes, and bagoong, along with a dip of kalamansi lime juice and chiles.

The marinade and flavors for dinaing na bangus or trout are equivalent to an adobo except that the fish is pan-fried rather than braised. For some, the belly is the best part of the bangus and some restaurants offer bangus belly as a specialty. I did not care for the belly, preferring instead the crispy tail and head, so I was a perfect eating companion for friends and family.

Vinegar

Vinegar defines adobo. Traditionally the Philippines produced a wide variety of fruit vinegars ranging in flavor and acidity, but over time commercial vinegars, which are primarily acetic acid, sprung up on supermarket shelves and eclipsed the natural, homespun varieties.

During my more recent travels, however, I've encountered some enterprising conservationists who are championing the revival of vinegar-making. In Manila, locally produced vinegars made from wild guava, duhat [Java plum], coconut, sukang Iloko [sugarcane, see page 121], bignay [Chinese laurel], and cashew were being sold. Sukang Paombong, a vinegar extracted from nipa [a type of palm], is still the most commonly used native vinegar in the Philippines. These fruit vinegars define a truly authentic adobo, but due to their scarcity, good substitutions have been found.

Here in the United States, I know Filipinos who use balsamic vinegar in their adobo for the sweetness it provides, but this strikes me as a poor use of the subtle flavors of good, costly balsamic. At Cendrillon, we use Japanese rice vinegar, French sherry vinegar, and, when we see it at natural food stores or Asian markets, organic coconut vinegar. Romy has also begun infusing his own vinegars. At home, I use organic, unfiltered apple cider vinegar for my adobos. When shopping for vinegar, avoid any containing malt or salt.

Filipino cooks have shared with me various superstitious beliefs regarding cooking with vinegar. The most common folk wisdom says that when cooking with vinegar, one must not stir the vinegar in the pot, as this will awaken its harsh aspects and prevent the dish from cooking properly. At first I thought this advice rather silly and ignored it, but after encountering this attitude repeatedly, I find myself taking heed. I've also noticed that the "un-cooked" taste of raw vinegar is disdained by many Filipinos—I suspect this stems from the need to integrate the flavor of vinegar into adobo. In a well-prepared adobo, the vinegar will have mellowed and blended with the other ingredients, yielding up its harsh sharpness.

ROMY'S FRUIT VINEGARS

This formula for lightly sweet, subtly flavored vinegar can be made with other acidic fruit purees such as mango, jackfruit, peach, or fresh passion fruit when available.

PINEAPPLE OR YELLOW TOMATO VINEGAR

MAKES 1 QUART

1   cup pureed fresh pineapple
    (from about 2 cups pineapple chunks)
    or
    pureed yellow tomatoes
    (from about 3 medium chopped tomatoes)
3   cups rice vinegar

Combine the fruit puree with the vinegar in a 1-quart jar. Refrigerate overnight. The next day, pour through a fine-mesh strainer set over a bowl. Transfer the vinegar to a container with a tightly fitting lid, and refrigerate until ready to use. Let rest overnight before using. The vinegar will keep, sealed in the refrigerator, for up to 2 months.

Sourness is at the heart of sinigang, a soupy concoction of indigenous fruits, seafood, meat, or chicken with taro, radish, leeks, onion, celery, tomatoes, bok choy, or water spinach [kangkong], and chiles. The simplicity of the recipe belies the nuanced balance of flavors in the finished dish. I love true sinigang, and always ask at restaurants in the Philippines how they prepare it, only to be proudly told that theirs is soured with an imported, MSG-laden flavor packet. The poor sinigang! This ubiquitous comfort food doesn't get the respect it deserves.

Classic chicken sinigang, sinampalukang manok [tamarind soured chicken] calls for green tamarind with its leaves and flowers, and chicken blood (common when chickens were slaughtered in one's backyard). Seafood sinigang is a simple broth soured with a fruit of choice (kamias and kalamansi lime are favored), chopped vegetables and shrimp, bangus [milkfish], pla-pla [tilapia], or lapu-lapu [grouper]. Meat sinigang, usually beef shank or pork belly, is boiled a day in advance to tenderize it. The next day, vegetables and roots are added and the meat and broth are soured. Filipinos generally season dishes like sinigang with a light hand, then offer sawsawan [dips], so diners can add fish sauce, kalamansi lime juice, and chiles according to their taste.

Traditional sinigang fruits are hard to find outside the Philippines, though the combination of lemon, lime, and tomatoes can do the job, too. I grew up eating kalamansi lime–soured sinigang in Manila, which, I've since learned, previous generations considered a shortcut, inferior to the more traditional and complex sourness of tamarind (the unripe pod, young leaves, and flowers are all used), kamias, siniguelas [Spanish plum], guava, or batuan [a small very sour green fruit unique to Visayan sinigang]. I fear that people in the Philippines take these fruits too much for granted. If not used for daily meals, they will lose their commercial value and become scarce—even in the home of sinigang!

Remnants of authentic sinigang culture remain. Claude Tayag, an artist-chef who hosted us in Angeles, Pampanga, told me about ordering corned beef sinigang in a restaurant. Before serving it the waiter brought out a demitasse of the sinigang broth. "Tikman ninyo ang asim, kung tama na" ("see if the sourness is right for you"), he said, and Claude replied, "kaunti pa" ("a little more sourness, please").

Guavas. Opposite: tinola [Visayan sinigang].

Sinigang

FISH SINIGANG

Doreen Fernandez considered sinigang the quintessential Filipino dish because it makes good use of the sour fruits that grow in the Philippines. I grew up eating pork and beef sinigang and was never too particular about the fish version until Romy came up with the idea of making a dry crust and pan-frying the fish fillets.

SERVES 4

Two 2-pound red snappers, cleaned and cut into 4 fillets (skin-on), head, tail, and bones reserved

Fish Stock:
Heads, tails, and bones from snapper

1	large carrot, cut into large pieces
3	leeks, green parts only, cut into large pieces
10	fresh tamarind pods or 2 ounces packaged tamarind pulp (not concentrate) soaked in 1 cup water
5	medium-ripe tomatoes, chopped
4	radishes, quartered
1	leek, white part only, sliced
2	ripe tomatoes, seeded and chopped
1	fresh green or red chile, sliced
1/4	cup fish sauce, or to taste

Kalamansi lime or lemon juice, to taste, if needed

Fish:

2	tablespoons Dijon mustard
3	radishes, finely chopped
2	leeks, white parts only, finely chopped
2	teaspoons fine cornmeal
4	tablespoons canola oil
2	bunches baby bok choy, cut into large pieces

1. For the stock, in a large pot over high heat, combine the fish heads, tails, and bones with the carrot, leek greens, tamarind pods or packaged pulp, medium-ripe tomatoes, and 10 cups water (9 cups if you're using the packaged tamarind pulp). Bring to a boil over high heat, then reduce the heat and simmer, uncovered, for 20 minutes. Skim the foam until the stock becomes clear. Strain. You can prepare the stock a day ahead, refrigerate, and reheat before serving.

2. Before serving, add the radishes, leek, seeded ripe tomatoes, and chile to the stock and simmer for 5 minutes to blend the flavors. Add the fish sauce. Taste and add lime juice and more fish sauce if needed.

3. For the fish, preheat the oven to 400° F. Rub 1/2 tablespoon mustard over the flesh side of each fillet to evenly coat. Combine the chopped leeks and radishes and press into the mustard in a thin layer. Sprinkle about 1/2 teaspoon cornmeal over each fillet. Heat 2 tablespoons oil in each of two large ovenproof skillets over medium-high heat. Pan-fry the fillets, skin side up, for about 3 minutes, or until lightly browned. Flip the fillets and place in the oven for about 5 minutes, or until the fillets are cooked through and the crust is lightly browned and crisp.

4. Divide the bok choy among 4 deep, wide serving bowls. Add about 1 1/2 cups steaming-hot stock (reserving any extra for later use), and place a fish fillet on top. Serve with additional fish sauce and lime juice on the side.

Tamarind pods.
Opposite: kamias.

FE'S SPECIAL PORK SINIGANG

"May I take your picture?" was how my uncle Dr. Victor Villadolid, an ophthalmologist, introduced himself to Fe Rael, a dietitian, in 1952, when he spotted her on the balcony of the Philippine General Hospital in Manila. Now married for fifty-one years, Victor still treasures this photo (right). Fe gave me this recipe, which is a winter favorite of the Villadolids that has kept the family warm and healthy during those long, cold nights they now encounter in New York. Victor's contribution to the dish is his encouragement to "cook with much love and imagination and your dish will always taste heavenly!"

SERVES 6

2   tablespoons canola oil
2   pounds boneless, country-style pork ribs,
      cut into 2 ½-by-1 ½-inch pieces
5   medium plum tomatoes, cored and diced
      (about 2 cups)
1   large onion, diced (about 2 cups)
1-2   jalapeño chiles, halved lengthwise and seeded
      (leave seeds in for a spicier version)
2   tablespoons freshly squeezed lemon juice
1½   teaspoons salt
½   teaspoon freshly ground black pepper
1   medium Chinese eggplant, cut into 1-inch pieces
1   cup peeled and sliced daikon radish
      (about ½ medium daikon)
1   bunch broccoli rabe, stems trimmed, flowers and
      stems cut into 2-inch pieces
Steamed white rice, for serving
1   bunch scallions, trimmed and thinly sliced,
      for serving

1. Bring a medium pot of water to a boil, then reduce the heat and keep at a steady simmer.

2. In a large, heavy saucepan over medium heat, warm the oil. Add the pork, tomatoes, and onion, and sauté until the pork turns light brown, 5 to 7 minutes. Stir in the jalapeños, lemon juice, salt, and pepper.

3. Add enough of the simmering water to the saucepan to cover the pork mixture. Partially cover and simmer until the pork is tender, 40 to 50 minutes. Taste and adjust the seasoning, if necessary.

4. Stir in the eggplant and daikon and simmer for 5 minutes, or until the vegetables are slightly softened. Add the broccoli rabe, cover, and simmer until the broccoli rabe, radish, and eggplant are tender, about 5 minutes. Serve over steamed rice, with the scallions on top.

Kinilaw

Halaan [clams].

Kinilaw is a Filipino tradition of immediacy and locality, a dish prepared and consumed the moment the products are harvested from the sea. It's a philosophy of matching the delicate texture of a raw, just-caught oyster, clam, shrimp, crab, or tuna with a tart dressing of vinegar, lime, or citrus juice, taking care not to "overcook" the fresh catch, then seasoning with ginger, onions, chiles, or coconut milk.

Kinilaw is probably the oldest known cooking method used by the early inhabitants of the Philippines. Archaeological digs in Butuan City, Mindanao, have unearthed "edible discards" of fishbones and remains of a fruit core called tabon-tabon from thousands of years ago. Today some regions in the Visayas and Mindanao still use prehistoric fruits like the tabon-tabon and dungon, grating, squeezing, and soaking the core of the fruit in water, then cleansing the fish in this fruit water before combining it with other ingredients, a process some claim makes kinilaw more digestible.

The usual technique is to clean the seafood, then rinse it, preferably in fresh sea water, to reawaken its flavors. The seafood is then bathed in a sour dressing that begins to firm the flesh, turning it from translucent to opaque. Then it is eaten, on the spot—letting it stand would destroy the supremely fresh texture and flavor and is unthinkable. The kinilaw treatment can extend to meat, usually beef or water buffalo, though these are not common. The term also embraces dishes like seared pork or grilled squid, which are cooked or half-cooked, then marinated in vinegar or lime.

TUNA AND OYSTER KINILAW

Marinate the raw fish for only a few minutes to avoid "cooking" it in its citrus marinade (this is what differentiates the kinilaw from a ceviche, which is purposely "cooked"). This dish must be assembled quickly, just before serving, to showcase the freshness of the kinilaw and its contrast with the icy granita. It's a perfect summer aperitif or intermezzo between courses.

SERVES 8

Citrus Marinade:

Freshly squeezed juice of 2 lemons
Freshly squeezed juice of 2 kalamansi limes
   or regular limes
Freshly squeezed juice of 1 orange
2   shallots, thinly sliced
1   tablespoon grated or very thinly sliced ginger
1   fresh green chile, such as jalapeño, seeded
       and thinly sliced
1   teaspoon salt, or to taste

Kinilaw:

1½   pounds sashimi-grade tuna, sliced against
       the grain ⅛-inch thick
24   Kumamoto, Olympia, or Fisher Island oysters
1 recipe Tomato Granita (recipe follows), for serving

Garnish:

16   cherry tomatoes, halved
4   red radishes, trimmed and thinly sliced
2   oranges, sectioned
2   grapefruits, sectioned
32   leaves fresh lemon basil or regular basil
8   sprigs fresh thyme
4   fresh red chiles, halved lengthwise (optional)

1. Place 8 soup plates or bowls in the refrigerator to chill.

2. In a large bowl, combine all the marinade ingredients. Place the tuna slices in the marinade, toss to coat, and let sit for 5 minutes.

3. Rinse the oysters in cold water and shuck them: Grip an oyster in a kitchen towel with one hand, and insert the tip of a strong, thin (preferably blunt-tipped) blade slightly into the shell near the hinge. Gripping the oyster without tipping it (you don't want to spill the liquid inside), twist the blade to pop open the shell. Slide the blade around the top half of the shell to detach it from the oyster (avoid inserting it deeply enough to cut the oyster). Pull off the top shell, and use a towel to dab away any grit on the oyster. Cut the adductor muscle, to detach the oyster from the shell, and lay it flat to hold as much liquor as possible.

4. To serve, spread about 2 tablespoons of the tomato granita in the center of each of the chilled soup plates. Use a slotted spoon to divide the tuna among the plates, laying it over the granita. Add the oysters in their shells to the plates. Divide the tomatoes, radishes, orange slices, and grapefruit slices evenly among the plates (see photo, page 49). Scoop about 3 more tablespoons of the tomato granita onto each plate. Garnish each plate with the basil leaves, thyme sprigs, and chile halves, if using. Serve immediately.

TOMATO GRANITA

This is a perfect base for ceviches or kinilaw during the late summer. Use freshly harvested, ripe local tomatoes, seeking out various shapes, sizes, and colors ranging from blood red, pale orange, and yellow to give the granita interesting colors.

MAKES ABOUT 2 PINTS

3   pounds (about 8 medium)
     ripe tomatoes
1   tablespoon grated fresh
     horseradish
1   tablespoon freshly
     squeezed lemon juice,
     or to taste
¾   teaspoon salt,
     or to taste
Sugar, if necessary

1. Bring a large pot of water to a boil over high heat and fill a bowl with water and ice. Using a paring knife, make a small "X" in the bottom of each tomatoes. Lower the tomatoes into the water, two at a time, and blanch until the skin at the bottom of the tomatoes begins to curl, about 30 seconds. Using a slotted spoon, immediately transfer the tomatoes to the ice water to cool. Repeat until all of the tomatoes have been blanched.

2. When cool enough to handle, remove the tomato skins with your hands or a paring knife. Slice the tomatoes in half, remove and discard the seeds, and chop the flesh into chunks. Place the tomatoes in a blender and puree until smooth, then strain through a medium-mesh strainer set over a bowl.

3. Add the horseradish, lemon juice, and salt. Taste the tomatoes, and add a little sugar if necessary. Taste again and add more salt and lemon juice, if needed.

4. Pour the tomato mixture into a shallow glass or ceramic dish and freeze for about 3 hours, stirring every 30 minutes to break up the crystals, until slushy but not too icy. If the granita becomes too solid, you can pulse it in a food processor before serving.

Opposite: oysters.
Below: heirloom tomatoes, lasona [small purple onions], scallops.

CHILLED LOBSTER KINILAW

This dish actually uses cooked lobster, so it will appeal to those who don't like the typical raw treatment of kinilaw.

SERVES 4

Two 1¼-pound lobsters, steamed, flesh cut
　　into bite-size pieces
1　large cucumber, peeled, seeded, and diced
1　cup diced honeydew melon
1　cup diced jicama
2　tablespoons chopped fresh cilantro or basil

Vinaigrette:
3　tablespoons olive oil
3　tablespoons kalamansi lime or regular lime juice
3　tablespoons rice vinegar
¼　teaspoon salt
Pinch of freshly ground black pepper

1 recipe Tomato Granita (at left), for serving

1. In a large serving bowl, combine the lobster meat, cucumber, melon, jicama, and cilantro.

2. To make the vinaigrette, place the oil in a medium bowl. Whisk in the kalamansi juice, vinegar, and salt and pepper.

3. Lightly dress the lobster mixture with the vinaigrette. Spoon about ½ cup of the tomato granita in each of 4 small dessert bowls or martini glasses. Top with the lobster mixture, and garnish with the remaining granita. Serve immediately.

Kinilaw Ingredients

Kinilaw is a selection of fresh products, soured and combined in the moment, specific to the exact moment and place. These vary with the season and region, and the dressing is unique to the person creating it. Still, the basic "pantry" of seafood, souring agents, fruits, and vegetables in the different regions of the Philippines can be condensed to the following:

⚬ **Seafood:** oysters, clams, crabs, small shrimps [suaje], abalone, sea cucumber, squid, and sea urchin

⚬ **Fish:** grouper, milkfish, tanigue, swordfish, pompano, tuna, kingfish, and dorade

⚬ **Vinegars:** coconut [tuba] and palm [paombong]

⚬ **Other souring agents:** kalamansi and dayap [different species of lime] and kamias

⚬ **Basic ingredients:** salt, ginger, chiles, onions, shallots, and coconut milk

⚬ **Fruits:** green mango, green papaya, cucumbers, banana blossoms, green siniguelas, and starfruit

⚬ **Vegetables and roots:** seaweeds, wild ferns, jicama, and radish

⚬ **Other additions:** salted duck eggs, tomatoes, tausi [salted black beans], and garlic

The Kinilaw Master

I grew up thinking all raw foods were dangerous. As a child, I watched my father down raw oysters doused with hot water in great fear that he would come down with cholera. So the discovery of this ancient tradition of eating pure and fresh raw seafood was an epiphany for me. I owe gratitude to the wonderful book on the topic by food writer Doreen Fernandez and Edilberto Alegre. Doreen organized a food tour of the Philippines for Romy and me, culminating in a visit to the second generation kinilaw master Enting Lobaton.

In 1999, I traveled to Sagay, a town on the northernmost tip of Negros Occidental. Sagay is a rarity, a minuscule piece of ocean and land free of commercial trawlers from nearby towns, which makes it possible to still savor a wide variety of kinilaw.

Early on that perfect September day we set out from Old Sagay on a partially covered pumpboat, heading toward a sandbar in Kabingabingahan, the marine reserve of Sagay. Enting Lobaton, a second-generation kinilaw master, set out rows of his red and blue plastic basins filled with strips of fish. He prepared the kinilaw, which we ate right on the boat.

Our first course was taclobo, giant clam. Lifting its fist-sized meat from the foot-long, beautifully sculpted shell, Enting split it down the middle, carefully removing and puncturing its bile sac. He flavored half of the clam meat with its own bile, a bitter taste that many Filipinos savor and yearn for. Our enjoyment of this sensual feast was dampened when he announced that the taclobo was near extinction!

Next came a profligate amount of seafood: parrotfish, squid, crab, and easily a dozen local fish of different sizes. Enting reached for vinegars variously flavored with lemongrass, garlic, ginger, and chiles, and, the one he favored most, coconut. Choosing the right dressing for each seafood, he shared some basic rules: for scallops, use kalamansi lime juice, not vinegar, which will make it tough; parrotfish, with its soft, white meat can withstand a vinegar marinade; some vinegar marinades are softened with lime and sugar; and depending on the type of seafood, flavors such as salted black beans, grated green mangoes, and coconut milk can be used.

Every now and then he would dip a small blue plastic basin over the side of the boat and scoop up fresh seawater to wash the fish in. We moved from one texture to another, his seasonings and vinegar preparations deepening with the flavors of the fish. At the end we were challenged by a daunting shipworm, a mollusk that bores into the side of wooden boats, which was quite crunchy and chewy. Miniature pineapples bursting with sweetness were a perfect close to the meal.

BANANA HEART KINILAW

Fernando "Fern" Aracama is a well-known chef in Manila (page 179). This is one of his favorite side dishes at home. He explains how the banana heart is treated in his house:

> The pakla (astringent or bitter) aftertaste of the banana heart is a fickle issue. Some people find it overbearing, but most don't. Our family cook doesn't thread the hearts (a process that makes the heart easier to cook and eat). Threading is usually done if the heart is shredded for guinataan [coconut milk–based stews] or guinisa dishes [dishes sautéed with garlic, onions, and tomato]. For sinigang or kare kare, it is usually just cut into eight sections, then soaked in water until it is added to the pot. Use a stainless steel knife, as carbon steel knives immediately stain the banana heart.

You may, indeed, find the banana heart quite bitter, so we suggest following the method described below for removing the bitterness.

SERVES 4 AS A SIDE DISH

Salt

4   fresh banana hearts (do not use canned)

4   shallots, thinly sliced

2   tablespoons coconut milk

Freshly squeezed juice of 1 lime, or to taste

½   hot red chile, thinly sliced

1   medium tomato, thinly sliced, for garnish

1. Fill a bowl with about 6 cups water and 2 tablespoons salt. Swirl to dissolve the salt. Peel the outer layers of the banana hearts until you reach the pale-colored heart. Finely chop the banana hearts and immediately place in the water. Massage the pieces with your hands for about 3 minutes to remove the bitter sap. Discard the soapy-looking liquid that emerges. Drain in a fine-mesh strainer, rinse, and repeat the whole process. Taste a small piece and if there is any bitterness remaining, wash the banana hearts again.

2. Fill a large bowl with water and ice. Bring a medium pot of water to a boil over high heat. Add the banana hearts and blanch very briefly, about 10 seconds. Strain through a fine-mesh strainer and place in the ice water for about 1 minute to cool. Drain thoroughly and pat dry with paper towels, then place in a serving bowl. Add the shallots, coconut milk, lime juice, chile, and ¼ teaspoon salt, and stir to combine. Taste and add more salt or lime juice if needed. If the mixture looks dry, add more coconut milk. Garnish with the tomato slices and serve.

Opposite: Banana hearts.

Kare Kare

Kare kare is one of those dishes that Filipinos will claim ownership to. According to Alan Davidson in *The Oxford Companion to Food*, the word *kari* is a Tamil word meaning spiced sauce. These sauces were stewlike dressings with small quantities of poultry or meat to put on rice. Through the centuries, the word and dish traveled to Europe, and the Portuguese, Dutch, and English helped it evolve into the present term, *curry*. The original kari was a soupy dressing flavored with a simple spice such as black pepper. It was only later that chiles and other spices such as cumin, coriander, and mustard seeds were added.

The Filipino kare kare (the Malay love to repeat words) is closer to the original Malay soupy stew. The sauce is devoid of seasonings, spices, or chiles, and is thickened with pounded toasted rice and peanuts (though peanut butter is a fine substitute). The kare kare of an older generation was usually cooked with pata [calf's foot], which produced a gelatinous sauce.

The classic condiment that is paired with kare kare is the bagoong na alamang, fermented shrimp paste, a condiment we also share with our Southeast Asian neighbors.

OXTAIL KARE KARE

I got this recipe from a good friend, Mila Manalac, while I was a student staying with her in Philadelphia. Mila was obsessed with cooking, and to this day, food is still her passion.

This version is made with oxtail along with longbeans, banana heart, and eggplant. Be sure to serve this with sautéed bagoong na alamang [fermented shrimp paste]. I like to mix my bagoong with kalamansi lime juice and a little bit of vinegar to soften the salt level.

Note that it is necessary to refrigerate the oxtail overnight to separate out the fat (which will be used for cooking).

SERVES 6

2   pounds oxtail, cut into 2-inch pieces
5   tablespoons oxtail fat or canola oil
1   small head garlic, cloves peeled and mashed
2   medium onions, chopped
6   plum tomatoes, quartered
¾   cup peanut butter (or ⅓ cup ground toasted rice [see Note] and ½ cup ground dry-roasted unsalted peanuts)
2   teaspoons salt, plus additional if using banana heart
1   small banana heart (optional)
20   longbeans, cut into 2-inch pieces
3   Chinese eggplants, quartered lengthwise and cut into 2-inch pieces
2   tablespoons achuete seeds, soaked in ¼ cup hot water for 20 minutes and strained (optional)
Steamed white rice, for serving
Bagoong na alamang [fermented shrimp paste], for serving

1. Wash the oxtails thoroughly and place them in a large saucepan with water to cover. Place over high heat and bring to a boil, then reduce the heat and simmer until the oxtails are fork-tender and falling off the bone, about 90 minutes. Let cool in the cooking liquid, cover the pot, and refrigerate overnight to separate the fat.

2. Skim and reserve the fat. Take the oxtails from the broth and reserve the broth.

3. In a large saucepan over medium heat, warm 5 tablespoons of the oxtail fat (make up the quantity with canola oil, if needed). Add the garlic and onions and sauté until softened, about 5 minutes. Add the tomatoes and peanut butter, if using, and cook for 2 minutes, or until the tomatoes have softened. Add the reserved broth and cook for 15 minutes to blend the flavors. Add the oxtail and cook, uncovered, for 20 minutes, until the broth has reduced partially (do not simmer off all the liquid).

4. If using the banana heart, fill a bowl with about 3 cups water and 1 tablespoon salt. Swirl to dissolve the salt. Peel the outer layers of the banana heart until you reach the pale-colored heart. Cut the banana heart into eight sections and immediately place in the water. Massage the pieces with your hands for about 3 minutes to remove the bitter sap. Discard the soapy-looking liquid that emerges. Drain in a fine-mesh strainer, rinse, and repeat the whole process. Taste a small piece and if there is any bitterness remaining, wash the banana heart again.

5. Add the banana heart to the pan and cook for 3 minutes, or until softened. Add the longbeans and eggplants, cover, and cook until tender, about 10 minutes. Add the ground rice, peanuts, and achuete water, if using, and cook for about 5 minutes, until the stew is the right consistency – not too thick but not too soupy. Serve over rice with the bagoong.

Note: To toast rice, place the rice in a skillet over medium heat. Toast, stirring constantly, until lightly browned and aromatic, about 5 minutes. Cool, then finely grind in a spice mill or food processor.

Grinding rice and peanuts.

Rice defines and localizes me. Growing up in Manila and living for several decades in New York City, there are times when I need to figure out who I am. Every time I reach out for rice, it tells me that I am Asian—specifically, I am Filipino. The reflexive gesture informs me that the proper seasoning and flavors of the accompanying dishes can only be negotiated when eaten with rice.

No Filipino can survive without rice. It is the center point of the meal, defining the final taste of everything consumed with it. It is not a side dish. We do not like it parboiled, nor do we like it dressed like a potato with butter or salt. We like it properly steamed, not dry, not mushy. And we eat rice at breakfast, lunch, merienda, and dinner. Leftover cooked rice is fried with garlic in the morning, and freshly simmered and steamed rice accompanies other meals. Filipino cooks turn to rice when adapting borrowed recipes, as in the ground rice that replaces corn in Filipino tamales (page 130) and empanadas (pages 98–101).

Rice exists in a variety of grain sizes, and can range from red and purple to brown. Rice in the Philippines is generally classified as regular [bigas] or glutinous [malagkit in Tagalog, pilit in Visayan]. The highest quality rice is milagrosa, its tiny, moist, delicate grains offering a nuanced fragrance and the flavor of fresh grass. Violet-colored pirurutong (referred to as black rice in the United States) is ground and steamed in bamboo cylinders for puto bumbong, traditionally a Christmas treat, now offered year-round by many outlets in Manila.

Filipino noodles, or bihon, are made by extruding a wet rice dough through a plate with round holes in it, letting the noodles fall directly into boiling water. The noodles are par-cooked, drained, then used fresh or dried. Rice is the basis of native kakanin, the treats served for breakfast or merienda (page 60). It is ground dry for rice flour, or soaked and ground with water to make a batter called galapong, the basis for puto (pages 66–67) and bibingka (pages 63–65). Since rice flour is gluten free, it gives baked goods a tender texture.

Rice has medicinal uses as well. Lugao [rice porridge], made with rice boiled with a quantity of lightly salted water, is usually given to sick people. Am, the liquid by-product that settles on top when cooking rice, is collected and given to children, supposedly for its high nutritional value. Rice tea, made by steeping burnt rice grains, is used to treat upset stomach. I grew up eating and consuming all of these to facilitate a return to good health.

Rice terraces. Opposite: varieties of rice at market.

Rice

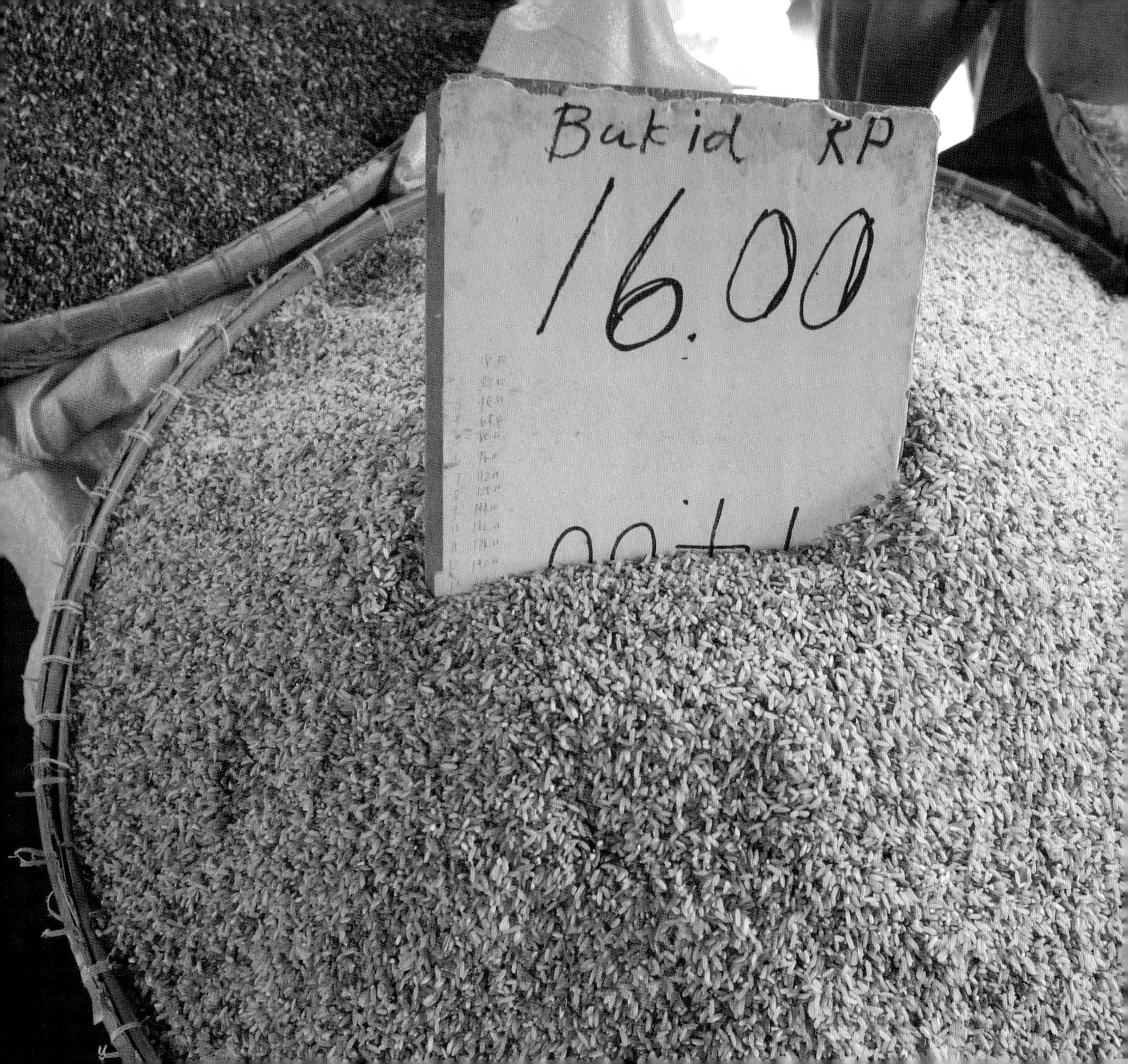
Bukid RP
16.00

Tutong

Traditionally rice was washed, then placed in a banana leaf-lined clay pot with water to the depth of the second line of the middle finger touching the rice. The covered pot would be simmered over a wood fire until the water was almost gone, then taken off the heat to let the rice settle at the final, critical stage, called in-in. This method was retained as stainless steel and gas or electric heat were adopted, but many people will tell you that even in this transition, much of the flavor and romance of rice disappeared.

Now that the rice cooker, with its even heat, has taken over, another major element of rice cookery has been lost: the tutong, the beloved crust that forms at the bottom of the pan (see Bringhe recipe, pages 126–27). Uro del Rosario, a cultural observer from Lucban, Quezon, remembers how his grandfather kept the grandchildren from fighting over this treat at the base of the rice pot:

"He would get cold rice and mix it with a little bit of water, then he would take out the big kawali [clay wok] and spread that rice so that you would have a whole kawali of tutong. Then the children were satisfied."

PINIPIG COOKIES

Pinipig are Philippine rice crispies. They are immature glutinous rice grains that are roasted and then pounded. Here in the United States, they can be found frozen in Asian markets. Pinipig can be dry-toasted in a wok or non-stick saucepan. Sprinkled with sugar, they can be eaten with milk as breakfast cereal. Pinipig is a favorite topping for the iced dessert Halo-halo (page 153). I put it on mango or purple yam ice cream for a simple dessert. It is also wonderful with hot chocolate for merienda, a treat that is popular during Christmas. In the Philippines, commercial ice cream-makers sell Pinipig Crunch, the pinipig mixed into the chocolate coating for ice cream on a stick.

These crisp, buttery cookies were the first cookies that I baked in the Philippines as a teenager. It's a very easy recipe to make, and the cookies most likely will be eaten as fast as you can bake them.

MAKES ABOUT 4 DOZEN COOKIES

1½   cups pinipig
½   cup (1 stick) unsalted butter, softened
¾   cup sugar
2   large eggs
½   teaspoon finely grated lemon zest
1   cup all-purpose flour
1   teaspoon baking powder
¼   teaspoon salt

1. Preheat the oven to 350° F and set racks in the upper and lower thirds of the oven. Grease 2 baking sheets.

2. Warm a medium skillet over medium heat. Add the pinipig and toast, stirring, until lightly browned and aromatic, about 5 minutes. Transfer to a plate to cool.

3. Cream the butter with the sugar until light and fluffy. Add the eggs, one at a time, and beat until incorporated. Beat in the lemon zest.

4. In a separate bowl, sift together the flour, baking powder, and salt. Gradually add the dry ingredients to the wet and stir to combine. Stir in the pinipig.

5. Drop the dough by heaping teaspoons onto the baking sheets 2 inches apart and press down with the tines of a fork. Bake the cookies in the upper and lower thirds of the oven, rotating the pans and switching the position of the baking sheets halfway through baking, until lightly browned around the edges, about 12 minutes. Let cool on the sheets for a couple of minutes, then transfer to wire racks to cool completely and bake the second batch on the cooled sheets.

Far left: rice cookers. Left: winnowing rice.

Kakanin

Kutsinta [rice cake]. Old stone rice grinder. Opposite (from top): suman, cassava bibingka, bibingka. Far right: steaming tupig.

Kakanin is a generic term for all native desserts, including puto, bibingka, and suman. The word is derived from the word *kanin*, which means cooked rice. Kanin is also related to the term *kain*, which means to eat. The majority of native desserts are made with rice, but cassava, saba [a cooking banana similar to the plantain], taro, and sweet potato are also used in certain regions. Filipinos generally eat kakanin for merienda, an in-between meal snack, and seldom for dessert after meals. They are usually steamed, boiled, or baked in makeshift ovens with heat on top. The best way to serve them is with muscovado sugar and freshly grated coconut. The best time to experience a wide selection of kakanin in the Philippines is during the Christmas season.

Making espasol in Bulacan.

ESPASOL

You can flavor this sticky rice dough with vanilla or lime (the lime or dayap flavor is the trademark of Bulacan, which is quite famous for espasol). They are soft, squishy confections formed into short logs or triangles. I first tasted espasol in my high school cafeteria in Maryknoll College in Quezon City. I remember that it only appeared a few times and then disappeared. That was why I searched for this recipe and made sure I watched the women of Barrio Maronquillo as they stirred the sticky dough in their huge vats to make their espasol.

SERVES 12

3	cups mochiko (sweet rice flour)
1	cup pinipig
Two	14-ounce cans coconut milk
1 ¼	cups sugar
½	teaspoon salt
1	tablespoon vanilla extract or 1 tablespoon lime juice plus 1 teaspoon grated lime zest
½	package (1 cup) unsweetened grated buko with juice

1. Warm a large skillet over medium heat. Add the mochiko and toast, stirring, until lightly browned. Transfer to a plate to cool. Place the pinipig in the same skillet and toast, stirring, until lightly browned and aromatic. Transfer to a separate plate to cool, then grind in a food processor until fine.

2. Sift the mochiko into a large bowl and whisk in the pinipig. Dust a large baking sheet with ½ cup of this mixture and reserve another ½ cup for rolling out the espasol.

3. In a large saucepan over medium-high heat, combine the coconut milk, sugar, and salt and bring to a boil. Lower the heat and simmer for 5 minutes, stirring to dissolve the sugar. Add the vanilla, if using.

4. Add the mochiko mixture and buko and cook, stirring continuously, until very thick and fairly dry, about 5 minutes. Add the lime juice and zest, if using.

5. Evenly spread the mixture over the prepared baking sheet and flatten and smooth with a rubber spatula. Let cool, then dust your hands with the remaining flour mixture (the batter is quite sticky) and work the espasol into shapes of your choice, such as logs, balls, and triangles. Dust the espasol with the remaining flour mixture to keep them from sticking to anything. Serve immediately or refrigerate for up to 3 days.

Bibingka

We have always translated *bibingka* as rice cake. While that is how most Filipinos will use it, it is not quite accurate. The majority of bibingkas are indeed made of ground rice and water, white sugar, baking powder, or yeast and often coconut milk for added luxury. But cassava bibingka, made with grated yucca, is another classic, well-loved dessert. The word refers not to rice but to a type of baking that requires very high heat at the top with low heat at the bottom, which gives bibingkas their characteristic caramelized tops. Since most people in the rural areas in the Philippines do not have ovens, many local bibingka makers form a makeshift oven. The bibingka is baked in a pan lined with banana leaf over a low fire, covered with a metal sheet with burning bunot [coconut husk], wood, pili shells, or hot coals heaped on top. This method defines the concept of bibingka.

In the restaurant, we use the top rack of a convection oven to bake our bibingka. The most efficient method I've seen is that of Glenda Rosales-Barretto. Outside her Oyster Bar restaurant in the Greenbelt section of Makati, Manila, she has an oven with several individual drawers that can bake one bibingka to order without heating the others. Served straight from the oven with a square of melting butter in the middle and topped with grated coconut, nothing can compare to Glenda's bibingka and puto bumbong (page 67).

Probably the most traditional bibingka that I have known is the biko, whole grain sweet rice cooked with coconut milk and anise-flavored sugar, then topped with a brown sugar and coconut milk mixture and finished by baking at high heat to caramelize the topping. It is conjectured that the most popular form of bibingka in the Manila area, bibingka sa galapong, which is based on a soaked, ground rice batter, was invented by an enterprising woman in Pampanga in the 1940s or 50s.

In the past, markets in the Philippines had stone grinders that produced galapong for bibingka and puto. Unfortunately, these days stone grinders have been replaced by motorized grinders fitted with plastic basins to catch the galapong.

The galapong is key. Different grinds and different textures with varying amounts of water determine how the cake will be cooked and how it will come out. However, the integrity of your ingredients is what really defines bibingka. When I was developing the bibingka for the restaurant, I realized that a good bibingka galapong has to taste of delicious rice. After going through batches of different rice, I settled on Japanese Nishiki short-grain rice because its flavor was delicate and its texture bridged that of sticky and regular rice.

Bibingka with salted duck egg.

BIBINGKA

This is the recipe that many of our customers have been waiting for. The bibingka's biggest following is, surprisingly, our Ukrainian and Russian customers who come regularly on the weekends and order them as appetizers.

I experimented with this recipe until I found the rice that suited my taste. I love Nishiki (short-grain rice) for this recipe, but other types such as jasmine rice will work as well. The bibingka should amplify the nuanced flavors of rice. Experiment by mixing black rice with the white rice or changing the flavorings from sweet to savory. Instead of cheese and sugar, Romy sometimes makes variations using leeks, mushrooms, and bits of pork tocino.

If you don't have the specified pan size, line giant or regular muffin tins with banana leaves and use those, reducing the baking time slightly. They are great served this way at cocktail parties.

MAKES FOUR 6-INCH CAKES TO SERVE 4

Galapong (rice batter):

1³⁄₄ cups short-grain rice

Bibingka:

Softened unsalted butter for the pie shells
Four 6-inch banana leaf rounds to line the pans

1¹⁄₄ cups all-purpose flour
¹⁄₄ cup plus 4 teaspoons sugar
1 tablespoon baking powder
¹⁄₂ teaspoon salt
1¹⁄₂ cups galapong
4 eggs, separated
³⁄₄ cup coconut milk
¹⁄₄ cup whole milk
1 salted duck egg, quartered (optional)
¹⁄₂ cup grated Gouda cheese
¹⁄₂ cup crumbled feta cheese
4 tablespoons unsalted butter, melted, for brushing
¹⁄₂ cup freshly grated coconut

1. For the galapong, rinse the rice under cold running water, drain, and place in a medium bowl with cold water to cover. Refrigerate overnight. Drain and rinse again, then drain in a colander for 30 minutes. Transfer to a food processor and process until the mixture is finely ground, about 1 minute, scraping the sides of the processor as needed. Work through a coarse sieve. Return the solids that did not go through the sieve to the food processor and process again, then work again through the sieve. You should have about 1¹⁄₂ cups galapong.

2. For the bibingka, preheat the oven to 450° F. Brush four 6-inch pie or tart shells with softened butter and line with banana leaf rounds.

3. Sift together the flour, ¹⁄₄ cup sugar, baking powder, and salt into a large bowl. Whisk in the galapong and make a well in the center. With a whisk, beat the egg yolks, coconut milk, and milk in a separate bowl. Pour into the well and with a rubber spatula mix slowly until smooth.

4. In the clean bowl of an electric mixer fitted with the whisk attachment, beat the egg whites until stiff but not dry. Fold the whites into the galapong mixture.

5. Divide the mixture among the lined pans. If you're using the duck eggs, nestle a quarter into the middle of each cake. Sprinkle each cake with 2 tablespoons of the Gouda, followed by 2 tablespoons of the feta, and finally 1 teaspoon of the sugar.

6. Set the cakes on the top rack of the oven and bake until firm and set and lightly browned on top, about 20 minutes. If the bibingka are set but not browned, preheat the broiler and broil them about 6 inches from the heat source, watching carefully, until bubbly and lightly browned, about 3 minutes.

7. Brush the bibingka with the melted butter while still warm. Unmold each bibingka onto a serving plate. Serve with the grated coconut.

CASSAVA BIBINGKA

This is the easiest bibingka recipe to make, and it is simply delicious. It should have the consistency of a firm custard. One variation is to add sliced jackfruit and a little bit of jackfruit syrup into the batter. Some people actually stuff the batter with chunks of cheddar cheese. The best cassava bibingka I have ever tasted in the Philippines was the one that Teresing Mendesona's cook in Cebu prepared for us, which used yellow cassava instead of white.

SERVES 10 TO 12

Bibingka:
2   large sections of banana leaf, for the pan
3   large eggs
4   large egg yolks
1½ cups sugar
2   tablespoons unsalted butter, melted
1   cup grated young coconut
4   cups grated frozen cassava, rinsed and squeezed dry
2   cups coconut milk
½   cup grated Gouda cheese

Topping:
1   cup dark brown sugar
¼   cup coconut milk
1   vanilla bean, split lengthwise, pulp scraped

1. Preheat the oven to 350° F. Line a 9-by-13-inch baking dish with a double layer of banana leaves.

2. In a large bowl, beat the eggs and yolks with the sugar until light and lemon-colored. Stir in the butter, coconut, cassava, and coconut milk. Mix well and pour into the prepared baking dish. Sprinkle with the cheese and bake until firm, about 25 minutes.

3. Meanwhile, for the topping, in a small saucepan over medium-low heat, combine the brown sugar, coconut milk, and vanilla bean pod and pulp. Cook, stirring often, until

the sugar has dissolved, 5 to 7 minutes. Take the pan from the heat, cover, and set aside until ready to use. Remove the vanilla pod before using.

4. Preheat the broiler. Reheat the brown sugar topping briefly if it has hardened, and pour it over the finished bibingka, spreading it evenly with a rubber spatula. Watching carefully, broil 6 inches from the heat element, turning the pan halfway through, until bubbly and crisp, 3 to 5 minutes. Serve warm or cold.

The Origin of Bibingka

No one really knows where the bibingka came from. We do know that there are sweet cakes in Goa called bibinca (or bebinca), and the term was also used for similar variations of the dessert in other Portuguese colonies such as Timor and Macau. The Goan dessert is described as a cake made by baking a batter of rice, sugar, and coconut milk, layer by layer, between spoonfuls of ghee. There are similarities to the Filipino bibingka in that the heat that cooks it comes from the top, not the bottom.

The Goan layered rice cake resembles the Indonesian and Malaysian dessert lapis legit or spekkoek, a Dutch term which, oddly, means "bacon cake." The Spanish, Portuguese, and Dutch colonizers of Southeast Asia were constantly sending ships back and forth, and Manila was a major port for trade and a melting pot of cultures, goods, and people.

My personal theory is that bibingka in the Philippines is a homegrown product, as rice and coconuts traditionally have been the main source of food and livelihood there. Bibingkas and countless variations of rice cakes are found everywhere in the Philippines. The term might have been applied to these Filipino cakes by Portuguese traders, who noted similarities to the bibinca of their colonies.

No matter where the term bibingka comes from, these native cakes are an integral part of our heritage and one cannot think of Philippine foodways without the bibingka.

Puto

Puto is the term for a class of rice cakes and their cooking method, steaming. Puto are usually round, but can vary greatly in size. Puto is one of the most challenging native dishes to make—I cringe if we are asked to do it at the restaurant. The big round puto (three to four feet in diameter or bigger), which we found in Pila, Laguna, was made with galapong [soaked ground rice], allowed to naturally ferment overnight and then mixed with ligia [lye water], wrapped in cheesecloth, and steamed. A few minutes before the cake was fully cooked, grated cheddar cheese was sprinkled on top.

Many Filipinos have resorted to making puto from a box, but those don't compare to the real thing. Even in the Philippines, good puto is hard to find. First of all, the type of rice used is critical. But what matters the most in making puto is the nuanced proportion of rice to water and the precise degree of fineness required for each galapong. One woman in Bulakan would look at a steady mass of galapong coming out of her grinder and sprinkle in a few drops of water now and then depending on the consistency she was getting. I had never seen puto galapong before and noticed how different it was from the bibingka galapong, which has more water in it. The puto galapong was finer, like thick whipped sour cream. Just looking at the texture told me exactly how that puto would taste and feel in my mouth.

Good puto must rise and become fluffy while maintaining its solid rice texture. Leavening methods vary from natural fermentation to using tuba [naturally fermented coconut sap], yeast, or baking powder. I have read accounts of people touting their secret family "lavadura," a sourdough starter-like mixture using ground rice (and probably flour), which is kept alive for years.

The most interesting method I saw was in Barrio Maronquillo, Bulakan, where Fely de Leon, a relative of our friend Hector Fernandez, would add five or six coconut husks to her galapong. She used equal weights of rice and sugar, let the galapong sit overnight, then added the cleaned coconut husks and let it rise again. As soon as it had risen, she removed the husks, added baking powder, and steamed the puto in four-inch rings lined with stretch cotton fabric. She sells the slim round cakes six in a batch, beautifully wrapped in very young banana leaves.

A major aspect of successful puto-making is the art of steaming. One needs to know the batter so well that you can accurately gauge how long it will take to steam. Lift the cover prematurely and all the heat escapes—you may as well start over. On the other hand, condensation accumulating under the cover can make the puto watery. Some experts prescribe sealing the steamer with towels and cheesecloth to maximize the steam and then, when the puto is nearly done, lifting the cover to drain the condensation and covering it again for the finishing touch.

Puto is so difficult to make that even famous puto makers almost invariably share their recipes, knowing that only those who live with their batter and steamer can do what they do so easily. Most great puto recipes are, indeed, passed from one generation to another. In Digos, a town outside Davao City in Mindanao, Mer's Food and Delicacies carries, in my opinion, the most delicious and authentic white puto one can hope to find. The late Mer, Gumercinda Sagolili-Cago, inherited the puto recipe from her mother, Antonina-Gaviola Sagolili, and her children now run the successful company.

Puto varies regionally. The most famous Visayan puto is from Manapla, north of Bacolod. Steamed in banana leaves, it is white, fluffy, soft, and moist. In Ilocos Sur, the putong Vigan are delicate little rice and coconut milk balls that melt in your mouth. In and around Manila, one can find ube [purple yam] and pandan [screwpine leaf] puto, compact, buttery muffins of rice heaven. Putong Pulo from Valenzuela, Bulakan, and Puto Binan from Binan, Laguna, are also famous and craved for by Filipinos abroad. Even the Chinese have a version of puto: lanson, which are white and sweet with an interesting texture, about an inch and a half high, steamed in big slabs and brushed with oil to prevent them from sticking. In New York's Chinatown, this puto is sold to Filipinos in huge quantities.

During my last trip to the Philippines the main revelations were the puto bumbong steamed in a bamboo tube and the cassava puto steamed in a funnel (page 163). Puto bumbong is made from malagkit and a small amount of pirurutong [black rice]. After soaking, the dough is wrapped in cheesecloth and put under weights. Then a few tablespoons are packed into a bamboo tube greased with coconut oil, and steamed. Puto bumbong must be eaten as soon as it is steamed. In Manila, on the patio outside her Makati Oyster Bar, Glenda Barretto serves the best puto bumbong. The hot steaming violet rolls are served with a chunk of soft butter and grated panocha [solid muscovado sugar]. Unfortunately, most commercially sold puto bumbong are no longer authentic, as many have replaced the pirurutong, an endangered species of rice, with purple yam flour.

In my readings of K. T. Achaya, author of *Indian Food: A Historical Companion*, I discovered the possibility that puto may have actually come from Kerala, India. Even the term is, for all purposes, the same—*puttu*—and his description of a Keralite breakfast of "rice grits and coconut shreds" layered in a bamboo tube and steamed recalls the puto bumbong method.

Opposite: puto. Above: making puto in Pila, Laguna. Below: pandan [screw pine] puto.

Suman

Among the kakanin of the Philippines, the suman most probably predates all other rice cakes. It is the most primitive and is prepared the most simply, without the soaking, grinding, and leavening used for bibingka and puto. *Suman* refers to any cake—of rice, grain, and/or roots—wrapped in banana or coconut leaves and boiled. Suman are boiled because the grains are, for the most part, used whole rather than ground. The most popular suman in the Philippines are the suman sa ibus (ibus means coconut leaves, and these are formed into a tube that contains the suman) and suman sa ligia [suman cooked with lye water].

It is possible that the suman originated from the concept of the puso [heart], a triangular weave of leaves used to hold and cook rice so that it was easily transportable. I was told that farmers would tie the puso around their waists to keep the meal convenient as they worked. Antonio Pigafetta, who was with Ferdinand Magellan when he discovered the Philippines in 1521, wrote of their first encounter with food offered to them by the natives, which most likely included the suman.

Most suman variations contain sticky rice, with the second largest contingent based on cassava. In Cebu and Dumaguete, millet is used for the suman called budbud kabog. In Irosin, Sorsogon, I learned of a recipe for suman sa kalabasa—squash mixed with sticky rice.

Suman come in countless shapes and sizes. The most common is the slim, rectangular shape of the suman sa ibus. Forming the coconut leaf into a suman container is a skilled art that only comes with practice. One deftly separates a part of the leaf from the midrib. The leaf is then wrapped around the rib to form a tube, into which the mixture of rice, coconut milk, salt, and sometimes anise is poured. The tube is sealed, its ends tied to those of other suman in a bunch, and the packages boiled for at least an hour and a half.

I have always associated the suman sa ibus with Iba, because my grandparents brought us neatly tied bunches of them as pasalubong [travel gifts] whenever they visited in Manila. At first we ate the suman for breakfast with mangoes, but if they lingered for a few days, then they would be fried in butter until they developed a crunchy crust and we would eat them dipped in lots of sugar.

SUMAN SA LIGIA

I love this recipe because I associate it with my father, Dr. Augusto Besa, an orthopedic surgeon and one of the kindest and most generous doctors in the Philippines. He set up a clinic in the first floor of our home in the Malate district of Manila, where he saw dozens of patients who regularly implored him to accept payment in kind. In exchange for fixing broken bones, we constantly received live chickens and all manner of native delicacies. My favorite patient was Mrs. Bourbon—I would always await her visit and the delectable suman sa ligia, which she brought without fail.

When we opened Cendrillon, this suman was immediately put on our brunch menu. It is a very simple recipe—all it requires is soaking sticky or glutinous rice, then draining it and mixing it with lye water. The use of lye water was always something of a curiosity for me. It is available in Chinatown stores in bottles, and safety precautions should be taken when handling it. The rural folk in the Philippines make lye water by soaking coal embers and straining the water. Gilda Cordero-Fernando, in her book *Philippine Food and Life*, says that one method was to put the water in a cracked earthen jar, letting it drip through the crack and catching the lye water underneath the jar.

MAKES ABOUT 16 SUMAN

2   cups short-grain sticky or glutinous rice
One 1-pound package banana leaves
2   tablespoons lye water (potassium carbonate
      and sodium bicarbonate solution)
Butter, for serving
Brown sugar, preferably muscovado, for serving
Ripe mangoes, for serving

1. Rinse the rice well, then place in a bowl and cover with water. Cover with plastic wrap and refrigerate overnight. The next day, drain the rice.

2. Mix the rice with the lye thoroughly and soak for 15 minutes—the rice will turn light yellow. Rinse, drain, and soak again in fresh water.

3. Clean the banana leaf sections by wiping them on both sides with a damp paper towel. Pass them over a medium flame on both sides to make them more pliable. Take the banana leaves and cut out sixteen 10-by-12-inch sections and sixteen 4-by-5-inch sections, removing the tough rib at the top of each banana leaf. You may want to cut out a couple extra in case of breakage. Cut another leaf crosswise into ¼-inch strips to use for tying the suman—you'll need to tie two or three of them together to make them long enough to fit around the suman bundles, so make about 25 strips. (Alternatively you can use kitchen twine.)

4. Place a large banana leaf section horizontally on your work surface. Place a smaller leaf section centered horizontally over the bottom of the larger leaf. Place 4 tablespoons of rice in the middle of the smaller leaf, flatten, and wrap by folding the leaf away from you and rolling, making sure that the rice is snug. Fold the two long ends over and set down, seam side down. Repeat until all the rice is used up. Using the banana leaf strips (or kitchen twine), stack the suman in pairs, with the folded ends facing in toward each other, and tie the suman together.

5. Bring a large pot of water to a boil. Add the suman, cover, reduce the heat, and cook until the rice is so sticky that it holds together, about 90 minutes.

6. The suman can be stored in the refrigerator for up to a week. Steam to reheat.

Opposite: suman sa Ibos, wrapped in coconut leaves. Below: suman sa ligia, wrapped in banana leaves.

Overleaf, clockwise from top left: siniguelas [Spanish plum], fish at market, marang, kamias, chicharron, sugpo [prawns], suman, lasonata, talangka crabs, banana heart, tomatoes, balimbing [star fruit].

chapter 3

From top to bottom: achuete, empanada, tamales, chiffon [angel food] cake. Opposite: making pancit in Malabon.

While Filipinos worked and tilled the soil, the main plot of the colonial political drama was propelled by the love-hate relationship between the Spanish and the Chinese. Eventually the Filipinos rebelled and cast off the oppressive yoke of the Spanish masters.

The processes by which China and Spain flavored Filipino cooking were vastly different. The Chinese came to the Philippines as traders, looking for wealth and new opportunities, settling as merchants in every town and village, starting from the bottom of the social ladder and working their way up. They had access to goods from China, and when they accumulated enough capital they were able to assimilate into every social stratum and economic class of the Philippines. There was no class status attached to the Chinese food available at the restaurants, called panciterias, of Chinatown. Everyone, including the Spanish elite who were the targeted clientele of the panciterias, ate Chinese food.

The term *panciteria* is a Hispanized version of the Filipino word *pancit* [noodle]. In fact, this process of giving essentially Chinese foods Spanish names to appeal to the Spanish is the genesis of comidas China—Chinese food reimagined as Spanish food. Escabeche (page 103), agri e dulce [sweet and sour fish], almondigas [pork balls in broth with soft noodles], camaron rebosado [battered deep-fried shrimp], and morisqueta tostada [fried rice] are all Chinese dishes, most likely renamed by savvy restaurateurs.

The Spanish came to the Philippines as colonizers. Spanish dishes became the food of the elite, fiesta food, rich with expensive ingredients like olive oil, chorizo, and ham. Whereas Chinese food became a part of the Filipino way of eating, as Ray Sokolov, in his book *Why We Eat What We Eat* explains, much of the food in the Philippines that now carries a Spanish name is simply native cuisine that the Spanish renamed, while other dishes are Filipino preparations of ingredients brought by the galleons from Mexico.

In the mid-twentieth century, American influence entered the scene in the form of a questionable devotion to convenience foods, a vague mission to increase the healthfulness of Filipino food, and a passion for 1950s-era Betty Crocker–style desserts. At the culinary crossroads of Chinese, Spanish, and American foods, the Filipinos took what they liked and made it their own.

The Chinese-Spanish Connection

Early historical documents show that the Chinese started coming to the Philippines around the tenth century, primarily to trade. However, it was not until the Spaniards arrived that the Chinese came and settled in increasing numbers. The galleon trade and the lure of Mexican silver brought Chinese junks to Manila harbor carrying silks, ivory combs, gold, and jade, which were highly valued in Europe.

A love-hate relationship between the Spaniards and the Chinese developed through the years. With the native islanders relegated to farming, the Chinese became the merchant class, providing goods to the colony. They also possessed the craftsmanship skills needed to build and fortify Intramuros, the walled city of Manila. As the Chinese community in Manila grew in size and wealth during the sixteenth century, the Spaniards became suspicious of the Chinese and felt vulnerable to rebellion. To maintain their control, the Spanish authorities created the Parian (from the Chinese word *palien,* meaning organization), an area outside the walls of the Intramuros, and forced the Chinese to live and do their business there. But the Spanish were so dependent on Chinese goods and services that they assigned one gate in the wall as the Parian gate, through which Chinese merchants could pass once a week to do business with the city.

As more Chinese arrived in Manila, the Parian became overcrowded. To resolve this problem, the Spanish established another community outside Intramuros called Binondo, where the Chinese could resettle. Only those willing to convert to Christianity and marry local Filipino women were allowed to live in Binondo. Thus a new class of Chinese-Filipino mestizos grew out of these intermarriages, eventually paving the way for Chinese assimilation into Filipino society.

These attempts at assimilation did not prevent a series of violent conflicts with the Spanish authorities. With the help of the native population, the Spanish massacred 30,000 Chinese in 1603 and 20,000 in 1639. Many Chinese attempted to shield themselves from further oppression by converting to Christianity. At baptism, many Chinese assumed the Spanish or Filipino name of their ninong [baptismal sponsor or godfather].

The Chinese Influence

Ask a Filipino to name typical Filipino dishes and he or she will invariably list pancit and lumpia. I encounter dumbfounded looks when I mention that these are Chinese in origin. Much of Filipino home cooking traces its roots to Chinese ingredients, cooking methods, and seasoning. The influence of the Chinese came with the traders who brought noodles, ducks, duck eggs, soy sauce, soybeans, sausages, and other affordable, accessible foods that could be eaten on a daily basis.

Since the sixteenth century, poverty and social upheaval in mainland China have caused a massive influx of Fujianese and Cantonese into the Philippines. As Chinese merchants and traders settled throughout the country establishing small businesses, they intermarried with Filipino women. It was a common practice among the Chinese who came to the Philippines to take a Filipino wife to gain acceptance within the community while maintaining a family in China. Today most Filipinos have Chinese blood in their veins and most Filipino cooking bears the traces of this legacy.

Whenever I enter a room where cigarette smoke and the smell of frying oil hangs heavy in the air, it brings me back to the panciterias of downtown Manila. During the 1950s and 60s, Ambrose Chiu, my uncle Gaudencio Besa's best friend, was a stockholder and corporate officer of Panciteria Moderna, which provided my earliest exposure to Chinese food and culture. My mother recalls the dishes there, among them nido [bird's nest] soup, sweet and sour pork, prawn and ham coated in batter and fried, steamed apahap [sea bass] fish in white sauce or fried with sweet and sour sauce (similar to escabeche), fried young pigeons served with crunchy kropec [shrimp-flavored crackers], fried rice, and different varieties of Chinese pancit.

The influence of Chinese cooking in the Philippines is primarily Fujianese-Cantonese. While the stir-fried, noodle-based Cantonese cuisine is easier to trace to its Chinese origins, Fujianese influences are more subtle. Fujianese cuisine is reliant on pork (and pork lard), as the area was very poor and mountainous and did not have enough land to produce vegetable oil.

Pancit

Above: garlic chives. Panciteria in Manila (left), yellow noodles (right). Opposite: pancit luglug.

The word *pancit* (or *pansit*) comes from the Hokkien words *pian-e-sit*, meaning something that is conveniently cooked. How this food of convenience came to mean only noodles is lost in the mix of history. What is more salient is that Filipinos saw the potential of the noodle, turning it into dishes made with ingredients readily available to them. The pancit Malabon, named after a fishing port north of Manila, is made with rice noodles topped with oysters, squid, and mussels. Inland towns tend to favor pancit luglug, which are rice noodles with a shrimp juice and ground pork sauce, garnished with fried garlic, fried tofu, hard-boiled egg, crushed chicharron, smoked fish, chopped scallions, and boiled shrimp.

Filipinos use a variety of noodles made from egg [Canton], rice [bihon], mung bean [sotanghon], wheat [misua], and whole wheat [miki]. They are usually sautéed with vegetables, as in pancit guisado and pancit bihon.

PANCIT LUGLUG

This is the most universally loved merienda item for Filipinos wherever they may be. The term *luglug* is Tagalog for immersing anything in water. It describes the process of cooking the rice noodles in boiling water in a sieve or strainer, allowing the cook to accurately gauge whether the noodles are done. This dish is oftentimes called pancit palabok, which refers to the shrimp juice-achuete sauce that is spread on top of the steaming hot noodles before it is garnished.

SERVES 4 TO 6

Sauce:

½   pound large shrimp with heads and shells
2   tablespoons canola oil
1   medium onion, diced
4   garlic cloves, minced
1   pound ground pork
1   tablespoon achuete seeds soaked in ½ cup hot water for 20 minutes and drained
2   tablespoons sweet potato starch or cornstarch mixed with ¼ cup cold water
1½   tablespoons fish sauce, or to taste
¼   teaspoon freshly ground black pepper, or to taste

1 pound dry thick tubular rice noodles, soaked in warm water for 15 minutes

Garnishes:

½   cup canola oil
6   garlic cloves, peeled and sliced
¾   cup ½-inch pieces firm tofu (about 6 ounces), patted dry
12   large shrimp, peeled and deveined
2   hard-boiled eggs, shelled and cut into wedges
½   cup flaked smoked trout
4   scallions, chopped
Lime or lemon wedges, for serving
Fish sauce, for serving

1. For the shrimp juice, cut the heads off the shrimp and peel off the shells. Place the heads and shells in a food processor with 1 cup water. Process until the heads and shells have broken down. Transfer to a bowl, cover with plastic, and refrigerate for 1 hour. Strain through a fine-mesh strainer, pressing down on the solids to remove all the juice. Cover and refrigerate until ready to use. Coarsely chop the shrimp bodies and set aside.

2. To prepare the sauce, warm the oil in a large skillet or wok over medium heat. Add the onions and garlic and sauté for about 3 minutes, until softened. Add the pork and cook until it turns white, about 5 minutes. Add the shrimp juice, achuete water, and sweet potato starch mixture. Cook, stirring, until thickened, about 3 minutes. Add the shrimp and cook for 3 minutes, or until they turn pink. Add the fish sauce and black pepper. Taste and add additional fish sauce and black pepper if needed. Set the sauce aside while you prepare the garnishes.

3. To prepare the garnishes, in a small nonstick skillet over low heat, warm the oil. Add the garlic slices and cook over low heat until lightly browned, about 5 minutes. Use a slotted spoon to transfer the garlic to a paper towel-lined plate. Raise the heat to medium-high and add the tofu squares. Fry for about 5 minutes, or until lightly browned and crisp on all sides. Use a slotted spoon to transfer the tofu to a paper towel-lined plate. Bring a large saucepan of water to a boil, add the shrimp, and cook until they turn pink and are cooked through, 3 to 5 minutes.

4. Meanwhile, bring a large pot of water to a boil, add the rice noodles, and cook until softened, about 5 minutes, depending on the size of the noodles. Drain.

5. To serve, place the noodles in a serving bowl. Briefly reheat the sauce and pour it over the noodles. Arrange the garnishes on top and serve with the lime wedges and fish sauce on the side.

Above: tinapa [smoked, dried fish]. Achuete seeds. Opposite: making sauce for pancit Malabon.

PANCIT MALABON

This recipe was given to us by our dear friend and accomplished cook Reggie Aguinaldo.

SERVES 4 TO 6

Sauce:
2 tablespoons canola oil
1 small garlic clove, peeled and minced
1½ cups shrimp juice (page 87)
2 tablespoons all-purpose flour
1 tablespoon achuete seeds, soaked in ½ cup water for 20 minutes
¼ teaspoon salt, or to taste
¼ teaspoon freshly ground black pepper, or to taste
1 tablespoon fish sauce, or to taste

Pancit:
1 pound dry thick tubular rice noodles, soaked in warm water for 15 minutes
1 cup chopped fresh pechay or bok choy, boiled for 30 seconds and drained
1 cup small shrimp, peeled and deveined, boiled until light pink (about 3 minutes)
1 cup shucked oysters, gently simmered with their liquor until their edges curl, about 3 minutes
1 cup squid, cut into 1-inch pieces and sautéed in 1 tablespoon canola oil until firm, 3 to 5 minutes
½ cup flaked smoked tinapa, trout, or mackerel
½ cup crushed fried pork rind (chicharron)
3 cloves fried garlic (recipe at left)
2 scallions, thinly sliced
½ cup chopped wansoy or cilantro
2 hard-boiled eggs, sliced
6 kalamansi or other limes, halved and seeded
¼ cup fish sauce
2 tablespoons kalamansi or regular lime juice

FRIED GARLIC

This is one of our favorite garnishes, and we also like to use it as a garnish for our fresh lumpia dishes.

½ cup olive oil
6 garlic cloves, thinly sliced

Heat the oil in a small skillet over low heat. Add the garlic and fry until nicely browned, about 5 minutes. Use a slotted spoon to transfer the garlic to a paper towel–lined plate. Reserve the oil and use it in place of your usual oil to add flavor to sautéed dishes and the like. Romy likes to use the oil to baste roast suckling pig.

1. For the sauce, in a medium saucepan over medium-high heat, warm the oil. Add the garlic and cook, stirring, until fragrant, about 1 minute.

2. In a small bowl, whisk together the shrimp juice and flour until mostly smooth. Add this mixture to the saucepan with the garlic. Cook over medium-high heat, whisking, until slightly thickened and smooth, 3 to 5 minutes.

3. Press the achuete seeds in the water until the water turns deep red. Discard the seeds and add the water to the saucepan. Cook, stirring, until the sauce is thick enough to coat the back of a spoon, about 5 minutes. Add the salt, pepper, and fish sauce. Taste and add more salt, pepper, or fish sauce if needed. The sauce can be made a day in advance. Store in a tightly sealed container and refrigerate until ready to use. Reheat over low heat to serve.

4. For the pancit, bring a large pot of salted water to a boil. Add the noodles and cook until softened, about 5 minutes, depending on the thickness of the noodles. Drain and transfer to a large bowl. Pour about a third of the sauce over the noodles. Add about ⅔ cup of the blanched penchay to the noodles. Reserve a few of the cooked shrimp, oysters, squid, tinapa, and chicharron for garnish. Add the rest to the noodles and gently stir. Transfer to a serving platter and pour the remaining sauce over all. Garnish with the remaining penchay and the reserved seafood. Sprinkle the fried garlic, scallions, and wonsoy on top. Arrange the sliced eggs over the top and place kalamansi halves around the sides of the platter. Serve with the fish sauce, mixed with kalamansi juice, on the side.

Pancit Memories

I asked our friend Danny Maclan to give us his memories on his hometown's most famous dish:

I remember my mom preparing the pancit using a buslo [sieve] with a long handle. She would soak the noodles in cold water, then when visitors arrived, she would dip the noodles in boiling water. The boiling time was critical—too long and the pancit were "malabsa" [overcooked], too short, and "matigas ang loob ng pancit" [too hard]. The warm pancit noodles were made tasty with chicharron, tinapa [smoked milkfish], squid, sugpo [prawns], boiled egg, and talaba [oyster].

Making Pancit Malabon. Opposite: hibe [dried shrimp].

TATA SING'S BAM-I

Mona and Carlos Lu stress that you seek out the specified brands of noodles if at all possible. Other pancit Canton noodles, they say, taste medicinal, and other mung bean vermicelli tend to disintegrate when stir-fried.

SERVES 8

Noodles:

1 package (250 grams) Longkou brand vermicelli mung bean noodles, halved lengthwise
1 package (8 ounces) Excellent brand Pancit Canton noodles

Broth:

2 whole, bone-in chicken breasts, (about 2 pounds)
2 teaspoons salt

Sahog:

1/3 cup canola oil
4 Chinese sausages, thinly sliced diagonally
1 large onion, diced
8 garlic cloves, peeled and finely chopped
6 dried shiitake mushrooms, soaked in warm water for 1 hour, drained, and thinly sliced
3 large carrots, thinly sliced diagonally
1 medium head green cabbage, halved, cored, and sliced crosswise 1/2-inch thick
1 tablespoon salt
3/4 teaspoon freshly ground black pepper
2 tablespoons soy sauce, plus additional to taste
1 bunch scallions, sliced

Lemon wedges, for serving

1. Place the vermicelli noodles in a large bowl and cover with hot water. Let soak for 30 minutes, then drain.

2. Meanwhile, to make the chicken stock, place the chicken breast in a large pot and add 8 to 10 cups water (just enough to cover the chicken) and 2 teaspoons salt.

Bring the liquid to a boil over high heat, then reduce the heat and simmer until the chicken is cooked through, 15 to 20 minutes. Transfer the chicken to a plate to cool. When the chicken is cool enough to handle, shred into bite-size pieces and set aside.

3. Strain the broth through a fine-mesh strainer, and return to the pot over low heat. Continue to keep at a steady simmer while you cook the sahong.

4. Heat the oil in a wok over medium-high heat. Add the sausage and cook, stirring, for 3 minutes, or until lightly browned. Add the onion and garlic and sauté for 2 minutes, until softened.

5. Add the mushrooms, carrots, and ½ cup chicken broth and cook until the carrots are softened but still crisp, about 2 minutes.

6. Add the cabbage and cook for 2 minutes, until the cabbage has softened slightly. Add the shredded chicken, salt, and ground pepper and cook just to warm through, 3 to 5 minutes. Set the sahog aside. Cover and keep warm.

7. Increase the heat under the broth and bring it to a boil. Add the Pancit Canton noodles and cook until tender but al dente, about 2 minutes. Add the sahog and mix with the noodles. Continue cooking on medium-high until the broth is absorbed by the noodles. Season with soy sauce. Gently toss in half of the chopped scallions. Taste and adjust the seasoning, if necessary. Garnish with the remaining scallions, and serve with lemon wedges.

A Classic Noodle Dish from Cebu

Mona and Carlos Lu, along with their children, have been regulars of the restaurant since we opened in 1995. When Mona Lu came to the United States from Manila in 1989, her mother, Tata Sing (Resing Luyao Corcuera), followed, as Mona was expecting her second child at the time. Between Tata Sing and Yaya (Lourdes Ebon), Mona's trusted nanny and cook, a great collaboration of minds and cooking talent ensued. Tata Sing taught this classic Cebuano noodle dish to Yaya.

Yaya helped raised Mona's three children in Connecticut, and has proven to be a wonderful cook. Mona discovered that Yaya's father, Mang Demit (short for Demetrio), was a famous cook who was hired from town to town when fiestas were celebrated in Antique, Panay. These days, Yaya is constantly requested by Mona's friends to cook their favorite Filipino dishes, but Tata Sing's Bam-i is the dish that has made her famous. Bam-i is a Visayan derivation of the Hokkien words *ba*, which means meat, and *mee*, noodles. According to Mona, when the children's friends visit their home in Greenwich, they refuse to go home without a baon, or doggy bag, of leftover Bam-i.

Pancit Bihon

The recipe for this favorite merienda item is exactly the same as that for bam-i, except that instead of using pancit Canton noodles and mung bean vermicelli, equal weights of rice noodles or rice vermicelli [bihon] are used. One of our regular customers, Rose Megur, a Cebuana, says she loves to add hibe or dried shrimp to her bam-i and pancit bihon. Soak the dried shrimp in water for several hours and sauté them with garlic, onion, and Chinese sausage.

Lumpia

Lumpia are spring rolls, either deep-fried or fresh. Deep-fried lumpia filled with ground pork are called lumpia Shanghai (the pork filling in all probability generated its Chinese nomenclature). Other versions filled with a combination of vegetables (usually cabbage, carrots, green beans, and sometimes bean sprouts) and flavored with pork and shrimp are generically called lumpia. Lumpia Shanghai are served with a sweet and sour dipping sauce, while other lumpia are dipped in vinegar and minced garlic, sometimes spiked with ground black pepper or chopped chiles.

Fresh lumpia, or lumpia sariwa, are usually served during fiestas or special occasions, as they are more labor-intensive to prepare. A good lumpia sariwa must be wrapped with a freshly made, delicate crêpe made with flour (or cornstarch), water, and eggs (some recipes call for duck eggs, which make the wrapper more resilient). The filling is a combination of sautéed vegetables such as cabbage, carrots, snow peas, or green beans flavored with shrimp, pork pieces, shrimp juice, and fish sauce. In the Visayas, fresh lumpia is a luxury item filled with ubod, fresh hearts of coconut— an expensive delicacy (see Lumpia Ubod, page 181). The traditional sauce for lumpia sariwa is a sweet and salty sauce topped with minced fresh garlic and ground peanuts.

Creative cooks have always gone beyond the traditional fillings and sauces. I have tasted spring rolls filled with bangus [milkfish], mushrooms, and crabmeat in Manila cafés and bistros. At Cendrillon, we have served fresh lumpia filled with lobster, fresh bamboo shoots, seasonal vegetables from the green market such as ramps [wild leeks], and fresh mushrooms such as shiitakes, chanterelles, and morels. In place of the traditional soy, vinegar, sugar, and cornstarch sauce for fresh lumpia, we make a peanut-lemongrass-garlic sauce. When we serve a seafood lumpia (filled with shrimp, scallops, crab, or lobster), we use a talangka sauce made from the fat of tiny crabs. These miniature crabs are washed, brined, and squeezed for their fat.

Rolling lumpia in Pampanga. Opposite: fresh lumpia (recipe, page 206); far right: Making lumpia wrappers in Silay.

Rolling Lumpia

Rolling lumpia is a perfect group activity. Whenever our friends Reggie Aguinaldo and Stephen Young return home to the Philippines, they always look forward to the Chinese-style fresh lumpia that Stephen's mother, Mercedes Dee Young, prepares for the family. She arranges the fresh lumpia wrappers, sautéed filling, sauce, and garnishes on the table and lets everyone roll and season his or her own fresh lumpia roll.

LUMPIA SHANGHAI

No one can do these as well as Romy's brother, Danny Dorotan, who comes to the restaurant two or three times a week to help us. Our friend Marc Rakotomalala was so impressed with these spring rolls that he came in at 8 A.M. one morning to videotape Danny's technique. One secret is to remove as much moisture from the vegetables as possible by squeezing them with paper towels. The hardest part is rolling them into perfectly shaped rolls that will not break open when fried.

Just like many of the foreign-inspired dishes that are a part of the Filipino repertoire, this spring roll has nothing to do with Shanghai. The addition of jicama, mushrooms, and bean thread noodles to the ground pork makes it a more flavorful and lighter filling.

MAKES ABOUT 50 LUMPIA

Filling:

4 cups coarsely grated jicama (about 2 small jicama)

1 cup coarsely grated onion (about 2 medium onions)

2 medium carrots, coarsely grated

2 pounds ground pork

2 egg yolks

Half of a 250-gram package sotanghon (bean thread noodles), soaked in hot water for 30 minutes

$3/4$ cup tree ear mushrooms, soaked in hot water for 1 hour, drained, and finely sliced

1 teaspoon freshly ground black pepper

2 teaspoons salt

1 tablespoon sugar

About sixty-five 8-inch egg roll wrappers (you'll need a few extra in case of breakage)

Water or egg whites, to seal the wrappers

Canola oil, for frying

Pineapple Sweet and Sour Sauce (recipe follows)

1. For the filling, squeeze the jicama, onions, and carrots with your hands to remove excess water, then pat dry with paper towels to remove as much moisture as possible. Combine all the filling ingredients in a large bowl and toss well.

2. Cut 14 of the spring roll wrappers in quarters so they form 4 equal rectangles. Wrap them in a damp kitchen towel so they don't dry out. Place the whole wrappers in a separate damp kitchen towel.

3. Place one whole wrapper in front of you with a corner pointed toward you, like a diamond. Place one of the smaller squares in the middle of the wrapper and spoon 1 heaping tablespoon of filling onto the center of the small square. Lifting the corner pointing toward you, fold the wrapper over the filling, tucking the end underneath the edge of the smaller square. Fold the right and left sides over the filling. Use a pastry brush to dab the edges of the rolls with beaten egg white to seal, then finish rolling. Transfer the completed rolls to the baking sheet and keep covered with a damp kitchen towel to prevent them from drying out. If you're not frying the lumpia right away, freeze them and fry them straight from the freezer.

4. Fill a wide, heavy saucepan with 4 inches of oil. Place over medium-high heat and heat until the oil registers 350° F on a cooking thermometer, then fry about 4 lumpia at a time (don't crowd the pan), turning with a slotted spoon, until golden brown, 3 to 5 minutes. Transfer to a strainer to drain. Serve hot with the Pineapple Sweet and Sour Sauce.

PINEAPPLE SWEET AND SOUR SAUCE

MAKES ABOUT 2 CUPS

½ medium pineapple, peeled, cored, and minced
½ medium onion, minced (about ⅓ cup)
1 medium carrot, grated (about ½ cup)
1 tablespoon minced ginger
½ cup rice vinegar
½ cup pineapple juice
1 red birdseye chile, minced
¼ cup sugar
½ teaspoon salt
2 tablespoons cornstarch dissolved in 4 tablespoons water

Combine all the ingredients except the cornstarch mixture in a medium saucepan. Bring to a simmer over medium heat and simmer until the pineapple has softened, about 5 minutes. Slowly stir in the cornstarch mixture. Simmer, stirring, until the sauce coats the back of a metal spoon, about 5 minutes. Cool to room temperature before serving. The sauce can be made a day ahead, refrigerated, and brought to room temperature before serving.

AMY'S SPRING ROLLS

This is one of the most enduring recipes that my grandmother Nanay left us. I loved these spring rolls so much that when I was in grade school I used to pack them for lunch. When I came to the United States, I reconstructed the recipe from memory, and it has been on our restaurant menu from the day we opened.

MAKES ABOUT 24 SPRING ROLLS

Filling:

½	pound pork loin, with a little fat
½	small onion
1	celery stalk, cut into 3-inch pieces
¾	teaspoon salt
¾	teaspoon freshly ground black pepper
½	pound large, whole shrimp, unshelled
6	tablespoons canola oil
One	8-ounce package firm tofu, pressed (see Note)
½	cup finely chopped onion
4	garlic cloves, finely chopped
½	cup shredded green cabbage
½	cup julienned carrot
½	cup trimmed and julienned string beans
1	teaspoon fish sauce
½	cup julienned jicama

Assembly:

About thirty (8-inch) square spring roll wrappers
2   large egg yolks, beaten
Canola oil, for frying

Dipping Sauce:

1	cup rice vinegar
2-3	minced garlic cloves
1-2	thinly sliced fresh chiles, to taste

Tofu. Below: Amy's spring rolls. Opposite: shredded vegetables for lumpia filling.

1. The day before you want to assemble the spring rolls, make the filling: In a medium saucepan over high heat, bring 6 cups of water to a boil. Add the pork, onion half, celery, ½ teaspoon salt, and ½ teaspoon black pepper. Simmer until the pork is just cooked through, about 20 minutes. Transfer the pork to a plate and let cool. Pour the broth through a strainer set over a bowl and reserve the liquid. When the pork has cooled completely, slice it into cubes.

2. Cut the heads off the shrimp and peel off the shells. Place the heads and shells in a food processor with ½ cup water. Process until the heads and shells have broken down. Transfer to a bowl and cover with plastic. Refrigerate for 1 hour. Strain through a fine-mesh strainer, pressing down on the solids to remove all the juice. Cover and refrigerate until ready to use. Devein and julienne the shrimp bodies and set aside.

3. Heat 4 tablespoons of the oil in a deep skillet or wok over medium-high heat. Add the pork and cook, stirring often, until browned and crisp, about 5 minutes. Use a slotted spoon to transfer the pork to a paper towel–lined plate to drain.

4. Heat the oil in which you cooked the pork over medium-high heat, add the block of tofu, and sear until all sides are lightly browned and crisp, 2 to 3 minutes per side. Drain the tofu and pat dry with paper towels. Let cool, then slice the tofu into small cubes. Wipe the skillet with paper towels.

5. Heat the remaining 2 tablespoons oil in the skillet or wok over medium-high heat. Add the onion and garlic and sauté until slightly softened, about 2 minutes. Add the cabbage, carrot, and string beans, and sauté until slightly softened, about 2 minutes. Season with the remaining ¼ teaspoon salt and ¼ teaspoon pepper.

6. Pour in the reserved shrimp juice and pork broth and bring to a simmer. Add the fish sauce, pork, shrimp, tofu, and jicama. Cook about 3 more minutes, or until the shrimp are cooked through. Taste and adjust the seasoning, if necessary, and transfer to a bowl to cool. The filling will be very moist.

7. Once the filling has cooled, transfer it to a container and refrigerate for at least 1 hour or overnight.

8. The next day, to assemble the spring rolls, remove the filling from the refrigerator and drain the mixture through a fine-mesh strainer, pressing on the solids to remove as much moisture as possible.

9. Place all of the spring roll wrappers on a baking sheet and cover with a damp dish towel to prevent drying as you work. Transfer a stack of 6 wrappers to a clean work surface, and cut into equal quarters, making 24 squares. Return the squares to the baking sheet and cover with the towel.

10. Place one whole wrapper in front of you with a corner pointed toward you, like a diamond. Place one of the smaller squares in the middle of the wrapper and put 3 tablespoons of filling onto the center of the small square. Lifting the corner pointing toward you, fold the wrapper over the filling, tucking the end underneath the edge of the smaller square. Fold the right and left sides over the filling. Use a pastry brush to dab the edges of the rolls with beaten egg yolk to seal, then finish rolling. Transfer the completed spring rolls to the baking sheet and keep covered.

11. Fill a wide sauté pan over medium-high heat with at least 1 inch of oil and heat until hot but not smoking. The oil should register 365° F on a cooking thermometer. (If you don't have a frying or candy thermometer, sprinkle a few drops of water into the oil. When the water has sizzled away, the oil is ready.)

12. Fry the rolls in batches, to avoid overcrowding the pan. Cook, turning once, until golden brown, 3 to 4 minutes per side. Transfer the rolls to a paper towel–lined plate to drain. Fry all the batches, letting the oil come back up to temperature between batches.

13. In a bowl, combine the vinegar, garlic, and chiles and serve this dipping sauce with the hot rolls.

Note: To press the excess moisture from the tofu, place it between two inverted plates, put a heavy can on top, and let drain for 15 to 20 minutes, then pat dry.

Fresh Shrimp Juice

Shrimp juice and diced shrimp were in almost every vegetable dish I ate as a child in Manila. Fresh shrimp are easier to get on the islands than here in the United States. I remember the shock of once again tasting freshly caught suahe [small shrimp] in Iba, Zambales, that were stir-fried alive and jumping in the carajay. They were so sweet– the true flavor of shrimp, so unlike the taste of chlorine that is used to preserve frozen shrimp in the United States. Shrimp juice is the most delicious flavoring agent for Philippine-style sautéed vegetables. Even the most bland squashes like patola or bottleneck gourds become delicious if shrimp juice is added to them while cooking.

There are several ways of extracting shrimp juice. The traditional way is to mash the shrimp heads and tails in a big mortar and pestle and then soak them briefly in luke-warm water before straining and extracting the liquid. Others mash them and then boil the shells and heads very briefly in a small amount of water and strain the liquid. Of course, you could extract the juice in a food processor, as we describe in Amy's Spring Rolls recipe.

If you have access to very fresh shrimps with heads on, I would recommend that you make a big batch of shrimp juice and freeze it in small portions for future use.

The Pig

Drying chicharron [pork rinds].
Opposite: crispy pata [pork knuckle]
and lechon kawali [pork belly].

Next to fish, the pig is the most important and accessible source of food for Filipinos. It is not unusual in cities and towns outside Manila to find beef in the markets only once a week, but pork is always available as fresh meat or as pork preparations such as longaniza [sausages], tocino [cured pork], lechon [roast pork], and chicharron [cracklings]. Culinary influences from Spain and China (both prodigious pork eaters) and the absence of any religious taboos on food (the Filipinos are predominantly Christian) have made pork an indispensable ingredient in the Filipino diet.

As children, my brothers and I loved all the extremities of the pig. Whenever lechon is served, I look for the crunchy, toasted parts, usually the skin, ears, and tails. Brandishing a tail and chewing on the skin is my trophy after an exciting afternoon of watching a pig turn on the spit.

The lechon is the inspiration for many pork dishes. When roasting a whole pig, what does one do with all the parts that no one eats during the feast? Sisig is a dish of the pork cheeks, snout, and ears. They are chopped up using two cleavers, chopping with both hands in a rhythmic fashion, then deep fried and sprinkled with lemon juice, vinegar, and chopped chiles. Tokwa't baboy [bean curd and pork] is made with cut-up pieces of boiled pork ears and fried tofu marinated in vinegar, soy sauce, rice wine, chopped red onions, and chiles.

My favorite pork dish is crispy pata. Deep-fried pig trotters became the rage in the 1960s in the Philippines. The trotters are first boiled in salted water, then air-dried for several hours (or days), before being deep-fried to perfection. The joy of eating this is breaking all the knuckles apart to savor every bit of skin and cartilage dipped in a vinegar and soy sauce dip. Lechon Kawali (page 91), deep-fried pork belly, is made similarly and is equally popular among Filipinos.

Lechon Stories

It was in Sagay, a small coastal town on the northern tip of the island of Negros Occidental in the Visayas, in 1999, where I would say without any qualification that I had the best lechon I had ever tasted. Hosted by the Maranon family (the mayor of Sagay and the Governor of Negros were both Maranons then) and my cousin Lyn Besa-Gamboa, we boarded a pumpboat to taste a lechon by "Enting Lobaton," the Master Lechonero of Bacolod and Silay.

We broke out with wild cheers as we approached the waving advance team sent by Enting to transform an empty sandbar into a full-blown picnic area. When we arrived, people crowded around the lechon scene — a steel drum cut lengthwise packed with carefully placed coal embers and a five-month-old native pig about forty pounds on a long, slender bamboo spit rotating on metal stands.

A master lechonero! At first the concept seemed ludicrous to me. But the stories that came to me convinced me that people with such skills and knowledge are few and quite revered by their followers.

On my last trip back home, I went to Cebu for its lechon. There I would meet a private master lechonero who cooks his lechon only for his family and friends. My hosts, the Escaño and Unchuan families, arranged for me to taste Richie Unchuan's special lechon. Richie, who learned much from his paternal grandmother's lechonero in Camiguin Island off northern Mindanao, told me that the secret to a good lechon is the wood fire and the management of the heat. Coal is

integrated with the wood and the pig is never put on top of the fire.

The techniques of lechon are often contradictory and differ greatly among its practitioners — from seasoning, prepping the pig, and the stuffing, to where the fire should be placed and how the heat is managed. While Richie's fire is built to surround the pig, Enting likes to use hot coals directly under the pig. Richie bathes the pig with anisado [anise-flavored gin], while Enting leaves the skin alone.

Exactly four years after the Sagay lechon, we asked Enting to re-create that lechon in my cousin Lyn's garden in Silay. Enting worked fast, rotating the pig over the hot coals in the drum. Enting likes to use local native pigs. The mystique of the native pig led my photographer, Neal Oshima, to do some of his own research on pig sourcing once we returned to Manila. It seems that a wife of a very famous Philippine architect is a master lechonera herself and researches the pedigree of the piglets that she buys from specific pig farms in Marinduque, an island province west of Luzon. Once she hits pay dirt, she makes sure that she corners all of that sow's progeny.

What I learned was that everyone's methods work. Every lechon we tasted was outstanding and finely nuanced in its basting flavors and stuffing. Even the roast suckling pig that Rosebud Sala bought for us from a company that ships roast pigs all over the country was crisp, nicely salted, and moist.

On that extraordinary day on the sandbar off Sagay many years ago, I remember that I was a laggard in the crush to grab the first spoils of the lechon. I inched my way inside the crowd, more out of curiosity to see what the stuffing looked like than to get a bite. Inside the pig were dozens of neatly bundled lemongrass stalks, the famous trademark of the Visayan lechon.

I broke off a piece of the skin and meat near the leg. I took my bite. There was none of that off-putting distinct taste of pork, but instead a sweet, moist meat with a hint of lemon oil that was quite new to me. The skin was crisp and salted enough to taste of salt, but not too much. There was hardly any fat on the skin or meat, and yet it was utterly flavorful and tender. The piece was soon gone, and so was most of the pig.

LECHON KAWALI

This is one dish that most Filipinos cannot resist and is often the subject of Filipino food cravings. It requires boiling, air-drying, and proper frying if you want the skin to be crisp. The Ilocano version of lechon kawali is bagnet, which looks like a giant chicharron. The skin of the pork belly is not only crisp, but is fried to puff up like chicharron.

The steps of this recipe need to be spread out over three days, so plan accordingly.

SERVES 4

4	pieces bone-in pork belly with skin, about 1 pound each
½	cup plus 2 tablespoons salt
3	bay leaves
2	tablespoons black peppercorns
1	head garlic, cloves separated, peeled, and halved crosswise
1	large onion, quartered
½	cup rice vinegar, or as needed to coat the pork belly

Canola oil, for frying

1. Rub the pork with 2 tablespoons of the salt, wrap tightly in plastic wrap, and refrigerate overnight.

2. The next day, rinse the pork, and place it in a large covered pot or Dutch oven with cold water to cover by 2 inches. Bring to a boil over high heat, skimming off any foam that rises to the top. Add the remaining salt, bay leaves, peppercorns, garlic, and onion. Reduce the heat to medium and simmer, covered, until the meat is tender and almost falling off the bone, 45 minutes to 1 hour, adding additional boiling water to keep the meat covered if necessary.

3. While simmering the pork, preheat the oven to 400° F. Using tongs, transfer the pork to a roasting pan fitted with a wire rack, pat the pork dry with paper towels, and brush on both sides with the vinegar. Transfer to the oven and roast for 20 to 30 minutes to dry, turning once with tongs. Remove from oven and keep in a cool place to dry for another 4 hours.

4. Wipe the pork dry with paper towels. Fill a large pot or wok with about 4 inches of oil, enough to submerge the pork belly pieces. Using a frying thermometer, bring the oil to 360° F over medium-high heat. Add the pork and fry until the skin is blistered and crisp, 5 to 7 minutes. Using tongs, transfer the pork belly to paper towels to drain. Pull the meat from the bone and cut into 2-inch slices. Serve warm.

Variation

For Crispy Pata (Deep-Fried Pigs' Trotters), the process is the same:

Use four 6-inch trotters. The trotters need to be boiled a bit longer on the stovetop –1½ to 2 hours, depending on the size. The roasting and frying are the same.

Opposite, top: lechon. Opposite bottom: tanglad [lemongrass]. Above: chicharron.

The Chinese brought mung beans to the Philippines and primarily use it as a sweet filling for the Chinese round cakes enclosed in flaky dough called hopia. The Filipinos eat it as an iced dessert called mongo con hielo [mung beans with shaved ice, milk, and sugar], a variation of Halo-halo (page 153). Although technically mung beans are a legume rather than a vegetable, this dish was served at home as a vegetable dish to complement meat and fish dishes.

I encountered mongo guisado in many interviews with Filipinos, who talked about the concept of food pairing when they put a meal together. In the Tagalog region, including Manila and provinces surrounding it, the term was *terno-terno* [match-match] and in the Visayas, the Ilonggo term for it is *sampat na pagkaon* [complementariness in eating]. Among the dishes mentioned as a perfect food pair for the mongo dish were adobo, paksiw na isda [fish poached in vinegar], and grilled or fried pork chop.

MONGO GUISADO

The traditional way of cooking mongo guisado is to flavor it with pork pieces or dried fish. There is also a Visayan variation called tinonoang mongo [mung beans cooked with coconut milk]. For me, this is the perfect way to use up leftover lechon kawali. Vegetarians can skip the pork, replacing the fat with canola oil, and still come up with a wonderful comfort food to pair with their other main courses.

SERVES 4 TO 6

1   cup dried mung beans

1½   cups water

1   teaspoon salt

¼   pound pork belly, cut into ½-inch pieces

3   garlic cloves, peeled and mashed

1   medium onion, diced

2   medium plum tomatoes, chopped (optional)

1   tablespoon bagoong or fish sauce, or to taste

2   cups spinach or chile leaves (available frozen in Asian markets)

1. Place the mung beans, 1½ cups water, and salt in a medium saucepan over medium-high heat. Bring to a boil, then reduce the heat and simmer for 30 to 40 minutes, or until the mung beans split. At this point you can mash the mung beans if desired.

2. Place the pork belly pieces in a large skillet and add ½ cup water. Place over medium-high heat and cook until the water evaporates and the fat is rendered, 7 to 10 minutes.

3. Fry the pork pieces in the fat until browned on all sides, about 5 minutes. Remove the pork with a slotted spoon and drain on paper towels.

4. Reduce the heat to medium, add the garlic and onion to the remaining fat in the skillet and sauté until softened, about 5 minutes. Add the tomatoes and cook for 1 minute, until softened. Add the mung beans and cook for another 10 minutes, or until the mung beans begin to break down.

5. Return the pork pieces to the mixture, add the bagoong, and cook for 5 minutes to blend the flavors. Add the spinach or chile leaves, cover, and cook until wilted, about 2 minutes. Taste and add more salt or bagoong, if needed.

PORK TOCINO

At Cendrillon, we use a combination of salt, sugar, and powdered achuete to cure our tocino. This is a big brunch favorite—we serve it with garlic-fried rice, eggs, and grilled plantains.

SERVES 6

3   pounds pork butt, frozen for 1 hour to firm up
     and sliced ¼-inch thick

Spice Rub
½   cup salt
¼   cup sugar
2   teaspoons freshly ground black pepper
One ⅓-ounce bag (4 teaspoons) annatto powder

12 cloves garlic, thinly sliced
2 tablespoons canola oil, plus more as needed

1. To make the spice rub, combine the salt, sugar, pepper, and annatto powder in a medium bowl. Sprinkle about 1 teaspoon of the spice rub over both sides of each pork slice. Press 2 or 3 garlic cloves into the top of each slice.

2. Stack the slices in a large storage container, cover, and refrigerate overnight.

3. Warm the oil in a large skillet over medium-high heat. Add some of the pork slices and pan-fry for 2 to 3 minutes on each side, until nicely browned and crisp; remove to a serving platter. Continue to fry the remaining pork slices, adding more oil to the skillet as needed. Alternatively you can grill the pork slices for 2 to 3 minutes on each side.

Above left: a variety of beans. Above right: making tocino in Tarlac. Burong isda [rice-fermented fish] (left) and burong baboy [rice-fermented pork].

**The Burong Baboy
of Tarlac**

I went home to my father's hometown, Tarlac, Tarlac, in Central Luzon, to hunt for the burong baboy of my youth. The burong baboy is the Kapangpangan version of the tocino—cured and fermented pork slices that are eaten for breakfast with fried rice and eggs [tosilog, short for tocino, sinangag at itlog]. Burong baboy differs from tocino in that in place of thin pork slices, it is made with huge slabs of butter-flied pieces of pork belly with a cross section of skin, fat, meat, and bone. The pork is layered with a cooked rice and salt mixture in a nonreactive container and allowed to ferment for several days to a week depending upon people's preferences. To cook, the burong baboy is first simmered in water to render its fat and then sugar is added to produce caramelized pork with hints of sourness.

However, I discovered that the burong baboy was not made in Tarlac City, but in Concepcion, another town in Tarlac. What was locally made in Tarlac was the tocino.

My cousin Isabel Besa-Morales brought me to the public market to visit Beth Buan, who has been making tocino for twenty years now. She told me that although a lot of people buy the pork freshly marinated, true Kapampangans like to age it for three days. She uses pork butt and chops because she says pork belly is hardly available anymore—the lechon kawali and chicharron business most likely has cornered the market in pork belly.

The Spanish-Mexican Connection

Top left: making tamales, Angeles, Pampanga. Top right: tocino del cielo, Arayat, Pampanga. Below: tamales, San Fernando, Pampanga.

The Spanish food that was brought to the Philippines beginning in the late 1500s was a Mediterranean melting pot, a fusion of indigenous European food and substantial culinary influences from the Arabs and Sephardic Jews. The Arabs were responsible for bringing important crops to Europe and cultivating them. Many of these still carry their Arabic names: sugar [azucar / al-sukkar], saffron [zafaran / al-zafran], rice [arroz / al-ruzz], and many citrus fruits and vegetables, including lemon [limon / laymun], orange [naranja / naranj], and spinach [espinaca / sbanikh]. Spain brought its passion for pork (chorizo and ham) to Manila via the galleon trade (in order to ferret out Jews during the Spanish Inquisition, the Catholic Church mandated the use and consumption of pork and pork products).

Filipinos acquired a taste for olive oil, tomatoes, eggplant, garbanzos, hard-boiled eggs, sweet red peppers, paprika, and saffron—all evidence of Spanish influences. These dishes and ingredients were transplanted into Philippine society without much of the subtext of their origins. Initially these foods were brought in to satisfy the culinary demands of expatriate Spaniards (government officials, soldiers, and priests). As these ingredients were assimilated by a growing class of mestizos, they became an emblem of colonial power, signaling Eurocentric superiority. Filipinos adapted them to a cuisine that stood for elite, fiesta fare based on expensive ingredients beyond the reach of others.

Spanish dishes are recognizable through their names and method of preparation. Rellenos are anything that can conceivably be stuffed: poultry (chicken, turkey, quail), seafood (fish, squid), and vegetables (eggplant, bell peppers). Tomato-based dishes that are fried first and simmered in tomato sauce are called afritada (*frito* means to fry). Morcon [beef flank] and embutido [ground pork] are stuffed rolled meat simmered in tomato sauce. Chorizos and hams are used to add robust flavor to soups and stews and as stuffing for chickens and turkeys.

The Galleon Trade

Looking beyond the festive Spanish dishes on the Philippine table, the culinary experience of the Philippines bears a more significant impact from the flavors of Mexico. The Philippines was a distant colony and Spain relied on its government bureaucracy in Mexico to rule the islands (it is often claimed that "the Philippines was a colony of a colony").

The galleon trade from 1565 to 1815 between Manila and Acapulco brought about an exchange between people, goods, and food. Pilipino, the national language of the Philippines, is primarily based on Tagalog. Tagalog words that are traced back to Nahuatl (Aztec) origins include *nanay* [mother], *tatay* [father], *tamales*, *calabaza*, *camote* [sweet potato], *sili* [chile], chocolate, *singkamas* [jicama], *tiangui* or *tiyangge* [market], and *tocayo* [namesake]. Among the many fruits, vegetables, and root crops that came to the Philippines from Mexico are tomatoes, potatoes, cassava, corn, peanuts, bell peppers, chiles, pineapple, papaya, guava, kaimito, avocados, jicama, chayote, cacao, guyabano, chico, and achuete. In return, the Philippines sent mangoes, tamarind, rice, and tuba [coconut toddy or wine] to Mexico. One finds tuba and tuba vinegar [coconut vinegar] mentioned in Mexican cookbooks today.

Many common Filipino dishes, such as the adobado [marinated in vinegar and spices], asado [vinegar and tomatoes], and estofado [sugar and vinegar stews] arrived via Mexico. While the Mexican terms refer to generic cooking methods—*adobado* refers to meats marinated in spices, *asado* means grilled, and *estofado* includes all manner of stews—the words have been applied to specific Filipino dishes based on these methods.

From left to right: guyabano [soursop], turrones de casuy, chiles, potatoes.

APRITADA

The root word of *apritada* (or *afritada* in Spanish) is *fritada*, which means fried. This dish, redolent with the flavor of tomatoes, garlic, and olive oil, can be made with pork, beef, or chicken. The essence of the dish is browned meat or poultry simmered in tomatoes, finished with fried or oven-roasted potatoes and onions. You can use pork belly, spare ribs, or pork chops here, or for a beef version, short ribs, but I find pork neck bones impart the best flavor to the dish and are the most fun to eat. Guajillo chiles, sold in stores with a Mexican clientele, give the sauce a mild smoky flavor. Like most Filipino stew dishes, this is excellent eaten the next day.

SERVES 4 TO 6

4   russet potatoes, peeled and cut into eighths
1   cup plus 2 tablespoons olive oil
Salt
3   large white onions, peeled and cut into eighths
3   pounds pork neck bones or spare ribs
2   heads of garlic, cloves peeled and lightly smashed
15   ripe plum tomatoes, seeded and quartered
Freshly ground black pepper
1   tablespoon fish sauce, or to taste
1   whole fresh chile, such as jalapeño
2   whole dried guajillo chiles (optional)
2   red bell peppers, seeded and cut into large rectangular pieces
½   cup pitted Spanish olives (optional)

1. Preheat the oven to 425° F. In a bowl, toss the potatoes with 2 tablespoons of the olive oil and ½ teaspoon salt. Spread in a single layer on a rimmed baking sheet and roast in the lower third of the oven, tossing occasionally, until well browned all over, about 45 minutes.

2. In a large Dutch oven over medium-high heat, warm the remaining cup of oil. Brown the onions in the oil, stirring occasionally so that the onion layers separate and evenly brown (adjust the heat as necessary to avoid over-darkening), 10 to 12 minutes. Use a slotted spoon to transfer the onions to a strainer set over a bowl and ilet drain.

3. Clean and pat dry the pork neck bones or ribs. Pour any accumulated oil from the onions back into the pan and warm over medium-high heat. Working in batches, and adding a little more oil to the pan if necessary, brown the pork bones on all sides, 2 to 3 minutes per side. Transfer the browned pork to a plate.

4. Reduce the heat to medium, add the garlic, and sauté until lightly colored, about 2 minutes. Add the tomatoes and simmer for about 5 minutes to break them down. Season with salt and pepper to taste.

5. Add the browned pork, fish sauce, fresh chiles, and dried chiles, if using, and bring to a boil. Lower the heat and simmer, covered, basting the pork regularly with the tomato sauce until it is cooked, about 45 minutes.

7. Once the meat is tender, add the bell peppers and cook until the peppers have begun to soften but retain some crunch, about 10 minutes. Taste the tomato sauce and season with additional fish sauce and ground black pepper if necessary.

8. Just before serving, stir in the onions, potatoes, and olives, if using, and heat until warmed through. Remove the chiles before serving.

MENUDO

I had always thought the term *menudo* to mean small diced things because the menudo I grew up with was a dish with pork, liver, and potatoes all uniformly diced. The name actually comes from a Mexican stew that uses tripe and white hominy. Romy reconstructed this dish from memory several years ago and he served it as a sauce to go with longaniza (pork sausage) on one of our Mother's Day menus. It is meant to be a main course, but, as we discovered, it can serve as a side dish or a food pairing with other dishes. This recipe uses chicken stock with tomatoes as a base for the sauce, which we prefer to the standard tomato puree.

SERVES 4

- ¼ cup extra-virgin olive oil
- ½ large onion, finely chopped (about 1 cup)
- 3 garlic cloves, chopped
- 2 large tomatoes, seeded and cut into ¼-inch cubes
- ½ pound pork loin, cut into ¼-inch cubes
- 1½ cups chicken stock
- 1 large potato, peeled and cut into ¼-inch cubes (about 2 cups)
- 1 large red bell pepper, cut into ¼-inch cubes
- ½ pound calf's liver, cut into ¼-inch cubes
- 1½ teaspoons salt or 1 tablespoon fish sauce, or more to taste
- ½ teaspoon freshly ground black pepper, or more to taste

1. In a large saucepan over medium heat, warm the oil. Add the onion and garlic and sauté for about 5 minutes, until the onion is translucent. Add the tomatoes and cook, stirring, for 1 minute. Add the cubed pork and cook until it turns white, about 5 minutes. Add the chicken stock, increase the heat to high, and bring to a boil.

2. Add the potato and red bell pepper. Bring the mixture back to a boil, then reduce the heat and simmer, uncovered, until the potatoes have softened, 6 to 8 minutes.

3. Add the liver and cook until it darkens in color and is cooked through, about 2 minutes. Season with the salt or fish sauce and pepper to taste.

Left: plum tomatoes. Below: Menudo.

Empanadas
of the Philippines

Empanadas are delicate turnovers that are a great favorite among Filipinos for merienda. The most common filling is ground beef sautéed with onions, peas, raisins, and potatoes. The filling is encased in crust and deep-fried or baked. Fillings vary: My cousin Betty Ann Besa-Quirino remembers fondly her Auntie Tacing's chicken empanada made of diced chicken, potatoes, and cream of mushroom soup filling and a flaky crust.

There are quite a few very interesting regional variations of the empanada. In Silay, Negros Occidental, I found the panara, a vegetarian-inspired version of the empanada filled with sautéed green papaya, squash, or newly sprouted mung beans. The authentic panara crust is made with corn flour [masa harina] and has a grittier texture. It is mixed with achuete water, which gives it an orange hue. But the more popular empanada in Silay is the empanada developed by Emma Lacson and now sold by her daughter, Nora "Baby" Lacson. This empanada has trademark ridges on the outer crust called *hojaldre*. The filling is made with ground pork, potatoes, onions, garbanzos, and raisins; the crust is brushed with beaten egg to give it some color before deep-frying.

Vigan, Ilocos Sur, is famous for empanadas that are quite different from most I had previously tasted. The dough is made with ground rice flour and cooked on the stove. The result is similar to a crunchy taco shell, which leads me to believe that this was a direct influence of Mexico. The Plaza in the center of Vigan is filled with empanada vendors and lines of hungry people waiting their turn. The special Vigan empanada filling is made with sautéed green papaya and Vigan sausage. Before the dough is sealed and deep-fried, the vendor drops a raw egg onto the filling. The hot, steaming packet is handed to you straight from the huge wok of boiling oil. This is dipped in sukang Iloko [Ilocano native sugarcane vinegar] to cool it down. It is worth the long drive from Manila.

Bonito Singson, who also hosted us in Vigan, told me he was drawn into the intricacies of empanada-making at age ten. He would always see Nana Sayong, an old, stooped woman, pass by their house carrying her big pestle, with which the ground rice for the crust had to be pounded in a huge mortar. This produced gritty rice flour, which would be mixed with boiling water to make a stiff dough for the crust. It was tough work for an old woman, so Bonito would help pound the rice.

Above: Vigan empanadas.
Opposite: empanadas from Silay.

BEEF AND CHORIZO EMPANADITAS

These miniature empanadas make perfect appetizers or hors d'oeuvres for cocktail parties. Using this basic recipe, you can, in place of ground beef, use diced chicken, duck, goose, shrimp, crab, or lobster. For vegetarians, combine the sautéed potatoes with sliced green papaya, bean sprouts, and mushrooms. Make sure that the filling is properly drained before wrapping it in the dough.

Most empanadas found in the Philippines are deep-fried. These are baked, using a rich pastry that provides a tender, flaky crust. You can freeze some or all of the unbaked empanaditas before brushing with the egg wash. Brush with egg wash just before baking and add about 10 minutes to the baking time if using frozen empanaditas.

MAKES ABOUT 40 EMPANADITAS

- 2 tablespoons vegetable oil
- 1/3 pound black trumpet or shiitake mushrooms, diced small
- 1 small onion, diced small
- 1 medium carrot, diced small
- 1 pound ground beef
- 1 cup peeled and diced sweet potato (about 1/2 small)
- 3/4 cup peeled and diced russet potato (about 1 small)
- 3 tablespoons soy sauce
- 3 tablespoons rice wine
- 1 tablespoon rice vinegar, or to taste
- 1 large Spanish chorizo, diced small
- 3 tablespoons raisins
- 1/3 cup fresh or frozen green peas

Salt, to taste (optional)

All-purpose flour, for rolling

- 3 recipes Rich Pie Pastry, divided into 4 equal pieces, each flattened into a disc and wrapped in plastic wrap (see opposite)
- 40 fresh basil leaves (optional)
- 4 egg whites, whisked, for sealing
- 2 egg yolks, slightly beaten, for brushing
- 1/4 cup whole milk, for brushing

1. Preheat the oven to 375° F and set 2 racks on the upper and lower thirds of the oven.

2. To make the filling, in a large sauté pan over medium heat, warm the oil. Add the mushrooms, onion, and carrot, and sauté until the vegetables have softened, about 5 minutes.

3. Raise the heat to medium-high, add the ground beef, and cook, breaking up with a fork, until the meat starts to brown, about 5 minutes. Add the sweet potato, russet potato, soy sauce, rice wine, and rice vinegar. Reduce the heat to medium, cover, and cook until the potatoes have softened, about 15 minutes. Add the chorizo and raisins

and simmer until most of the liquid has evaporated, about 10 minutes. Stir in the green peas and heat just to cook through, about 3 minutes. Taste and add more vinegar and salt if necessary.

4. To assemble the empanaditas, remove 1 disc of the Rich Pie Pastry from the refrigerator. On a lightly floured surface with a lightly floured rolling pin, roll out the dough to about ⅛-inch thick. Using a 4-inch round cookie cutter, cut the dough into circles, saving the scraps to reroll at the end.

5. Using a spatula or your fingers, transfer the dough rounds to an ungreased baking sheet, setting the rounds 1 inch apart. (Alternatively, the dough can be rolled out and cut into rounds, then wrapped tightly in plastic wrap and refrigerated up to 1 day ahead.)

6. Spoon 1 heaping tablespoon of the filling into the center of each dough round and top with a basil leaf, if using. With a pastry brush, lightly dab the edges of the circle with the egg white. Fold the dough in half into a half moon, enclosing the filling. Crimp the folded edges decoratively with the tines of a fork, if desired, or gently press the edges together with your fingers to seal. Repeat this process, taking one disk of dough from the refrigerator at a time, and arranging the filled empanadas on 2 baking sheets, until all of the dough has been used, and the scraps have been rerolled.

7. In a small bowl, whisk together the egg yolks and milk. Brush the tops of each empanadita with the egg wash. Bake the empanaditas on the upper and lower thirds of the oven, switching the position of the sheets from top to bottom and back to front halfway through baking, until they are golden brown, about 25 minutes. Let cool slightly before serving warm or at room temperature.

RICH PIE PASTRY

MAKES ENOUGH FOR ONE SINGLE CRUST PIE OR ONE 10-INCH TART MOLD

1½ cups all-purpose flour
½ teaspoon salt
6 tablespoons chilled unsalted butter, cut into small pieces
1 large egg, beaten
Ice water, as needed

1. Sift the flour and salt into a large bowl. Cut the butter into the flour using your fingertips or a pastry blender (or pulse in a food processor) until the texture resembles coarse meal with visible bits of butter. Stir the egg into the flour mixture and stir or pulse until incorporated. Pinch off a small handful of dough; if it doesn't hold together, add ice water ½ tablespoon at a time, stirring or pulsing after each addition.

2. Turn the dough out onto a lightly floured work surface and pat into a disk about ½-inch thick. Wrap the disk in plastic wrap and refrigerate until firm, at least 1 hour or up to 2 days.

QUAIL RELLENO

In the Philippines, quail is known as *pugo,* which was traditionally cooked as an adobo. This tiny bird has almost disappeared from the culinary lexicon of Filipino cooks. We wanted to revisit the versatility of this bird, and came up with this recipe. You can also try making this with snipes, the tiny rice-field birds of Pampanga.

SERVES 6

Filling:

1	tablespoon olive oil
1	small onion, diced
1	small carrot, diced
¾	pound ground pork
1	small chorizo, diced
¼	pound calf's liver, minced
1	cup diced water chestnuts
1	large egg
1	tablespoon cornstarch
2	teaspoons salt
½	teaspoon freshly ground black pepper

Quail:

12	whole quails, deboned
	Salt and freshly ground black pepper
12	quail eggs, boiled for 2 minutes, drained, and peeled
6	tablespoons olive oil, or as needed
1	head garlic cloves, unpeeled
½	cup melted unsalted butter or olive oil
	Garlic Sauce (recipe follows, optional)

1. For the filling, in a large saucepan over medium heat, warm the oil. Add the onion and carrot and sauté until softened, about 3 minutes. Transfer to a large bowl and let cool. When the mixture has cooled, add the pork, chorizo, liver, water chestnuts, egg, cornstarch, and salt and pepper. Using clean hands, mix well until thoroughly combined.

2. Preheat the oven to 425° F. Season each quail with salt and pepper and place on a work surface breast side up. Close the neck opening of each quail by inserting a toothpick under the wings and through the top of the body cavity. Stuff each quail with about ¼ cup of the filling, nestling 1 quail egg in the center. Tie the legs.

3. In a large saucepan over medium-high heat, warm 2 tablespoons of the oil. Add 4 of the quail and sear until lightly browned on all sides, about 5 minutes. Transfer to a large roasting pan. Repeat with the remaining quail, in two more batches, adding more oil to the pan as needed.

4. Scatter the garlic cloves around the quail. Brush with the melted butter or oil. Roast, turning once, until the quail are nicely browned on both sides and the internal temperature of the filling reaches 165° F, about 25 minutes. Serve garnished with the roasted garlic cloves, or use the garlic cloves to make a sauce.

GARLIC SAUCE

2	cups chicken stock
	Roasted garlic cloves from the quail
1	tablespoon unsalted butter
1	teaspoon lime juice, or to taste
	Salt, to taste
	Freshly ground black pepper, to taste

While the quail roasting pan is hot, pour in the chicken stock and stir and scrape up the browned juices from the pan. Transfer the liquid to a medium skillet. Squeeze out the roasted garlic and add to the skillet. Cook over medium-high heat, stirring to incorporate the garlic, until the liquid is reduced by a third, about 5 minutes. Stir in the butter and lime juice and season with salt and pepper. Serve warm.

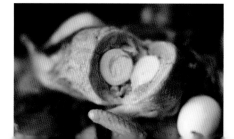

ESCABECHE

Today's escabeche is a fried fish dish with a sweet and sour sauce that is more Chinese than Spanish. This recipe for fried mackerel in a sweet and sour sauce is adapted from Glenda Rosales-Barretto's book *Flavors of the Philippines*, and is called Tanguigue Escabeche [Mackerel in Garlic-Turmeric Sauce]. If whole sea bass or snapper are unavailable, an equal weight of mackerel steaks can be substituted. Score both sides of the whole fish before dredging in flour and deep frying.

SERVES 4

Sauce:

One 1-inch piece fresh turmeric, peeled and finely chopped (optional)

¼ cup canola oil, plus additional for frying

3 garlic cloves, peeled and thinly sliced

1 large onion, thinly sliced

1 red bell pepper, cored and julienned

1 green bell pepper, cored and julienned

One 1-inch piece ginger, peeled and julienned

1 cup fish stock or water

¼ cup rice vinegar

1 tablespoon sugar

Fish:

One 4-pound whole sea bass or snapper, or four ½-pound tanguigue [mackerel] steaks

All-purpose flour, for dredging

Sea salt

Freshly ground black pepper

2 tablespoons freshly squeezed kalamansi lime juice or lemon juice

1. Using a mortar and pestle, pulverize the turmeric, then add a few drops of water and press to extract the juice. Pour the juice through cheesecloth or a fine-mesh strainer into another bowl.

2. In a large saucepan over medium heat, warm the oil. Add the garlic, and cook, stirring, until lightly browned and crisp, about 3 minutes. Using a slotted spoon, transfer the garlic to a paper towel–lined plate to drain.

3. Add the onion, bell peppers, and ginger to the pan, and sauté until softened, about 3 minutes. Add the stock or water, turmeric juice, vinegar, and sugar. Increase the heat and bring to a boil. Reduce the heat and simmer for 5 minutes, then taste and adjust the seasoning if necessary. Return the garlic to the pan, stir to combine, and keep the sauce warm.

4. While the sauce simmers, prepare the fish: Mound flour in a large, shallow bowl. Season the fish with salt and pepper, and sprinkle the fish with the kalamansi juice. Dredge the fish in the flour, turning to coat evenly, then transfer the fish to a plate.

5. Fill a large sauté pan with enough oil to come halfway up the sides of the fish. Place the pan over medium-high heat. When the oil is very hot, but not smoking, add the fish and fry until crisp on the outside and cooked through (about 10 minutes per inch of thickness).

6. Transfer the fish to a serving plate, pour the sauce over, and serve.

The Origins of Escabeche

The word *escabeche* is the Spanish word for ceviche. In the Philippines, it originally meant pickled fish. The 1919 cookbook *Aklat ng Pagluluto* (literally "book for cooking"), which documented, preserved, and translated into Tagalog the European-influenced dishes in the Philippines, describes the method for preparing escabeche de pescado. A whole fish is soaked in hot oil, then cooled; it is then topped off with vinegar, bay leaves, oregano, salt, and water. In 1941, a compilation of recipes from Cebu and other parts of the country called *Our Favorite Recipes* included a recipe for fish that was first fried, then marinated for several days, and served cold.

The American Influence:
Transformations

In the early half of the twentieth century, nutritionists and dieticians became the authority on what Americans should consume to be healthy and fit. The manufacturing of processed food became part of this campaign and made the promotion, exportation, and distribution of American taste and culture throughout the world much easier. The Philippines became an American colony in 1901, and for the next forty-five years, the Americans eagerly remade their only colony in their image. When it came to the Philippine diet, the Americans had much goodwill to share. They were worried about the poor nutrition that they saw in the Filipino meal of rice and fish and sought dietary improvements by introducing Filipinos to dairy products, canned meats, vegetables, and fruits from the United States.

The Philippine government took an active role in changing the diet of the Filipinos. Cooking classes in the public school system taught young girls and women how to cook American dishes. The Bureau of Education "Bulletin on Housekeeping and Household: A Manual for Girls in the Elementary Grade in the Philippine Islands" listed recipes prepared in a 1912 cooking class, including biscuits, candies, doughnuts, fried chicken, muffins, ice cream, hot cakes, puddings, and pound cakes. Ironically, most of the recipes taught would not qualify as nutritious today. There were a few attempts to integrate local ingredients in recipes such as banana fritters, goat stew, guyabano desserts, rice cakes, and preserved fruits.

The pervasive influence of American food and culture on the Philippines affected all classes of Filipinos. The American canned product is oftentimes more valued than fresh fruits, fish, and meats from the local markets. Spam, corned beef, Vienna sausage, canned peaches, fruit cocktail, and Nestlé's cream appear in many recipes for everyday food, and they hover above our better senses as comfort food.

As a teenager, I will never forget the humbling generosity of a family who offered us shelter from a storm while we were vacationing on one of the beaches of northern Luzon. The family was very poor and lived in a nipa hut. As we climbed into the small space and sat on the floor, they put before us one deliciously steamed pompano. Pompano was rarely available in Manila markets at the time and was often expensive. As I looked with wonder at the miracle meal placed before us, they profusely apologized that they had no canned goods to offer us.

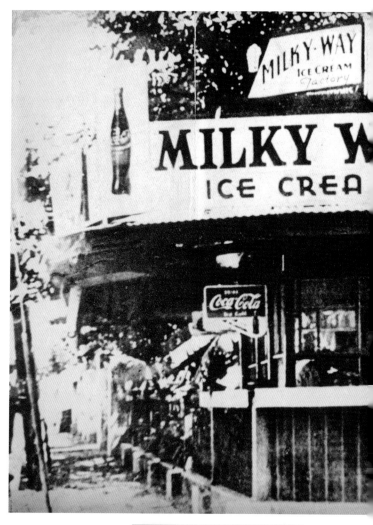

Cooking Demonstrations

Televised cooking shows in the 1950s were a perfect medium for food manufacturers to promote their products. Companies including Nestlé and Knorr were joined by Manila Gas (which was then owned by Americans) to sponsor these shows, featuring recognized personalities. Mrs. Virginia Gonzalez (Mrs. Virginia Perez at the time) was recruited by Nora Daza (famous cook, author, and restaurateur) to run the show in the 1960s. She developed hundreds of recipes using products like powdered, evaporated, and condensed milk, bouillon cubes, and powdered coffee. A generation of Filipinos watched these shows avidly, learning how to cook from TV personalities in place of the grandmothers, mothers, and nannies who had traditionally handed down family recipes.

NANGKA (JACKFRUIT) DELIGHT CHIFFON CAKE

This cake was adapted from a recipe belonging to a Mrs. Flora C. Moran that was one of the finalists in the 1960 *Manila Chronicle* Cooking Demonstrations' White King chiffon cake contest.

MAKES ONE 10-INCH TUBE CAKE

2¼   cups cake flour
1½   cups sugar
1   tablespoon baking powder
1   teaspoon salt
½   cup canola oil
6   large eggs, separated
½   teaspoon lemon extract
1   tablespoon grated lemon zest
¼   teaspoon cream of tartar
Nangka Frosting (recipe follows)

1. Preheat the oven to 325° F.

2. Sift the flour, 1 cup of the sugar, the baking powder, and salt into a large bowl.

3. In a separate bowl, whisk together the oil, egg yolks, ¾ cup water, lemon extract, and lemon zest. Add the dry ingredients and beat until well blended, about 2 minutes.

4. In the clean bowl of an electric mixer fitted with the whisk attachment, beat the egg whites with the cream of tartar until soft peaks are formed. Gradually add the remaining ½ cup sugar and continue beating until stiff peaks are formed. Gently fold the egg whites into the batter and pour the batter into an ungreased 10-inch tube pan.

5. Bake for 50 to 60 minutes, or until the top springs back when lightly pressed and a toothpick inserted into the center comes out clean. Invert the pan by inserting a thin-necked bottle through the hole in the tube. Let cool completely.

6. Run a knife around the outside edge and around the tube, turn the pan upside down, and tap it a few times to release the cake onto a plate. Frost the cake with the Nangka Frosting.

NANGKA FROSTING

MAKES 1 CUP

2   cups confectioners' sugar, sifted
4   tablespoons (½ stick) unsalted butter, softened
6   tablespoons nangka juice (see Note)
1   teaspoon vanilla extract
Pinch of salt

Place all the frosting ingredients in the bowl of an electric mixer fitted with the whisk attachment. Beat on medium speed to a smooth, spreadable consistency.

Note: Nangka juice is the liquid extracted from jackfruit pulp. To make your own, puree a can of jackfruit in syrup and strain through a fine-mesh strainer. Add water to thin out the juice.

Banana vendor. Overleaf, clockwise from top left: fresh noodles, longaniza, tripe, guyabano [soursop], cucumber, eggplant, tofu, pineapple.

The Chiffon: An Imported Classic Cake

The best-loved desserts in the Philippines were traditionally derived from Spanish and French classics: flan, brazo, tocino del cielo, yemas, and sans rival (a local version of the French dacquoise). But with the influx of U.S. products, advertising, and mass information at the start of the twentieth century, American cakes—in particular, the chiffon cake—became the dessert Filipino matrons used to demonstrate their baking prowess. In place of the dense, rich European cakes, the light, airy American cakes and breads became the standard by which baked products were judged. Today, chiffon cakes are still baked in Filipino homes and are sold in mass quantities at bakeries all over the country.

BANANA CREAM PIE

Banana cream pie was my favorite dessert whenever we would visit Camp John Hay in Baguio, the summer capital of the Philippines, about 150 miles north of Manila. Eating at the main clubroom overlooking the golf course was one of summer's promises that I always treasured. The thought of eating "American" banana cream pie was just a dream come true.

MAKES ONE 9-INCH PIE

½   recipe Basic Pie Pastry (recipe follows)
8   large egg yolks
½   cup sugar
¼   teaspoon salt
3   tablespoons cornstarch
2½ cups whole milk
1¼ cups heavy cream
2   tablespoons unsalted butter, cut into pieces
1   tablespoon vanilla extract
2   ripe bananas, sliced

1. For the crust, roll the dough out on a lightly floured work surface into a 13-inch circle that measures about ⅛-inch

thick. Transfer to a 9-inch pie pan, pressing the pastry into the sides and bottom of the pan and trimming, rolling under, and fluting the edges. Cover with plastic wrap and refrigerate for at least 1 hour or overnight.

2. Preheat the oven to 350° F. Using a kitchen fork, randomly prick the bottom of the pastry. Line the pie shell with enough parchment paper to cover the bottom of the pan and come up the sides. Fill the bottom of the pan with pie weights or dried beans to prevent the pastry from puffing during baking.

3. Place the pie shell in the oven and bake until set and lightly browned around the edges, about 15 minutes, removing the parchment paper and weights about 3 minutes before the pastry is baked to ensure that it is evenly browned. Let cool completely on a wire rack.

4. To make the pastry cream, place the egg yolks, sugar, and salt in a large heatproof bowl and whisk until well blended. Whisk in the cornstarch.

5. In a heavy-bottomed medium saucepan over medium-high heat, scald the milk, then slowly whisk it into the egg-yolk mixture until smooth.

6. Return the mixture to the pot and cook over medium-low heat, whisking constantly, until it starts to bubble in the center, about 3 minutes. Take the pan off the heat and whisk in ¼ cup of the heavy cream, the butter, and 2 teaspoons of the vanilla.

7. Slice the bananas over the bottom of the pie crust. Pour the pastry cream over the pie crust, smooth out the surface with a rubber spatula, and cover the surface of the pastry cream with plastic wrap. Refrigerate until thoroughly chilled, about 2 hours.

8. For the topping, whip the remaining 1 cup of heavy cream with the remaining 1 teaspoon vanilla until the cream holds its shape. Spoon the whipped cream over the top of the pie and serve.

BASIC PIE PASTRY

Makes enough for one 9-inch double pie crust

2¼ cups all-purpose flour
½   teaspoon salt
¼   teaspoon baking powder
½   pound (2 sticks) unsalted butter, cut into small pieces and chilled
4 to 6 tablespoons ice water

1. Sift the flour, salt, and baking powder into a large bowl. Cut the butter into the flour using your fingertips or a pastry blender (or pulse in a food processor) until the texture resembles coarse meal with visible bits of butter. Drizzle 4 tablespoons ice water evenly over the mixture and gently stir with a fork or pulse until incorporated. Pinch off a small handful of dough; if it doesn't hold together, add more water, ½ tablespoon at a time, stirring or pulsing after each addition.

2. Turn the dough out onto a lightly floured work surface. Divide the ball of dough in half, and pat into disks about ½-inch thick. Wrap each disk in plastic wrap and refrigerate until firm, at least 1 hour or up to 2 days.

chapter 4

We have always believed that the best Filipino food is found in the homes of families with a tradition of good cooking and appreciation of fresh ingredients found locally. With this in mind, we decided that the best way to discover what Filipino food is all about would be to talk to as many families as we could and ask them what they eat and how they cook these dishes. Coming from a culture where family recipes are kept close to the vest, we were surprised at the general outpouring of support and enthusiasm from the families we approached. We wanted a sampling of regional variation, so we visited families from Ilocos, Tarlac, Pampanga, Bulacan, Laguna, Quezon, Bicol, Samar, Cebu, Iloilo, and Bacolod/Silay, and they have contributed recipes to this book. Though we've compiled a good number of recipes, we feel that this book does not do justice to all the regions of the Philippines—hopefully there will be future opportunities to further showcase the wonderful home cooking of the Philippines.

Ilocos
The Wild West of the Philippines

In the 1960s and 70s, Wild West stories of shootouts between clans made the Ilocos region seem barren and hostile. But a few decades later, regional tours of the Philippines became de rigueur, and Vigan, Ilocos Sur, one of the "noble cities," began to attract local tourists with its centuries-old bahay na bato [stone houses], museums, churches, and food.

Ilocanos will inform you that they triumph because of the harshness of the area, which lacks the lush vegetation of the south or the flat, fertile valleys of Central Luzon. They are

known as tight-fisted and thrifty. (It was in the Syquia Mansion that I tried cow's womb. Boiled for hours, but still rubbery, it was interesting, but not too tasty.)

Limited natural resources haven't hindered the development of Vigan and Laoag as important trade centers. Market days (usually Sundays) are wild with bright orange squash, shades of green saluyot [Jew's mallow], malunggay [leaves of the horseradish tree], katuray or katuday [West Indian pea, a hooklike flower used in salads], amorgozo [a bitter melon variety], watermelons, bitter melon blossoms, lemongrass bundles, and twitching bunches of frogs tied to bamboo. The freshest vegetables go into the famed Ilocos Pinakbet (page 114). A common salad is made of peeled katuday and kangkong [water spinach], both blanched, mixed with chopped tomatoes and minced ginger, and sprinkled with kalamansi lime juice.

At the Laoag market, I saw a remarkable variety of seaweed gathered from the Ilocos Norte and Cagayan area of Northeast Luzon, including gammet, a black seaweed sold in flat round sheets from Burgos, used in soups such as sinigang, and kulot [first-class seaweed] from Bangui (between Burgos and Pagudpud), washed and served as salad with tomatoes and bagoong.

The region is also known for longaniza [sausage] marinated in sukang Iloko [sugarcane vinegar] and bagnet, a dramatic version of the lechon kawali [huge pork belly pieces with puffed skin]. Bagoong monamon, a fermented fish paste, is preferred over salt by Ilocano cooks. Some dishes call for the fish sauce that rises to the top of the bottle. For pinakbet, the monamon is usually strained, and naturally the Ilocano finds a thrifty recipe for using the remaining fish particles.

Opposite: Cooking innards stew in Laoag Market, Ilocos Norte. Above: bagnet, Vigan. Bottom left: making kalamay in Candon, Ilocos Sur. Bottom right: Vigan market.

Families That Hosted Us

We decided to take the ten-hour drive to Laoag, Ilocos Norte, from Manila, where Annette Ablan's cook showed us how to make the traditional pinakbet and dinuguan. There we met Bonito Singson, a prominent businessman of Vigan, Ilocos Sur, who invited us to his home in Vigan, which had a huge high-ceilinged kitchen renovated in the style of the old bahay-na-bato home. On our way to Vigan, we stopped at Dingras to visit the Puruganan house and watch Glezy Valencia make the most delicious puto and tupig [Ilocano sticky rice cakes] I had ever eaten. Carla Pacis, a descendant of the Syquia family, hosted several meals at the Syquia Mansion. Both Bonito and Carla had longtime cooks renowned for their delicious rendering of traditional Ilocano cooking.

PINAKBET

This recipe was developed at Cendrillon using vegetables more commonly available in local markets. The principle is the same. Make sure the vegetables are not over-cooked. Vegetarians can skip the pork and bagoong and season with sea salt.

SERVES 6 TO 8

¼   cup bagoong monamon [fish sauce] or alamang [small shrimp]
½   medium kabocha squash, peeled, seeds removed, and cut into 2-inch chunks
1-inch piece of ginger, peeled and thinly sliced
2   large tomatoes, cut into ¼-inch slices
1   large red onion, cut into ½-inch slices
2   medium bitter melons, halved, seeds and pulp removed, and cut into 1-inch slices
3   Chinese eggplants, halved lengthwise and cut into 2-inch pieces
10 pieces okra, stems trimmed
15 longbeans, cut into 2-inch pieces
1   large yellow summer squash, cut into 2-inch slices
1   large zucchini, cut into 2-inch slices
1   section Lechon Kawali (page 91), cut into 2-inch pieces, optional

Combine the bagoong with 1 cup water and stir to break up any chunks. Pour the mixture into a large saucepan. Add the kabocha squash, spreading it out to make a bottom layer. Add the remaining ingredients and place the pot over medium-high heat. Bring to a boil, then reduce the heat, cover, and simmer without stirring until the vegetables have softened a bit, 10 to 15 minutes. Remove the cover and simmer without stirring until the vegetables are cooked through but still al dente, about 5 minutes. Taste and add more bagoong if needed.

The Authentic Ilocano Pinakbet

Pinakbet is the traditional vegetable dish of the Ilocanos. It has been adapted and replicated with variations all over the country, so no dish could claim to be more Filipino than this mélange of local vegetables that comes close to the Western ratatouille.

We traveled to Laoag, Ilocos Norte, to taste the Ablan family's seriously authentic Ilocano cooking. While in Laoag, we stayed at Palazzo de Laoag, owned by Manuel "Nonong" Ablan, our host Annette Ablan's uncle. On our first night at the Palazzo, Nonong Ablan regaled us with stories about the land and its food. He opened a small bottle of duhat [Java plum] wine during our dinner of insarabasab [grilled pork loin], seaweed salad, and the pinakbet.

The following morning, Annette Ablan introduced us to their cook, who has been with her grandmother and her family since 1968. She cooked the pinakbet for us using baby eggplants, baby bitter melon, squash blossoms, katuray, okra, tomatoes, bagnet slices, and bagoong monamon. Using a tall stockpot, she put a layer of bagnet slices, cut-up tomatoes, and ginger at the bottom. Then she put the vegetables in layer by layer. She poured in a half bottle of strained bagoong monamon. Covering the pot and making sure it was securely sealed, she turned the heat on high and let it steam for about 10 minutes.

When making pinakbet, one must remember not to stir the vegetables in the pot with a spoon. The vegetables are steamed in their own juices and the pot is physically shaken twice to mix the vegetables and its flavors. The Ilocanos like their pinakbet vegetables intact and al dente.

Squash blossoms (left); katuray [West Indian pea] (right).

DINUGUAN

Dinuguan is, at heart, an adobo. For people squeamish about innards, regular pork meat is used instead of organ meats. The meat is cooked with garlic, bay leaves, lemongrass, and salt, then a pork blood-vinegar mixture is added. When done properly and skillfully, the dinuguan is absolutely delicious. The classic pairing for dinuguan is steamed white puto — a black and white culinary masterpiece. This is the Cendrillon recipe, created by Romy's brother Danny Dorotan.

SERVES 8

3   pounds pork butt, cut into ½-inch cubes
1   lemongrass stalk, trimmed, cut crosswise into 4 pieces, and crushed
3   garlic cloves, chopped
6   bay leaves
1   teaspoon freshly ground black pepper
1   cup pig's blood, strained
½   cup coconut milk (optional)
¼   cup rice vinegar, or to taste
2   teaspoons salt, or to taste
½   green or red chile, chopped (optional)

1. In a large pot over high heat, combine the pork, lemongrass, garlic, bay leaves, and pepper with 4 cups water. Bring the mixture to a boil, then lower the heat and simmer, skimming occasionally, until the pork is tender and most of the water is absorbed, about 30 minutes.

2. Remove the lemongrass and bay leaves. Add the blood, coconut milk, vinegar, salt, and chile, if using. Cook for 5 minutes, or until the stew thickens. Taste and add more vinegar and salt, if needed.

A Popular Everyday Dish

Dinuguan is blood and innard stew (*dugo* means blood). A dish made with innards and blood may sound challenging to some, yet it is surprisingly accessible and easy to like. It was a revelation to discover in my travels that the dinuguan has widespread popularity as an everyday dish throughout the Philippines. Families were eager to share what they claimed was the best dinuguan recipe in the region. In my later interviews, I had to stop collecting recipes, as I was accumulating too many (see page 128 for the Arayat, Pampagnan, version of ground beef in pork blood, Tidtad Baca), and I instead noted only interesting regional variations. In Laguna and Bicol, I found recipes using cow's blood, an ingredient many had disavowed as too greasy. In Bicol, they like to add coconut milk to the blood. And in New York City, of all places, I discovered goat dinuguan. In Sta. Rita, Pampanga, the Guanzon family prefers to let the blood coagulate and adds it as chunks to the stew, calling it white dinuguan (pork blood needs to be mixed with vinegar to prevent it from coagulating). In Laoag, Ilocos Norte, the Ablan family uses the classic vinegar-blood mixture, but continues to cook the stew until it is almost dry. The result is a thickly coated stew, almost like a dry-fried dinuguan.

TOMATO AND SALTED DUCK EGG SALAD

This is the classic Filipino salad—it is eaten on a daily basis and is also served at parties. It is a perfect accompaniment to fried fish and pork dishes. The strong flavor of the salted duck eggs contrasts with fresh, juicy tomatoes and savory red onion.

Salted duck eggs are found in many Chinese and Thai stores in Chinatowns. If salted duck eggs are not available, hard-boiled chicken eggs can be used as a substitute.

SERVES 4

4   large heirloom tomatoes (3 to 4 pounds), cored and chopped

½   teaspoon salt

2   salted duck eggs, peeled and cut into wedges

½   small red onion or 1 shallot, minced

2   tablespoons rice vinegar or sugarcane vinegar

2   tablespoons chopped garlic chives or 1 tablespoon chopped scallions

2   teaspoons chopped fresh cilantro

Place the tomatoes in a large bowl and sprinkle them with the salt. Add the duck eggs, red onion, and vinegar, and toss together to combine. Taste and add more salt and vinegar, if needed. Sprinkle the chopped chives and cilantro over the salad and serve at room temperature.

Salted Duck Eggs

In the Philippines, salted duck eggs are available already cooked (hard-boiled) and they are called itlog na pula [red egg]. Their shells tinted in distinctive reddish-mauve coloring, they are instantly recognizable as ready to be used in salads or as a garnish for bibingkas and other kakanin. Here in the United States, they are available in Chinatown stores uncooked either in brine or packed in Styrofoam cartons with a photo on the label showing a cross section of the orange-red yolk. To use uncooked salted duck eggs in recipes, boil the eggs for at least 20 minutes. A duck egg connoisseur once informed me that the best salted duck egg was one that is boiled and then simmered for at least an hour and a half, cooking the egg until the yolk takes on a gritty and oily texture. Many accomplished chefs in Manila have used mashed salted duck egg yolks as a secret ingredient in their famous vinaigrettes.

GRILLED EGGPLANT SALAD WITH PAPAYA-MISO SAUCE

In the Philippines, we would grill our small, slender, local eggplants on a parilla [small grill] over a fire on top of the stove. Here we use an innovative sauce—ripe papaya mixed with miso—to serve with the grilled eggplant.

SERVES 6 TO 8

Papaya-Miso Sauce:
One small ripe papaya (1 to 1 ½ pounds), peeled, seeded, and cut into pieces

½   cup light miso (preferably organic)

¼   cup rice vinegar

2   tablespoons olive oil

¼   teaspoon minced ginger

Eggplant:
8   Chinese eggplants

2   tablespoons olive oil

12   cherry tomatoes, halved

1. For the sauce, place all the ingredients in a blender or food processor and blend until smooth. If the sauce is too thick, add water as needed.

2. For the eggplant, preheat the broiler. Place the eggplants on a broiler pan and broil 6 inches from the heat source, turning once with tongs, until blackened on all sides, 6 to 8 minutes, depending on the size of the eggplants. Let cool until just cool enough to handle (it's easier to remove the skins when the eggplants are still steamy). Remove the skin from the eggplant using your hands. Cut the eggplants in half lengthwise and flatten each half. Arrange the eggplants on a platter and drizzle with olive oil. Scatter the tomatoes over the platter.

3. Serve with the Papaya-Miso Sauce on the side. You can serve any leftover sauce with grilled vegetables, squid, or shrimp.

KANGKONG SALAD

Kangkong is a green leafy vegetable with a hollow stalk. Also known as water spinach, it is available in Chinatowns. Chinese restaurants with big Filipino followings know that Filipinos like theirs served with bagoong.

My mother got this recipe from Mrs. Dela Rosa, the mother of a former faculty member of the biochemistry department at the University of the Philippines. This is a popular item on my mother's table at our home in Malate, Manila. When guests are over, they inevitably ask her for the recipe before the end of the evening.

Depending on your preferences, you may change the dressing into a typical vinaigrette by increasing the amount of olive oil and decreasing the amount of water.

SERVES 4

Dressing:

⅓	cup rice vinegar or apple cider vinegar
4½	teaspoons sugar
2	teaspoons prepared mustard
1	teaspoon olive oil
½	teaspoon salt
½	teaspoon chili sauce (either Tabasco, sriracha, or Thai chili sauce)
⅛	teaspoon freshly ground black pepper

Salad:

1	pound kangkong leaves and stalks, stems trimmed and cut into 2-inch pieces
2	medium tomatoes, cut into wedges
½	small red onion, diced
2	salted duck eggs, peeled and cut into wedges (opposite), or 2 hard-boiled chicken eggs

1. Combine all the dressing ingredients in a medium bowl with ¼ cup of water.

2. Bring a large saucepan of salted water to a boil over high heat. Add the kangkong and cook until slightly wilted, about 1 minute. Drain and arrange the blanched kangkong on a platter. Decorate with the tomatoes, red onions, and salted duck eggs. Whisk the dressing and dress the salad, reserving any extra dressing for future use.

Vegetables in the Filipino Diet

During my childhood, my mother avoided serving salads and raw vegetables for fear of contamination, so we ate a variety of cooked vegetables using a method of preparation called the guisado (see Mongo Guisado, page 92), which uses a base of fried garlic, onions, and tomatoes, to which shrimp, then a vegetable, was added. The dish was seasoned with shrimp juice, fish sauce, and sometimes with bagoong. We ate a lot of chayote, upo [gourd], kalabasa [squash], sigadillas [winged-beans], and sitao [longbeans]. The few times we ate a salad, usually made with cucumbers or blanched greens like water spinach, the salad dressing would not be like the traditional oil and vinegar combination found in the West, but rather a vinegar-water-sugar combination. When I came to the United States, I had to get used to eating salads coated in oil.

From left to right: patola [squash], calabaza and camote [sweet potato] tops, seaweed, sigadillas [winged beans].

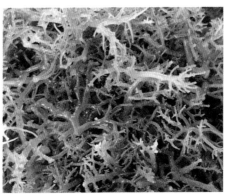

Nostalgia for Bagoong

Carla Mendoza Pacis is the granddaughter of Petronila Syquia (Mamang Nila) and Vicente Mendoza. She is presently one of the trustees responsible for the preservation and care of the family ancestral home, the Syquia Mansion, one of the highlights of any tour of the noble city of Vigan, Ilocos Sur. This is her account.

Childhood summers began when my grandmother, Mamang Nila, planned our yearly trip from Manila to Vigan, her beloved hometown. Mamang loved to travel with most of her large family in tow. Departure time, length of stay, number of cars, people in each car (titas, titos, siblings, cousins, friends, yayas, and drivers), luggage, food, and where to stop were planned with military precision. As soon as school was over, I looked forward to conjuring up the family ghosts at the old Syquia Mansion, built in 1830 by my great-great-great-grandfather Vicente Angco—and to eating the best Ilocano food anywhere in the country.

We'd depart at four A.M., younger children still asleep in pajamas bundled into cars. We drove northward single file, like camels in a caravan, the ten-hour trip punctuated by stops at each major town market, where my grandmother haggled like a true Ilocana for biscocho in Bulacan, tocino in Pampanga, and tupig, a sticky roll of coconut and molasses, in Pangasinan. In La Union, we'd make a detour to Damortis for fresh capiz [windowpane oyster] shells, to be added to the dinengdeng immediately when we arrived in Vigan, with perfect timing, for a late lunch.

Mamang's arrival was a major event. The windows on the second floor were opened, the grand staircase and floors polished, the yellow damask curtains hung. On a table long enough to seat three generations, we would start our Ilocano food fest.

Sinanglaw, my grandmother's favorite, a piping hot stew of blood cubes, eyes, ears, and snout of a most unfortunate pig, was a nourishing brew always served after a long trip or a long night of revelry. Those of us who could not quite share in her pleasure would have pinakbet (page 114), vegetables like ampalaya [bitter melon], eggplant, okra, and patane [lima beans] heaped into a bowl with bagnet, large chunks of pork with thick layers of fried, crispy skin. For the children, there would be the spicy Vigan longaniza and scrambled eggs with tomatoes, a treat we would have again for breakfast.

Evenings the house was at its prettiest: the heat was replaced with a cool breeze, chandeliers glittered like large diamond earrings, and the blue lamp by the chapel glowed like sapphire. Dinner was more formal—the best silverware was brought out and more of the family's favorite dishes served. For appetizers, we usually had crispy ukoy, a mixture of milled rice, eggs, small purple onions, lagdaw or baby shrimp, tomatoes, lasona, and kutchay [chives]. Laid out across the table were large bowls of pancit musiko or dinengdeng. The other Syquia favorite, chicken pipian (right), was a welcome change from all the bagoong-flavored dishes.

Dinner lasted for hours, colored by lively conversations. Memories of past Vigan sojourns would be relived and the food relished. A whole year would pass before these flavors would be encountered again. With full stomachs and contented hearts, we would move to the ante-sala to repose and discuss the next day's activities and meals.

The Syquia Family of Vigan, Ilocos Sur

(as told by Carla M. Pacis)

The nineteenth century was a turbulent time in China, with several waves of migrations to the developing Asian countries. In 1829, Sy Qui Ah, only twelve years old, left his hometown of Am Thau in Amoy to live with relatives in the Chinese enclave of Binondo, Manila, where he lived and worked for many years as a clerk and salesman. In 1848, he found himself in the old Spanish town of Vigan, a

province of Ilocos north of Manila and a major trading port. There he fell in love with Petronila Singson Encarnacion, a member of the Vigan aristocracy. In order to marry her, he was asked to embrace Christianity, so he was baptized and given the Christian name of Vicente Romero Syquia.

Gregorio, the eldest son of Vicente and Petronila, managed his father's interests in Vigan. He was a shrewd businessman and made the most of what he had inherited from his father, planting crops such as tobacco, indigo, cotton, and rice. It is said that during the time of harvest, the crops lined the street outside the house and turned the block.

Although of Chinese heritage, the Syquia family did not speak any Chinese and, in fact, spoke Spanish and Ilocano. Gregorio was such a loyal Spanish subject that he received the Isabela La Catolica medal, an honor awarded to subjects who have contributed greatly to the honor and grandeur of Spain.

CHICKEN PIPIAN

The pipian is, in essence, a chicken version of the Filipino kare kare. In Mexico, pipian is a sauce thickened with ground toasted pepitas [pumpkin seeds]; in the Philippines, ground toasted rice is used instead. We adapted this dish from the pipian cooked by Rusty Ponce, the resident cook at the Syquia Mansion in Vigan. The main flavoring agent is the epazote, called *pasotes* in Ilocos. The pasotes plant, found only in Ilocos Sur, was probably transported from Mexico on one of the galleons that regularly sailed to Vigan. Rusty mixes his with a small amount of pork, but we prefer an all-chicken dish.

There is an undertone of tartness to this dish, which comes from the kamias. If kamias is not available, lime juice is a good substitute.

SERVES 4 TO 6

⅓   cup raw white rice
3   tablespoons vegetable oil
One 3 ¼-pound chicken, cut up
1   medium onion, chopped
3   garlic cloves, mashed
3   medium tomatoes, chopped
Strained pulp from 3 to 4 fresh kamias (see Note),
       or ¼ cup fresh lime or lemon juice
1   tablespoon fish sauce or 2 teaspoons rock salt
       or sea salt
2   teaspoons achuete (annatto) seeds soaked
       in ½ cup hot water for 30 minutes
1   tablespoon dried crumbled epazote leaves
1   tablespoon rice wine (optional)

1. In a dry wok over medium heat, toast the rice, tossing constantly, until browned, about 5 minutes. Transfer to a plate to cool, then grind to a powder in a spice grinder (or using a mortar and pestle). Place in a small bowl.

(continued)

2. In a large heavy-bottomed saucepan over medium-high heat, warm the oil. Add the chicken pieces and brown on both sides, about 5 minutes per side. Transfer the chicken to a plate.

3. Add the onions and garlic to the pan and sauté for 3 minutes, then add the tomatoes and sauté for 1 more minute. Return the chicken to the pan with 3 cups of water, bring to a boil, then reduce the heat, cover, and simmer, until the chicken is tender, about 30 minutes. Skim several times while cooking to remove any scum.

4. Add the kamias pulp or 3 tablespoons lime or lemon juice. Season with fish sauce or rock salt.

5. Strain the achuete seeds and mix this liquid into the toasted ground rice until smooth. Add this mixture to the chicken and cook until the ground rice tastes cooked and the stew is thickened, about 5 minutes.

6. Add the epazote and the rice wine, if using. Cook for 3 more minutes to finish the dish. Add the remaining lime or lemon juice. Taste and add more salt or lime/lemon juice if needed.

Note: Fresh Kamias Pulp
If you have access to fresh kamias, cut the kamias into pieces and boil in about ½ cup of water. When soft, mash the kamias and strain. Add the strained kamias pulp into the chicken.

Above: dinuyduy and pinapaitan, Vigan. Opposite, top left: tying rice cakes; top right: steaming puto; bottom left: kitchen of Puruganan home; bottom right: burnay for fermenting vinegar.

Memories of Vigan Kitchens

Dishes Carla Pacis describes from her childhood trips to Vigan, and those we saw prepared by Bonito Singson's chef, Digna Claudio Mercado, map out the traditional flavors of the Ilocos region.

Dinengdeng: A soupy dish of malunggay, squash blossoms, saluyot, and rosangis [pinhead-sized clams], seasoned with bagoong.

Dinuyduy: A dish made by simmering pork pieces in water until the lard is rendered, sautéing garlic in the lard with the pork pieces, seasoning with bagoong monamon, then adding thinly sliced calabaza squash and water.

Lomo-lomo: A soupy version of dinuguan (page 115) to which sautéed chopped pork meat, heart, liver, kidney, and, at the end, coagulated cubed pork blood, chives, and fish sauce are added.

Pancit musiko: A soup of miki [wheat flour noodles], pork, and chicken sautéed in garlic, achuete, and paminta [black peppercorns].

Pinapaitan: Pait means bitter and the traditional pinapaitan is goat cooked in its bile. The Vigan version uses beef that is simmered until soft. Onions and ginger are sautéed in suet, to which the simmered beef, bile, water, vinegar, and chiles are added.

Poki-poki: Long, narrow native eggplants are grilled, peeled, and mashed, It is sautéed in garlic, onion, tomatoes, and a beaten egg.

Salads: Made of blanched sitao [longbeans] and labong [bamboo shoots] dressed in vinegar, sugar, water, and ground black pepper.

Tinegteg: Chopped beef sautéed with tomatoes, lasona [small purple onions], and potatoes.

Dingras: The Granary
of Northern Ilocos

Lestie Fronteras every so often tries to make the long ten-hour trip back home from Manila to Dingras, 20 kilometers southeast of Laoag, Ilocos Norte. Dingras is a historic town built in 1598 by the Spanish in the classic tradition, with the Catholic Church built on one end of the plaza and homes of prominent families around the square. Lestie is a Puruganan, and their ancestral home stands behind the statue of the martyred Josefa Llanes Escoda, executed by the Japanese during World War II.

I met Lestie through her brother Emil, who came to eat at the restaurant one day. When I told him I was in search of old homes, old kitchens, and traditional home cooking, he embarked on a tireless campaign to get me to Dingras. Known as the rice granary of northern Ilocos, Dingras is also a big corn producer. The most famous local product is cornix—dried corn kernels boiled twice with lye, deep-fried, and seasoned with salt and garlic. The technique was probably brought over from Mexico, and the result is addictive.

The Puruganan ancestral home is a huge house of wood and white stone built in the Spanish-era bahay-na-bato style. As you walk through the gate, you are actually entering the ground floor, where one can see the huge trunks of trees that were used as foundation for the house.

We spent some time next door with Glezy Valencia, who demonstrated her tupig, puto, and patupat [Ilocano rice delicacies] for us. And we met Leonora Rocimo, who was busy chopping up meat to prepare the traditional family breakfast of yusi, a soup made from pork, liver, heart, garlic, soy sauce, and chives. Leonora started learning how to cook from Lestie's grandmother, Maria Rivera Puruganan, when she was seventeen. Lestie remembers the two women always in the kitchen, cooking pinakbet, arroz caldo, and chicken soup.

Pampanga
The Rice Heartland of Luzon

Above: carabao [water buffalo] milk. Top: sorting rice, rice-fermented fish and pork, Talangka crabs. Opposite: burong dalag (mudfish fermented with rice then deep fried).

Pampanga is one of the oldest provinces of the Philippines with a history that is very much intertwined with that of Manila. It is known for its food, and Kapampangan cooks are highly respected by Filipinos. I visited the Guanzon family in Sta. Rita, Pampanga, where we were able to photograph that day's batch of turrones de casuy and sans rival (pages 132–33) by the Lansang Delicacies bakery. Then I was off to stay a few days with Claude Tayag and his wife, Mary Ann, in Angeles, Pampanga. Claude built his beautiful home from wood and other material he rescued from churches and old homes that were being demolished.

He introduced Mary Ann's family cook, Juana Tuazon Miranda, who showed us how to make tamales. I have included a section here on the food and memories of Marc Medina from Arayat, Pampanga. Marc Medina is a writer who decided to follow his passion and has been devoting his time to the promotion and preservation of the foods of Pampanga.

Although I was not able to visit Marc, my photographer, Neal Oshima, spent a day with him in his home, feasting on food made from his family's treasured recipes.

The Arayat Kitchen

Susan Calo Medina visited Cendrillon in 1999 while traveling with then-Secretary of the Philippine Department of Tourism, Gemma Cruz-Araneta, who assisted us in our food tour of the Philippines that year. Since then, I've gotten to know Susan's son, Marc, who recalls the life and food of his hometown, Arayat:

The kitchen is the oldest part of my grandmother's house: wooden slats as floors, thin rattan walls, a bamboo and nipa roof held up by hardwood pillars half-eaten by termites. At the far end facing the adobe steps are four clay stoves on a long hardwood table. Underneath are stacks of wood, clay pots, and tin pans; onions, garlic, tomatoes, and oil; bowls of rock salt and ground pepper; misshapen knives and worn-out cleavers; and a long bamboo tube. One of my most vivid childhood memories is watching my grandmother's cook (aunt of my father's present cook) puff through that long piece of bamboo to control the flames. Clay pots black with soot sat four in a row, filled with boiling meats, simmering rice, or frying vegetables.

The wood-fire stove is still the heart of the house. For my grandfather Dr. Esteban Medina, it was wood fire or nothing. It was actually my grandfather who had a passionate love affair with food, and he was first and foremost a culinary purist. His breakfast was a frothy cup of hot chocolate made with ground peanuts and native cacao, slowly boiled and whisked with fresh carabao's milk, with the light green grains of premature fragrant rice sprinkled on top. He also relished the exotica of Pampango cuisine: adobong camaru [mole crickets fried in garlic and chile], ebun barag [boiled eggs of large swamp lizards], dumará [wild ducks braised in onions, olives, and white wine], and burong talangka [live small freshwater crabs doused in boiling water and fermented overnight in salt].

There were as many as four cooks in the kitchen at one time, with a half-dozen assistants, yet my grandmother's everyday table was straightforward and decidedly lowbrow. By the time she married, she had mastered a handful of everyday Pampango dishes, including "pang aldo-aldo," as they say in the local vernacular, or tidtad bigac [pork loin stewed in its own blood], tidtad baca [a soup of ground beef and pig's blood], afritada [chicken and pork braised in vinegar, tomatoes, and red peppers], suam mais [a thick soup of native corn and squash blossoms], asado [chicken and pork soured with vinegar, tomatoes, and soy sauce], estofado [pig's trotters braised with sugar and herbs], and burong asan [fermented soft rice and fish].

Every dish had a corresponding tiltilan [condiment]: atsara [shredded pickled green papaya], burong asan [fermented rice and fish], bagoong, kalamansi lime juice and patis, kamias and soy sauce. One of my grandmother's favorites was a sauce for grilled fish made of sour tamarinds boiled and ground to a pulp and mixed with grilled green chiles, spiked with bagoong. When mangoes were in season, my grandmother's cook would slice the young, fragrant mango leaves and serve them with thin shavings of green, unripe mangoes and bagoong to accompany fish, which, in landlocked Pampanga, was invariably freshwater hito [catfish] or dalag [mudfish].

My mother loves to tell of her first meals with her in-laws. Having come from Mindanao, where fish was served with vinegar, patis, or soy sauce, the variety of sauces for fish was baffling. Shortly after their marriage, my grandmother sent her chief cook to teach my mother the rudiments of Pampango cooking. Thirty-nine years later, my mother refuses to cook Pampango food, simply because it never turns out as good as her mother-in-law's (who has been dead for more than twenty years).

My mother did learn some secrets, though. She makes an impeccable begucan, pork loin boiled in vinegar and bagoong and fried in its own fat with tomatoes. It is neither too sour nor too salty, the richness of the flavors tempered by the ripe bananas with which it is always served. The strips of pork and innards in her menudo, a fiesta favorite, are boiled in

Making biscocho for lechon sauce.
Left: Squeezing coconut milk.

vinegar, then removed and refried until the fat rises to the surface. She also learned a few desserts, which no genuine Pampango would ever do without. Her silken, lime-scented leche flan depends on fresh carabao's milk and the rind of a local lime called dalayap.

Over the years, I've realized that the secrets to my grandmother's cooking can be found in two simple rules. One, cook slowly and patiently. The lowly chicken and pork adobo, in our family made without soy sauce, with chicken gizzards, liver, and generous amounts of garlic, should be boiled in vinegar then double-fried, ever so slowly, until golden brown. Both afritada and asado should simmer undisturbed over a very low fire, until the sauce, rich and robust, settles beneath the oil.

Two, use only the freshest ingredients. My grandmother's cooks went to the market every morning. Tidtad bigac works well only with fresh pig's blood, which forms a thin black sauce that separates from the oil. Sauce for the spit-roasted lechon can only be made from fresh pork liver. The tartness of the vinegar in the sauce is balanced by a generous helping of white sugar.

My grandmother's cooking was disciplined, down to earth, and rarely high concept. Pork estofado, one of my grandfather's favorites, was cooked in a clay pot, the pig's trotters braised slowly on a tray of bamboo set an inch or so above the bottom, with the onions, garlic, vinegar, brown sugar, and sangkot-sangkot [oregano and other local herbs] slowly flavoring the layers of pork fat and cartilage. "When sour becomes sweet, and sweet becomes sour," one of my grandmother's cooks used to say, "stop adding the sugar."

My grandmother did have a few innovations. Among my personal favorites is pancit langlang, a hefty noodle soup similar to the Tagalog pancit luglug. The sauce, red-orange from achuete seeds, is made from the juice of raw shrimp heads and pig's cheeks, simmered slowly and mixed constantly. Pancit langlang is eaten in a soup bowl, the sauce poured over white vermicelli, garnished at the table with crushed pork cracklings, toasted garlic, spring onions, and hard-boiled eggs, and accompanied by sisig babi, a sweet-sour dish made with the remaining pig snout, ear, and forehead, and soaked in vinegar, soy sauce, garlic, onions, sugar, and black pepper.

Today my father has a household staff of three: one to cook, one to clean, and another to watch the old house at night. We all eat at the kitchen table. The dishes are still prepared with attention and care, but my father's seventy-year-old cook, born and raised in the old house, often looks back at the gentle, pre-War days of my grandmother with nostalgia.

BRINGHE

Bringhe is a Filipino version of paella, made with glutinous rice and steamed in banana leaves.

SERVES 4 TO 6

One 3 ½-pound chicken
1   large onion, quartered
Banana leaf sections, for lining the wok
2   tablespoons canola oil
3   garlic cloves, sliced
1   medium onion, diced
1   red bell pepper, diced
1   large carrot, diced
1   large russet potato, peeled and diced
One 1-inch piece fresh turmeric, peeled and grated
      (or 1 teaspoon ground turmeric)
2   cups glutinous rice, soaked overnight in water
      to cover, drained well
About 2 cups coconut milk
4   tablespoons fish sauce, or to taste

1. Place the chicken and quartered onion in a large saucepan and add water to cover. Bring to a boil over high heat, then reduce the heat and simmer, uncovered, until the chicken is tender, about 40 minutes. Remove the chicken, strain, and reserve the broth. Set the chicken aside to cool, then remove the meat from the bones and shred it. Set aside.

2. Wipe the banana leaves with damp paper towels to clean them. Run them through a flame on both sides to soften them a bit. Grease a large wok (or 2 small woks) and line it with a double layer of banana leaves.

3. In a large sauté pan over medium heat, warm the oil. Add the garlic, diced onion, and bell pepper and sauté until the onion is translucent, about 5 minutes. Add the carrots and potatoes and cook until softened, about 5 minutes. Add the turmeric and stir for 1 minute, until

aromatic. Add the rice and cook, stirring, until thoroughly coated with the oil, about 5 minutes. Add 1 ½ cups of the coconut milk, 1 ½ cups of the reserved chicken stock, and the fish sauce. Bring to a simmer and cook, stirring frequently, until all the liquid is absorbed. Add another ½ cup coconut milk and ½ cup stock and continue to stir until the liquid is absorbed. This should take about 20 minutes—the rice should be tender but al dente. If the rice isn't cooked through, add more coconut milk and stock. Continue to cook, stirring, until the liquid is absorbed and the rice is cooked through. Add the shredded chicken and cook until warmed through, about 3 minutes.

4. Fill the prepared wok (or woks) with the rice mixture, smooth the top to create an even layer, cover with the lid or foil, and place over medium heat. Cook without stirring for 20 minutes, or until a golden brown crust that holds the dish together is formed at the bottom of the dish. If the crust hasn't formed, raise the heat to medium-high and cook for another 5 to 10 minutes to form the crust. Invert onto a large serving plate, remove the banana leaves, and serve.

Dilaw [tumeric].

A Family Heirloom Recipe

This is Marc Medina's family heirloom recipe, and I asked him to describe it:

Bringhe is an old party favorite among many families in Arayat. The procedure and ingredients are more or less the same from house to house, with variations only in the amount of coconut milk and water used and the cooking time. Some prefer a dry bringhe where the rice can easily be broken up with a fork, but our family prefers a bringhe where the rice sticks to both plate and palate. My grandmother's version uses chorizo as an added ingredient, and substitutes chile leaves for local turmeric as food coloring (the chile leaves are scraped on a sieve over the coconut milk). With my grandmother gone, local turmeric has become the standard, without the canned chorizos. Either way, the glutinous rice mixture must be stirred slowly and constantly over medium fire, until the grains are translucent, before covering it with banana leaves for steaming. This guarantees a bolder taste to the otherwise mild flavoring of the bringhe.

Bringhe is best cooked over wood fire, like a paella, and it doesn't have a very long shelf life—a day at most in the refrigerator. It makes an excellent partner for a lechon and the standard sweet-sour liver sauce.

TIDTAD BACA

This is another one of Marc Medina's family recipes.

SERVES 8

¼	cup canola oil
1	medium onion, chopped
4	garlic cloves, chopped
3	pounds ground beef
3	tablespoons fish sauce
1½	cups thinly sliced fresh or frozen kamias (about ½ pound)
1½	cups pig's blood, strained

1. In a large saucepan over medium heat, warm the oil. Add the onion and garlic and sauté until softened and translucent, about 5 minutes. Add the ground beef, raise the heat to medium-high, and cook, breaking the meat up with a fork, until the meat browns, about 5 minutes. Add the fish sauce.

2. Spread the kamias over the top of the meat, reduce the heat to medium-low, and cook without stirring until the kamias have softened and are slightly translucent, about 10 minutes.

3. Pour in 1 cup of water, raise the heat, and bring the mixture to a boil. Reduce the heat and simmer for 10 minutes, or until most of the liquid has been absorbed. Add the blood and cook for 5 minutes, or until the stew has thickened.

4. Taste and add more fish sauce, if needed, or kamias, if you prefer the dish a little more tart.

The Secret to a Good Tidtad Baca

Marc Medina recounts:

In Pampanga, the pig's blood stew [dinuguan] is called tidtad bigac. However, our family makes a soup of ground beef and pork blood, soured with green kamias instead of vinegar, called tid-tad baca (*baca* means cow). It is eaten in a soup bowl with rice and bagoong on the side. The secret to a good tidtad baca is using a generous amount of kamias.

No one seems to know the history of this soup, and my father's sixty-four-year old cook, Ate Lucia, says she has never seen it elsewhere in Arayat. Tidtad baca is similar to a popular dinuguan soup called tinumis in neighboring Nueva Ecija, another rice-growing province separated from Arayat by the Pampanga River. The "tidtad Medina" as Ate Lucia calls it, may have been inspired by the Nueva Ecija version.

Making turrones de casuy at the Lansang Delicacies in Sta. Rita. These nougat candies are traditionally made with almonds, but here cashews are used. Beloved throughout the Spanish-speaking world and especially popular for gift-giving at the holidays, they have a wafer coating referred to as "the host," because of its similarity to the communal wafer.

ARROZ CALDO

Arroz caldo is one of those dishes that is Spanish in name but really is in essence a Chinese dish—congee with chicken. There are two ways of making arroz caldo. One way is to sauté the chicken pieces and add the water and rice to the chicken and cook until the rice is done. I prefer making a chicken broth first, then shredding the chicken before adding both to the rice soup. Having extra broth on the side will allow you to decide how thick you want the arroz caldo to be. You will need to stir the rice continuously as it cooks.

SERVES 4 TO 6

Chicken Broth:

One 3½-pound chicken, skin-on, quartered

2   celery stalks, cut into large pieces

1   head garlic, cloves separated and peeled

1   medium onion, quartered

2   teaspoons sea salt or kosher salt

1   teaspoon whole black peppercorns

Arroz Caldo:

3   tablespoons canola oil

1   head garlic, cloves peeled and crushed

One 2-inch piece fresh ginger, peeled and julienned

1   medium onion, thinly sliced

½   cup uncooked short-grain rice

½   cup glutinous (sweet) rice

Chicken Broth, as needed

2   teaspoons fish sauce, or to taste

½   teaspoon freshly ground black pepper

Kalamansi lime juice or freshly squeezed lemon juice, to taste, for serving

½   cup chopped fresh parsley or fresh cilantro, for garnish (optional)

5   scallions, white and light green parts, thinly sliced for garnish (optional)

1. To make the chicken broth, combine all of the broth ingredients with 10 cups water in a large pot and bring to a boil over high heat. Reduce the heat and simmer until the chicken is tender, about 30 minutes. Use tongs to transfer the chicken pieces to a plate to cool. Strain the broth through a fine-mesh strainer into a very large, clean saucepan and bring to a gentle simmer over medium heat. Continue to simmer, adjusting the heat if necessary, while you make the arroz caldo.

2. When the chicken pieces have cooled, remove the skin, then use your fingers to remove the meat from the bones and shred it.

3. To make the arroz caldo, warm the oil in a large saucepan over medium heat. Add the crushed garlic cloves and cook in the oil until browned and crisp, about 4 minutes. Use a slotted spoon to transfer the garlic to a paper towel–lined plate to drain. Reserve for garnish.

4. Add the ginger and onion to the oil remaining in the pan and cook, stirring, until the onion is translucent, about 3 minutes. Add both regular and sweet rice and sauté until the rice is evenly coated with oil, about 2 minutes. Ladle in 1 cup of the warm chicken broth and cook, stirring, until most of the broth is absorbed. Continue adding chicken broth, 1 cup at a time, stirring frequently, until you've used up all the broth and the rice begins to break down, 35 to 40 minutes. If you like your arroz caldo thick, you can hold back some of the broth.

5. Add the shredded chicken, fish sauce, and black pepper. Taste and adjust the seasoning, if necessary. Place the fried garlic, kalamansi lime or lemon juice, and herbs and scallions, if using, in separate small bowls. Ladle the arroz caldo into serving bowls and serve, with the bowls of toppings on the side.

Stay for Some Arroz Caldo!

After spending a day eating under the shade of towering acacia trees in the elegant garden of Tess Guanzon in Sta. Rita, Pampanga, it was time to say good-bye. As I walked to my waiting car and driver, Mamang Guanzon, Tess's mother-in-law and also my host, held my arm to stop me from leaving. "But you have not had merienda yet. Stay for some arroz caldo!" My driver looked at me with sheer panic, protesting he could not eat another mouthful of food. But stay we did and the arroz caldo was sheer heaven. I am used to a thin rice soup, but this version was thicker than usual because they added malagkit [glutinous rice] to the rice mixture.

TAMALES

We learned this technique of making tamales from Mary Ann Tayag's family cook, Juana Tuazon Miranda, who cooked in Claude Tayag's beautifully reconstructed old-fashioned Filipino kitchen in Angeles, Pampanga. The word *tamales* is derived from the Mexican *tamal* (in the Philippines, it is never referred to as tamal, always tamales), but in place of the corn flour, Filipino tamales are made with ground rice.

MAKES 16 TAMALES

Half of a 3½-pound chicken
1   large onion, quartered
4   tablespoons achuete oil (page 17)
1   large onion, finely chopped
2   medium carrots, finely chopped
2   small chorizos, finely diced
1   tablespoon plus ½ teaspoon salt
¼   teaspoon freshly ground black pepper
4   cups short-grain rice, soaked overnight in water
     to cover
½   cup coconut milk
One 1-pound package banana leaves
16   quail eggs, boiled for 2 minutes, drained, and peeled

1. In a large saucepan over high heat, cover the chicken and quartered onion with 10 cups water and bring to a boil. Lower the heat and simmer, uncovered, until the chicken is tender, about 40 minutes. Strain, reserving the stock. When the chicken is cool enough to handle, remove the meat from the bones and shred it. Set aside.

2. In a medium skillet over medium heat, warm 2 tablespoons of the achuete oil. Add the onion and carrot and sauté until softened, about 3 minutes. Add the chorizos

and shredded chicken and cook to warm through, 3 to 5 minutes. Add ½ teaspoon of the salt and the pepper. Taste and add more salt and pepper if needed.

3. Drain the rice, place it in a food processor, and process until finely ground. Strain through a medium-mesh strainer. Take any solids that didn't go through the strainer and process them again until they are ground fine enough to fit through the strainer. You will have about 5 cups galapong [ground rice].

4. Combine the galapong with 7 cups of the chicken stock, the remaining 2 tablespoons achuete oil, and the remaining tablespoon salt. Bring to a boil over high heat. Reduce the heat to medium and cook, whisking constantly, until thickened (like polenta), 3 to 5 minutes. Add the coconut milk and whisk for another minute, until incorporated. Transfer to a large bowl and cool.

5. Clean the banana leaf sections by wiping them on both sides with a damp paper towel. Pass the leaves over a medium flame on both sides to soften. Cut out sixteen 10-by-12-inch sections and sixteen 5-by-5-inch sections, removing the tough rib at the top of the leaves. You may want to cut out extra in case of breakage. Cut a leaf crosswise into 32 quarter-inch strips to use for tying the tamales. (You can also use kitchen twine.)

6. Place a large banana leaf section horizontally on your work surface. Center a smaller leaf section on the larger leaf. Spread about ½ cup of the rice over the middle of the smaller leaf in a square formation and top with about ¼ cup of the chicken mixture. Nestle in a quail egg. Fold over the sides, first lengthwise, then widthwise. Place seam side down and tie the packages closed crosswise and lengthwise (like a present) with the banana leaf strips.

7. Bring 2 inches of water to a boil in a covered pot fitted with a steamer basket. Stand the tamales upright, cover, and steam until the banana leaves peel off easily, 10 to 15 minutes.

TOCINO DEL CIELO

Pampangos are famous for their rich desserts, and this is one of the richest.

MAKES 6

1   cup sugar
¼   cup unsalted butter, cut into small pieces
10   large egg yolks, beaten

1. Preheat the oven to 350° F. Have ready six 2-ounce ramekins.

2. To make the caramel base, place ½ cup of the sugar in a small, heavy saucepan. Drizzle 2 tablespoons water over the top. Place the pan over medium-high heat and cook, gently swirling the pan but not stirring, until the sugar has melted into a deep amber-colored syrup, 5 to 7 minutes. Quickly pour the mixture into the ramekins, tilting to evenly spread the caramel. Let cool.

3. While the caramel cools, in a separate saucepan combine the remaining ½ cup sugar with ¾ cup water. Cook over medium heat, stirring, until the sugar dissolves and the mixture reaches the soft ball stage, 235° F to 240° F. Whisk in the butter.

4. Whisk the egg yolks in a large heatproof bowl. Whisking constantly, very slowly pour the sugar-butter mixture into the egg yolks. Strain the mixture through a fine-mesh strainer into the ramekins.

5. Place the ramekins in a baking or roasting pan and add enough hot water to come halfway up their sides. Very loosely cover the baking pan with foil, poking the foil with a knife a few times to create air vents. Bake until set in the center, 50 minutes to an hour. Transfer the ramekins to a wire rack to cool, then cover and refrigerate overnight.

6. The next day, allow the Tocino del Cielo to come to room temperature. Run a sharp knife around the edges of the ramekins to loosen them. Place a small plate on top of each ramekin, and flip the plate over. Carefully lift off the ramekin.

Pork Fat of the Heavens

Marc Medina describes this heavenly dessert:

For most Pampangos, tocino is cured pork (page 93), but many old families all over the province have a recipe for a rich flan made with egg yolks, butter, and sugar called tocino del cielo [probable translation, "pork fat of the heavens"]. The flan does not take much technique or skill, but seems to have disappeared from the popular compendium of Pampango recipes. The procedure is fairly straightforward and holds no secrets, yet the few families that still make this recipe say theirs is the original. Perhaps the previous generation of cooks kept this popular dessert such a secret that they have taken the recipe to their graves.

For as long as my cousins and I can remember, this tocino del cielo, and its cousin the leche flan, were the standard ending of any party meal. Unlike the leche flan made with fresh carabao's milk and dalyap, tocino del cielo is made with ingredients easily obtainable in the city. It is sumptuous and rich, with golden brown syrup dripping over the buttery flan.

Both my aunt Hidelisa Medina Caguiat and my mother have, with a generosity uncommon among Pampango housewives, shared this recipe with many friends. Oddly enough, none of them, myself included, can cook it the way the women in the Medina family have done for more than half a century.

CHOCOLATE MACADAMIA SANS RIVAL

The sans rival is the royalty of all desserts in the Philippines, extremely rich and delicious. It is also a specialty of the town of Sta. Rita, Pampanga, where, through the intercession of Mamang Guanzon, we were able to watch the bakers of Lansang Delicacies make that day's batch of sans rival.

The cake is made up of layers of dacquoise, then iced with a buttercream frosting. This recipe, which we adapted from the *Frog Commissary Cookbook*, uses macadamias instead of cashews for the dacquoise and a chocolate rather than the plain buttercream frosting. Romy suggests working in a cool space when preparing this cake – if the room is too hot, the buttercream will melt and not spread as it should.

SERVES 12 TO 16

Meringue:

2½   cups (12 ounces) macadamia nuts
2   tablespoons cornstarch
1¼   cups sugar
7   egg whites, at room temperature
¼   teaspoon salt
½   teaspoon cream of tartar
2   teaspoons vanilla extract

Buttercream:

7   egg yolks
¾   cup sugar
½   cup heavy cream
6   ounces bittersweet chocolate, finely chopped
1   pound unsalted butter, at room temperature
2   teaspoons vanilla extract

Sugar or marzipan flowers, for decorating (optional)

1. To toast the macadamias, preheat the oven to 325° F. Spread the macadamias in a single layer on a rimmed baking ban. Toast until lightly golden and fragrant, 10 to 15 minutes. Set aside to cool. Raise the oven temperature to 400° F.

2. To prepare the meringues, lightly grease three 9-inch cake pans. Line with parchment circles, then grease and flour the parchment circles.

3. Place the macadamia nuts, cornstarch, and 1 cup of the sugar in a food processor and process until the nuts are finely ground into a paste.

4. In a clean bowl of an electric mixer fitted with the whisk attachment, beat the egg whites and salt until frothy. Add the cream of tartar. Continue beating, slowly adding the remaining ¼ cup sugar, until the whites are stiff but not dry.

5. Working in 3 additions, gently fold the beaten whites into the nut mixture. Spread the meringue evenly over the bottoms of the prepared cake pans. Transfer to the oven and immediately reduce the temperature to 275° F. Bake until dry on the sides and slightly soft in the center, 50 minutes to 1 hour. Cool for 15 minutes, then carefully remove the circles of meringue and completely cool on wire racks.

6. To prepare the buttercream, beat the egg yolks with the sugar in the bowl of an electric mixer fitted with a whisk attachment until light and lemon-colored. Place the heavy cream in a large saucepan and warm carefully over low heat until tiny bubbles appear around the sides. Whisk the heavy cream into the egg yolks and return to the saucepan. Stir over low heat until very thick, about 12 minutes. Do not boil or the custard will curdle. Take the pan off the heat, and let cool, strain into the same electric mixer bowl (that has been cleaned and wiped dry) through a fine-mesh strainer.

7. Melt the chocolate in a double boiler or small bowl set over simmering water. Let cool slightly.

8. With a paddle attachment, start adding the butter into the slightly cooled custard, bit by bit, beating each bit in until completely absorbed before adding the next. Beat in the vanilla extract. Place two-thirds of the mixture in a separate bowl and stir in the melted chocolate.

9. Place one of the meringues on a serving plate. Spread with a little less than half of the plain buttercream and top with a second layer of meringue. Spread with the remaining plain buttercream and top with the third meringue. Use the chocolate buttercream to cover the top and sides of the cake. (Reserve some of the buttercream for decoration, if desired, using a pastry bag fitted with a star tip.) Decorate with sugar or marzipan flowers if you like.

Laguna
Buko Pie Country

Laguna is part of a group of provinces south of Manila called Calabarzon (Cavite, Laguna, Batangas, Rizal, and Quezon). These provinces all share the same topography, culture, and history, and the entire region is very scenic and fertile because of several active volcanoes, including Taal Volcano, Mt. Makiling, and Mt. Banahaw. This is the start of coconut country, which continues down south to the Bicol region. Quezon and Batangas are known for lambanog, a spirit distilled from tuba [coconut toddy], while Laguna is famous for buko [young coconut] pie. Archaeological digs have unearthed old settlements in several areas, including those of Pila, Laguna. When the Spanish arrived in Pila, they found the people so highly civilized and cultured that they called it La Noble Villa de Pila — The Noble Town of Pila.

Left: coconut buds. Top left: kalamansi limes and singkamas [jicama]; top right: bukayo. Opposite: buko pie.

Loreto Del Mundo-Relova of Pila, Laguna

Loreto Del Mundo-Relova is descended from the Del Mundos of Marinduque and the Rivera clan of Pila, onto whose land the present town was relocated after floods obliterated the old site. Though frail and in her eighties now, she is still beautiful and regal. Her cooking has sustained the family through the decades. What her children consider a family tradition comes from her hands, and what family warmth they look back on comes from her presence. She told a compelling story of how she learned to cook during World War II.

When I was a dalaga [a young, unmarried woman], I did not know how to cook. So I decided to study French cooking. But when the war broke out, I stopped cooking and my recipes got lost. During the war, my aunt and her son from Marinduque evacuated here and hid in the attic because her son was being sought by the Japanese. She was a good cook and I learned from her.

The guerrillas started coming into the town and the Japanese rounded up all the men and put them in the church for nine days. On the third day, the Japanese captain who was searching for guerrillas came and asked if he and his men could use our bathroom. He happened to be educated in England and he was nice, very handsome, and tall. It turned out he loved to sing Tagalog songs, and when he learned that I played the piano he stopped investigating and just sang songs.

The guards at the church knew my husband, so they let him out to go home and take a bath. When it was time to leave, the Japanese cried. They loved it here because the people did not try to kill them. San Antonio is our patron saint—that's why they call this town Bayang Pinagpala, the Promised Town. All the other towns around us were burned and everyone from these areas had to evacuate. We fed everyone, using up our entire rice harvest.

Cora Relova

Cora Relova, Loreto Del Mundo-Relova's daughter, has but one memory that she would always keep with her—the memory of the dining table in their family home in Pila, Laguna, one hot afternoon around May in 1957. She says she was about ten years old then, and Frank Sinatra was singing "All the Way" on the radio. The view from the table—when the eight-foot-high sliding windows are pulled to the side—now reveals a profusion of pink bougainvilleas. But she distinctly remembers a makopa [Curacao apple] tree then.

Cora was profoundly moved by the Japanese movie *After Life*. "The movie is all about what happens when you die and you go to this temporary place like purgatory. You have to choose one memory of your life, which will be your forever memory. If I had to choose one memory, it would be here at this table, eating fried chicken. But what is more important is that my family was complete. No matter what problems in the world we were facing, the one constant was the table and Mama's cooking. You could always count on that no matter what."

PATA ESTOFADO

Pork estofado is a classic Tagalog dish popular in the provinces south of Manila. The traditional way of cooking this is in a clay pot in which the pig's trotters or knuckles in their marinade are covered with saba [plantain] and slices of bread, and the pot opening is sealed with a banana leaf and tied around the rim. The pot is left on a slow fire and the pork knuckles are simmered for several hours. The pot is usually opened the following day to let the flavors of the pork, vinegar, and caramel fully develop.

This recipe was shared with us by Loreto Del Mundo-Relova.

SERVES 4

1½   cups soy sauce
1   teaspoon freshly ground black pepper
5 ½   pounds pig's trotters, cut into 4-inch pieces
1   cup sugar
2   cups sugarcane vinegar or rice vinegar
6   tablespoons canola oil
1   head garlic, cloves peeled
4   shallots, quartered
2   ripe plantains, sliced lengthwise to get 4 pieces

1. Pour ½ cup of the soy sauce into a large nonreactive bowl and add the pepper. Add the trotters and turn to coat them in the soy sauce. Cover, refrigerate, and let marinate for at least 1 hour, or preferably overnight.

2. Place the sugar in a deep, large pot. Drizzle 2 tablespoons water over the top. Place the pan over medium-high heat and cook, gently swirling the pan but not stirring, until the sugar has melted into a deep amber-colored syrup (watch carefully, as this speeds up toward the end and you don't want to overdarken it—if you do, simply start again).

3. While the sugar is caramelizing, pour the vinegar into a separate pot. Place over medium-high heat and bring to a boil. Slowly add the boiling vinegar to the caramelized sugar—the mixture will spit, so take care and stand away from the pot as you pour. Swirl, then stir, to combine. Set aside.

4. Remove the trotters from the marinade, reserving the marinade. In a large sauté pan over medium-high heat, warm ¼ cup oil. Add the trotters to the pan, in batches, and sear until browned on all sides, about 5 minutes.

5. Add the trotters to the sugar-vinegar mixture. Add the reserved marinade, the remaining 1 cup soy sauce, the garlic, and shallots. Add water to cover. Bring to a boil, then reduce the heat, cover, and simmer for about 2 hours, or until the meat is tender and falling off the bone. Remove the trotters from the pot, raise the heat, and cook the sauce until reduced by half, about 20 minutes.

6. While the sauce is reducing, fry the plantains: Warm 2 tablespoons oil in a medium skillet over medium-high heat. Add the plantains and cook until softened and lightly browned on both sides, about 5 minutes.

7. When the sauce has thickened, return the trotters to the pot, add the plantains, and heat to warm through, about 5 minutes.

GUINATAANG HIPON RELOVA

When Cora Relova promised that her mother, Loreto Del Mundo-Relova, would make guinataang hipon for me, my friend Becky Villegas, a famous baker and cook in Manila, groaned with envy and pleaded to come with me. In my mind, guinataang hipon was shrimp cooked in coconut broth—like a Malaysian laksa—but to my surprise, it was really shrimp fried in latik, coconut milk cooked until the oil is extracted. It was not only delicious, but it came to the table beautifully browned and glazed in all its coconut goodness.

SERVES 4

16   large whole shrimp with shells and heads
4   cups coconut milk (preferably fresh or frozen)
6   frozen kamias, sliced
Salt, to taste
Steamed white rice, for serving
2   limes, cut into wedges

1. Clean the shrimp, leaving the heads on and trimming off the eyes, antennas, and sharp points from the tails. Using a sharp paring knife, slit open the backs of the shrimp and devein them, keeping the shells on.

2. Place the coconut milk in a wok or medium saucepan over medium-high heat. Cook for 20 to 25 minutes, stirring occasionally at first, and then constantly when the coconut milk starts to separate. The coconut milk will separate into oil and latik, which are solid particles. When the latik turns golden brown, add the shrimp to the pan. Fry the shrimp in this oil for 2 minutes, then add the kamias and continue frying until the shrimp are cooked through and the latik turns a darker, reddish shade (take care not to burn the latik). Season with salt to taste. Using a slotted spoon, scoop the shrimp, kamias, and latik onto a serving plate. Serve over rice, along with lime wedges.

*Top: guinataang hipon Relova.
Above: kamias.*

ACHARANG UBOD

In the Philippines, ubod refers to the heart of a coconut tree and is more commonly used in Visayan dishes, so I was quite surprised to get a recipe for ubod in Laguna. Here in the United States the closest equivalent to ubod is the heart of palm (pith of the sabal Palmetto) and they are available fresh, canned, or frozen.

This recipe was adapted from one by Mrs. Loreto Del Mundo-Relova.

MAKES ABOUT 1 QUART

2	cups rice vinegar
¾	cup sugar
1½	teaspoons salt
2	garlic cloves, thinly sliced
4	shallots, thinly sliced
1–2	birdseye chiles, to taste, thinly sliced
1	pound ubod or 8 pieces heart of palm, cut into thick matchsticks

1. Combine the vinegar, sugar, salt, garlic, shallots, and chiles in a large nonreactive saucepan. Bring to a boil over high heat, then reduce the heat to medium-low and simmer for 3 minutes to blend the flavors.

2. Transfer to a storage container, cool to room temperature, cover, and refrigerate for at least 1 hour to chill completely.

3. Add the ubod and stir to coat with the pickling solution. Refrigerate overnight before serving.

LECHE FLAN WITH CARAMELIZED MACAPUNO

We adapted this recipe from the leche flan that Joe Lat, Mrs. Relova's cook, prepared for us. The special surprise of the flan was the homemade macapuno that he spread over the bottom of the pan before the custard was poured in. When the flan was turned over on a platter, the caramelized macapuno would be on top of the flan. For this recipe, we decided that it would be easier to make the caramelized macapuno separately and serve it on the side.

Macapuno [coconut sport] are mutant coconuts that manufacture meat until their shells are entirely filled up (*puno* in Tagalog means filled up).

SERVES 6

Flan:

2 ¼ cups sugar
4   large eggs
8   large egg yolks
1 ¼ cups heavy cream
1 ¼ cups milk

Caramelized Macapuno:

Leftover caramel from the flan
½   cup coconut milk
½   cup heavy cream
One 16-ounce jar shredded macapuno

1. Preheat the oven to 350° F. To make the caramel base, have ready six 8-ounce ramekins. Place 1½ cups of the sugar in a small, heavy saucepan. Drizzle ¼ cup water over the top. Place the pan over medium-high heat and cook, gently swirling the pan but not stirring, until the sugar has melted into a deep amber-colored syrup, 5 to 7 minutes. Quickly pour the caramel into the bottom of the ramekins and let cool. Reserve the remaining caramel to make the macapuno.

2. To make the caramelized macapuno, add the coconut milk and heavy cream to the leftover caramel in the pan. Bring to a simmer over medium heat, whisking, for 2 minutes, until smooth. Add the macapuno and stir for 3 more minutes. Set aside to cool, then cover and refrigerate until ready to serve.

3. To make the flan custard, lightly beat the eggs and egg yolks together in a large bowl. In a medium saucepan, heat the heavy cream, milk, and remaining ¾ cup sugar, stirring until the sugar dissolves. Whisking constantly, slowly pour the scalded milk mixture into the beaten eggs. Strain through a fine-mesh strainer into a clean bowl. Pour the custard into the caramel-coated ramekins.

4. Place the ramekins in a large baking or roasting pan and add enough hot water to come halfway up the sides of the ramekins. Very loosely cover the pan with foil, poking the foil with a knife a few times to create air vents. Bake until the flans are just set in the center, about 1 hour and 20 minutes. Let cool, cover with plastic, and chill overnight.

5. To serve, run a small knife around the edges of the flans to loosen. Place a small serving plate on top of a ramekin and flip over. Carefully remove the ramekin. Repeat with the remaining ramekins and serve, topped with the caramelized macapuno.

BUKO PIE

This is the most famous dessert of the province of Laguna, south of Manila, where coconut country starts. We have many customers who come to the restaurant just for this dessert, and it is pure comfort food. We like to serve this pie with vanilla or purple-yam ice cream. You can make the filling a day ahead, refrigerate it, and let it come back to room temperature before proceeding.

MAKES ONE 9-INCH PIE

1 recipe Basic Pie Pastry (page 107), chilled

Filling:

1 cup young coconut juice

⅓ cup cornstarch

1 cup heavy cream

1½ cups sugar

Four 1-pound packages frozen grated unsweetened young coconut, thawed and drained (juice reserved) or 4 cups shredded young coconut, juice reserved

Egg wash:

1 large egg yolk

1 tablespoon milk

1. In a small bowl, whisk together the coconut juice and cornstarch until smooth.

2. In a large saucepan over medium heat, combine the heavy cream and sugar and bring just to a simmer, stirring to dissolve the sugar, about 3 minutes. Add the coconut and bring back to a simmer, stirring. Slowly pour in the coconut juice-cornstarch mixture, stirring constantly. Bring to a simmer and cook, stirring constantly, until thickened, about 2 minutes. Transfer to a bowl and let cool completely.

3. Preheat the oven to 425° F. To roll out the pie pastry, divide the dough in half and roll each piece out on a lightly floured work surface with a lightly floured rolling pin into two 14-inch circles (about ⅛-inch thick). Use one of the pastry circles to line a 9-inch pie pan, pressing the crust into the sides and bottom of the pan. Pour in the cooled buko filling, spreading the filling out evenly over the pastry. Fit the second dough circle on top of the pie and roll the edge of the top crust under the edge of the bottom crust, fluting the edges.

4. In a small bowl, beat the egg yolk with the milk to make the egg wash. Brush the top of the pie with the egg wash. Using a kitchen fork or a paring knife, prick 6 vent holes in the top of the pie.

5. Place the pie on a baking sheet and bake for 15 minutes, then lower the oven temperature to 350° F and bake until the crust is golden brown, 30 to 40 minutes. Cool on a wire rack before serving.

Buko [young coconut].

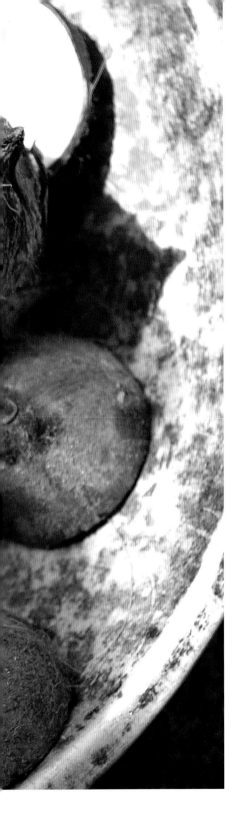

Lake Bulusan, Sorsogon, Bicol. Opposite: mature coconuts.

Bicol
The Heart of Coconut Country

I always recommend that people visit Bicol because its landscapes are beautiful and its food rich with the goodness of coconuts. Through the help of Marichi Francisco, mother of a good friend and regular customer, Monica Benares, we were able to visit Naga in Camarines Sur, Legazpi (where Mt. Mayon is located), Polangui, Albay, and Irosin in Sorsogon, Romy's hometown.

From top to bottom: buko, mature coconut, pancit buko. Opposite (at bottom): Tinutungan [chicken in burnt coconut crème].

The Coconut at Every Stage

Buko, the young coconut, is best eaten fresh, and young coconut juice is the healthiest drink nature can offer. The top of the buko is trimmed off in layers, leaving a soft pate of flesh on the top, which is punctured with a straw. If you are lucky, you will have enough of the meat to scrape inside the buko shell after you finish your drink. The buko meat is soft and delicate and is used for many Philippine desserts: buko pie, buko sorbets, and buko salads. It is also made into buko pancit and used as a substitute for noodles.

Lukadon, the in-between stage of the coconut, was an exciting discovery for me, as it is often mistaken for the buko. This is the stage when the coconut meat is still pliant and soft, but has enough body to withstand cooking. It is used in many sweets and desserts and is the main ingredient for bukayo, a coconut and brown sugar jam that is eaten by itself, put on pan de sal, or used as a filling for puto or suman. It is used in a sticky, chewy delicacy of Candon called calamay.

The mature coconut is the source of the coconut milk that is widely used in Southeast Asian cooking. Unlike buko juice, mature coconut milk is extracted from grated mature coconut meat. The first squeezing, without any water added, is called *kakang gata*, or pure coconut cream. The once-squeezed grated coconut can be mixed with water for a second and third extraction. The pure coconut cream is used the way heavy cream is used in Western desserts, and the water-added extractions are used primarily for cooking. Freshly grated coconut is also used for native desserts such as bibingka, puto, and suman.

When coconut milk is cooked continuously, the milk will separate into a solid called latik and its by-product, coconut oil. Latik is mixed with sticky rice for some suman and is also used as a topping for certain puddinglike snacks. Coconut oil is used for frying and cooking and is the basis for most vegetable cooking oil sold in the Philippines.

Burnt Coconut

One of my most exciting discoveries of Filipino cooking techniques happened where I least expected it, while in Tiaong, Quezon (a province south of Manila), visiting the famous potter Ugo Bigyan. I always try to go to Ugo's every time I am back in the Philippines because his home is a beautiful, self-made oasis that provides a moment of solitude from the tattered fabric of life in Manila. It feels like Bali in the small enclave of homemade bricks that line his pathways and form the foundation of his home. There, in one of his gazebos caressed by some northerly breeze, he lays out a lunch that is simply delicious: appetizers of clam soup, side dishes of banana hearts bathed in burnt coconut cream, grilled tilapia wrapped in banana leaves, lechon kawali, and local fruits of lanzones and bananas.

Bicol, the coconut capital of the Philippines, has always been known for its coconut-based dishes. When I started interviewing Ugo about the meal that he cooked for us, the banana heart dish with its tart, smoke-flavored coconut cream base stood out for several reasons. It showed me that provincial boundaries are arbitrary and that Quezon, along with Laguna and Bicol, formed one long unbroken strip of land filled with lush coconut groves. Quezon, as much as Bicol and Laguna, has a sophisticated sense and tradition of what to do with a coconut.

I had discovered the concept of burnt coconut several years ago through the Muslim cooking found down south in the Zamboanga area of Mindanao. Chunks of coconut meat were burnt on a grill until totally black. This charcoal-black coconut was pounded with spices such as cumin and turmeric to form a paste that would be used like curry in chicken or meat stews. This is called pinaitum (*itum* means black).

What Ugo taught me was different. Freshly grated coconut was returned to its husk and a live coal is placed in it to burn the grated coconut. Once the coconut is burnt and toasted, it is then squeezed with a little amount of water to produce a barbecue-flavored extract that can totally change the character of many traditional dishes such as adobo and kinilaw. To add another layer of flavor to the burnt coconut cream, Ugo suggests adding grated green mango or a little bit of vinegar and chopped chiles to the burnt coconut before extracting the cream. The coconut cream will give a delicately tart and smoky flavor and an undertone of heat to your dish.

For home cooks who would like to try using burnt coconut cream in their dishes, we highly recommend this safer procedure, which achieves a similar effect: Spread the freshly grated coconut on a baking pan and toast in a 350° F oven until golden brown or darker, depending on one's preference, 10 to 15 minutes. The coconut can be squeezed in a fine-mesh strainer or through cheesecloth.

CRABS IN COCONUT MILK

This recipe was inspired by our trip to Bohol, Visayas, in 1999. One late afternoon, we went to the public market to see what the bagsakan (the term used when fishermen drop off the day's catch at the market) would bring. I found a huge live mangrove crab that must have weighed five pounds, which I bought without any hesitation. I asked the kitchen staff at the Bohol Beach Club to cook it in coconut milk, lemongrass, a little bit of ginger, and some scallions. It was absolutely delicious!

Crabs and coconut milk are a natural combination. The resulting sauce of coconut milk, delicate herbs and spices, and crab juices is unforgettable.

SERVES 4

2	shallots, peeled and halved
8	cloves garlic, peeled

One 1-inch piece fresh ginger, peeled and thickly sliced

1	stalk lemongrass, trimmed, smashed, and cut into 2-inch pieces
5	cups coconut milk
2-3	chiles (birdseye, jalapeño, or serrano), slit down one side

One 1-inch piece fresh turmeric, thickly sliced, or 1 teaspoon dried turmeric

3	kaffir lime leaves

One 1-inch piece galangal, thickly sliced (optional)

2	live mud crabs, 2 Dungeness crabs, or 8 blue crabs, cleaned, gills removed, and cut in half
2	teaspoons fish sauce, or to taste
1	teaspoon lime or lemon juice, or to taste

1. In a large pot over medium-high heat, combine the shallots, garlic, ginger, lemongrass, coconut milk, chiles, turmeric, lime leaves, and galangal and bring to a simmer. Add the crabs, cover the pot, and quickly bring to a boil. Reduce the heat to medium and cook, covered, until the crabs are cooked through and the shells turn red, about 10 minutes, depending on the size of the crabs.

2. Transfer the crabs to a serving platter and return the pot to the stove. Cook over high heat, stirring often, until the liquid has reduced to the consistency of heavy cream, 5 to 10 minutes. Season with the fish sauce and lime juice. Taste and add more fish sauce or lime juice, if needed. Return the crabs to the sauce and cook over medium-high heat until warmed through, about 5 minutes. Remove and discard the chiles. Arrange the crabs on a large serving platter and pour the sauce over them.

BANANA HEARTS IN COCONUT MILK

Banana heart, a dark purple-leafed six-inch oblong blossom with a pointed end, is sold fresh and canned in Asian markets. Perry Mamaril, our resident artist and banana heart expert at Cendrillon, gave us this recipe. It is cooked in coconut milk, then drained and served as a salad.

SERVES 4 AS A SIDE DISH

Salt

2	banana hearts (available in Chinatowns, or substitute one 20-ounce can, drained)
2	teaspoons vegetable oil
1	large onion or 4 shallots, minced
1	cup coconut cream or ½ cup regular coconut milk
1	teaspoon lemon juice or kalamansi lime juice, or to taste
1	tablespoon chopped scallions, for serving
1	birdseye chile, thinly sliced, for serving (optional)

1. Fill a bowl with about 6 cups water and 2 tablespoons salt. Swirl to dissolve the salt. Peel the outer layers of the banana hearts until you reach the pale-colored heart. Finely chop the banana hearts and immediately place in

Clockwise from top: mud crabs in coconut milk, periwinkles in coconut milk (page 148), and banana hearts in coconut milk.

the water. Massage the pieces with your hands for about 3 minutes to remove the bitter sap. Discard the soapy-looking liquid that emerges. Drain in a fine-mesh strainer, rinse, and repeat the whole process. Taste a small piece and if there is any bitterness remaining, wash the banana hearts again.

2. In a medium saucepan over medium heat, warm the oil. Add the onion or shallots and sauté until softened, 3 to 5 minutes.

3. Add the banana hearts, 1/4 teaspoon salt, and the coconut cream or milk. Raise the heat, bring to a boil, then lower the heat and simmer, uncovered, until the hearts are tender, about 5 minutes.

4. Use a spider or slotted spoon to scoop the banana hearts into a serving dish. Season with the lemon or kalamansi juice and additional salt to taste. Garnish with the scallions and chiles.

Cleaning mud crabs.

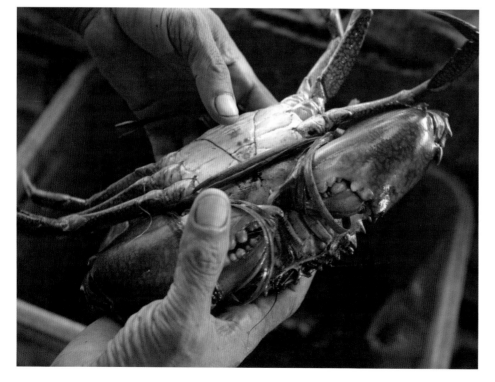

PERIWINKLES IN COCONUT MILK

Periwinkles are small snails and are called *cojol* in the Philippines. In Bicol, all kinds of snails are traditionally cooked in coconut milk to create a rich but delicate sauce laced with subtle heat from chiles. It is a culinary experience to successfully suck the snail out of the shell and retain one's composure. At the restaurant, Romy tactfully provides toothpicks for people who are seriously snail-challenged. Be sure to use the freshest periwinkles—you may need to special-order them from a reputable seafood supplier.

SERVES 6 TO 8

2   pounds periwinkles, tough ends trimmed
1   tablespoon olive oil
2   garlic cloves, thinly sliced
1   small shallot, minced
1-1½ cups coconut milk, as needed
1   fresh red chile, sliced
½   teaspoon salt, or to taste
¼   teaspoon freshly ground black pepper, or to taste
Freshly squeezed juice of ½ lemon, or to taste

1. Place the periwinkles in a large bowl. Cover with water and swish around to clean them. Drain, and repeat twice more. Place the periwinkles in a bowl and add enough water to cover. Set aside for at least 1 hour or up to 2 hours. Drain and rinse again.

2. Combine the oil, garlic, and shallot in a large skillet or wok. Cook over medium-high heat until lightly browned, 2 to 3 minutes. Add the periwinkles and increase the heat to high. Cook, stirring, for 1 minute. Pour in enough coconut milk to come halfway up the sides of the periwinkles. Add the chile. Bring to a boil and cook, stirring, for 2 to 3 minutes, or until you can easily remove a periwinkle from its shell with a toothpick. Do not overcook. Add the salt, pepper, and lemon juice. Pour into a bowl and serve.

Naga: Heartland of Bicol

It's easy to fall in love with Naga. Disembarking from the plane feels like going back to a Philippines that can only be found in old novels. As I looked at the quaint iron gate that separated the arrivals from the sparse crowd, I had to remind myself that I was no longer in that fabled, genteel colonial past of my grandparents' time. Despite the modern vigor and vitality that met me throughout my stay, I could not shake this feeling.

Aling Conching, a Naga restaurant run by Clara Verdadero, serves the recipes of Clara's mother, Consolacion David Verdadero, who was a Kapampangan from San Fernando, Pampanga. When Consolacion moved to Naga, she adapted the cooking of Pampanga to the ingredients found in Bicol. This influence is seen in the kare kare with freshly roasted and ground native peanuts and in their balo-balo, fermented rice wrapped in mustard leaves.

When I got to Aling Conching, a stand-alone stove and gas tank were set up in the middle of the restaurant to demonstrate classic Bicol dishes based on coconut milk. The next day, another cooking demo was held in the park, with young men from the local photography club trooping in for our photographer, Neal Oshima's autograph. As Neal brandished his light meter and camera, they followed every movement with great anticipation.

Bicol Classics

Kinunot is made with either pating [shark] or pagui [stingray] braised in vinegar and coconut milk. The very strong flavors of these fish are tempered by blanching, after which the fish is scaled and skinned and its meat shredded. Large strips of ginger are browned in oil, to which is added whole garlic cloves, diced red onions, tomatoes, the shredded shark or stingray, a cup of vinegar, coconut milk, chopped red and green chiles, and chile leaves. In Sorsogon, malunggay [leaves from the horseradish tree] are added to the kinunot.

Tabagwang [river snails] have long, straight, tapered, and ribbed black shells. They are soaked in several changes of water for at least one night to get rid of impurities. Before cooking, the tail is cut off so that one can suck the snail from the shell. To cook the snails, coconut milk is boiled with mashed garlic, slivers of ginger, and small onions, and is stirred constantly to prevent curdling. Once the coconut is flavored, the snails are added, the sauce reduced, and ferns [pako leaves] and sliced chiles are added.

Above: Naga market. Top: turo turo
[to point] in Naga market.

149

Right: taro leaves on pedicab. Below and right: pinangat of Naga.

The Taro Leaves of Bicol

Taro leaves [*gabi* in Tagalog, *natong* in Bicol] are used for everyday cooking all over the Bicol region. They can either be made into pinangat [taro purses] or laing [taro leaves cooked in coconut milk—see page 152]. The pinangat, according to Honesto General, author of *The Coconut Cookery of Bicol*, is the quintessential Bicolano dish. However, one will notice differences in how it is made as one drives farther south to Albay and to Sorsogon.

Naga's pinangat was the most luxurious, perhaps a sign of the abundance of the freshwater shrimp (*ulang* in Tagalog, *buyud* in Bicol) in Camarines Sur and the people's general ability to afford them. The Naga version contained pork, lukadon, freshwater shrimp meat and juice, and freshly salted alamang, seasoned with garlic, ginger, and lemongrass that are pounded together until fine. In Albay, the filling is a mixture of sliced taro leaves, pork, chicken, or dried fish. Down in Sorsogon, the purses are simply filled with sliced taro leaves with minimal seasoning. The purses are steamed in a wok on a bed of lemongrass. Once steamed, coconut sauce seasoned with garlic, onions, salt, and chiles is poured over them.

LAING

This is a classic Bicolano dish made of taro leaves cooked in coconut milk. At Cendrillon, we use fresh or dried taro leaves, depending on what is available. Dried taro leaves are available from Filipino stores and fresh taro leaves from stores that serve West Indian communities. Experienced Bicolano cooks recommend using dry leaves for two reasons: air-drying destroys the crystals that coat the leaf that cause itchiness to the tongue, and dry leaves do not disintegrate during cooking the way fresh leaves do.

SERVES 6 TO 8

1   tablespoon canola oil
1   large onion, diced
3   garlic cloves, crushed or sliced
1   fresh green or red chile, sliced (optional)
Three 14-ounce cans coconut milk
½   teaspoon salt
4   cups dried taro leaves

In a medium saucepan over medium heat, warm the oil. Add the onion, garlic, and chile, if using, and cook, stirring occasionally, until the onions are translucent, about 5 minutes. Add the coconut milk and salt, raise the heat to medium-high, and bring to a simmer. Add the taro leaves, bring back to a simmer, then reduce the heat and simmer, uncovered, for 20 minutes, stirring occasionally, until nicely thickened. Taste and add more salt if needed.

Origins of Halo-Halo

According to the Bicolanos, the halo-halo started from the simple mongo con hielo – boiled mung beans, milk, sugar, and shaved ice – sold by Japanese-owned soda shops in Naga, Camarines Sur. During World War II, these innocuous soda fountains took on a sinister role, as Danny Gerona recounts in his book *Naga: The Birth and Rebirth of a City*:

Almost five years before the Japanese invasion of the Philippines, the province of Camarines Sur registered a substantial number of Japanese residents. There were about eight retail stores owned by Japanese, most if not all of these were in Naga. Among the more prominent Japanese establishments in Naga were the Filipino Bazar [sic] and the K Mori refreshment parlor, which served the most desired cold drink of mongo con hielo. The residents of Naga and their Bicolano customers had no idea about the mission of these Japanese merchants until the Japanese Army arrived in Naga. To the residents' surprise, most of these Japanese merchants donned their military uniforms and turned out to be high-ranking officers in the Japanese Imperial Army.

Above left: shredded taro leaves.
Below: silag [sugar palm seeds].

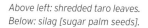

HALO-HALO

Halo-halo, which means "mix-mix," is the traditional iced dessert of the Philippines. It is an Asian parfait made with layers of sweetened red beans and native delicacies topped by shaved ice and milk. A more elaborate version (the halo-halo special) has extra toppings of leche flan, pinipig, and ice cream.

There are many variations of the halo-halo. At some establishments, bowls of every imaginable ingredient are laid out for people to pick and choose. Some regions include fresh fruits like cantaloupe, watermelon, mango, and papaya. In Pampanga, local purveyors add saba and pastillas de leche. In Bicol, grated cheddar cheese is sprinkled on top of all the other toppings for extra richness. At Cendrillon, we use fresh milk, although many Filipinos prefer using evaporated or condensed milk, having grown up with it.

For 1 serving:

1	tablespoon sweet red beans (or sweetened garbanzos or white beans)
1	tablespoon nata de coco (coconut gel, or use nata de piña, pineapple gel)
1	tablespoon kaong [palm seed]
1	tablespoon macapuno [coconut sport]
1	tablespoon jackfruit in syrup, thinly sliced
2	tablespoons gulaman (recipe follows)
2	cups ice cubes
1/2	cup whole milk, plus additional for drizzling
1	tablespoon haleyang ube (ube jam, optional)
1	scoop of ice cream (suggested flavors: purple yam, macapuno, or mango)

The first five ingredients listed above are sold in jars packed in syrup. You can vary amounts, omit, substitute, or add ingredients according to preference. To assemble, layer the first six ingredients in a tall parfait glass. In a blender, pulse the ice cubes and milk to the consistency

of shaved ice. Scoop the ice over the layers of sweet ingredients. Pour on more fresh milk, top with haleyang ube, if using, and a scoop of ice cream, and serve.

To make a more decadent halo-halo, sprinkle some toasted pinipig (page 59) over the halo-halo and top with a small serving of leche flan (custard) along with a scoop of ice cream.

Many non-Filipinos have missed out on the pleasures of this treat because they do not know how to eat it. Halo-halo should be mixed so that the sweetness of the ingredients will blend with the ice and other ingredients. The purple-yam jam [haleyang ube] gives the halo-halo a nice lavender color and flavor.

GULAMAN (AGAR-AGAR)

Dried gulaman or agar-agar is a gum extracted from seaweed. More and more chefs are using this as a vegetarian substitute for gelatin. It is available in Chinese and Japanese markets and in natural food stores. It is sold in colored or white bars. Gulaman can be eaten as is for dessert, but is primarily used as an ingredient in halo-halo, sago [tapioca pearl] drinks, and fruit salads.

MAKES ABOUT 12 SERVINGS

2/3 cup sugar
One 1/4-ounce bar gulaman [agar-agar], about 10 inches long, torn into small pieces

In a medium saucepan over medium-high heat, combine 2 2/3 cups water with the sugar, stirring to dissolve the sugar, and bring to a boil. Add the gulaman, bring to a boil, then reduce the heat and simmer, stirring or whisking constantly, until the gulaman is totally dissolved, 7 to 10 minutes. Strain through a fine-mesh strainer and pour into an 8-by-8-inch baking pan. Set aside to cool for about 1 hour to firm up, then refrigerate until ready to use.

BICOL EXPRESS

Romy adapted this recipe from a dish Carlos "Itos" Briones, a Manila City Information Officer, cooked for us in the beautiful Isarog Garden in Naga. The chile-laden Bicol Express was renamed after the train that started from the Tutuban Station in Manila to Legazpi, Albay (probably because of the speed at which the incendiary chiles sent one flying for water), and has since gained nationwide recognition, making it Bicol's best-known dish. To make this spicy condiment, pork is cooked in coconut milk seasoned with chopped ginger, garlic, onions, and lemongrass. Once the pork is soft, freshly salted bagoong and a substantial amount of chopped chiles are added. It is delicious with steamed rice and seafood and vegetable dishes.

MAKES ABOUT 6 CUPS (SERVES 8 TO 10)

1½ pounds pork butt, cut into ¼-inch strips
One 1-inch piece fresh ginger, peeled and thinly sliced
1   stalk lemongrass, smashed and cut into quarters
6   garlic cloves, sliced
1   large onion, thinly sliced
2   cups coconut milk
4   tablespoons shrimp bagoong
3   poblano chiles, seeded and cut into ¼-inch strips
5   jalapeño chiles, seeded and cut into ¼-inch strips
2   habanero or other fresh red chiles, seeded and cut
     into ¼-inch strips (optional)
3   New Mexico or other fresh green chiles, seeded
     and cut into strips
5   hot Thai chiles, thinly sliced (with seeds)

1. In a large saucepan over medium-high heat, stir together the pork, ginger, lemongrass, garlic, onion, and coconut milk. Bring to a boil, then lower the heat and simmer, uncovered, stirring occasionally, until the pork softens, 10 minutes.

2. Add the bagoong and chiles and cook until the chiles are softened but still al dente, 5 to 7 minutes.

Polangui: The Hunt for the Kurakding

"Oh good, we're going to Bicol," Neal fired back to me via e-mail as I informed him of our travel plans to photograph and research material for this book. "I want to hunt for the kurakding. I hear it's quite difficult to find." Kurakding is a wild mushroom that grows on the rotting bark of trees found at the foot of volcanoes and mountains. It is only available in the local markets if the people who live around mountainous areas forage for it. At that point, we did not even know that much. We asked our hosts in every part of Bicol that we traveled to, but all we got were shrugs or non-answers. We knew it existed, but in the world of the Philippines, reality is defined by different rules. If you are used to the precision of responses for directions and data that one normally expects in the West, you need to make serious adjustments in perspective once you get to this part of the world. Here, body language, long

Kurakding on taro leaves in Polangui market.

memories, immediacy of recognition, and richness of natural resources make the need
for precise definitions, names and genuses of flora, fauna, and in this case, wild and
intermittent fungi, unnecessary.

We eventually stumbled upon the kurakding in Polangui, a small town outside Legazpi
City, the capital of Albay in the Bicol region. Bicol is the southern tip of Luzon, a narrow
alley leading down to the southern islands of the Visayas. Legazpi is famous for Mt. Mayon,
one of the most perfectly shaped and beautiful volcanoes in the world. Possibly because
of its rich environment, Bicol is also one of the least economically developed regions of the
Philippines. As we drove through miles of lush and breathtaking scenes of coconut trees,
pili trees, and thousands of other botanical delights, I was secretly glad of its lack of
industrial development. True, the Filipinos in that part of the country were some of the
poorest, but were they really that poor when the land is still virgin, the air unpolluted, and
the trees still stand?

We drove into the town of Polangui at night after a traumatic visit to Mt. Mayon, where
I slipped, fell, and bloodied my arms and legs trying to climb up a rock to get a better photographic angle in one of the abandoned guesthouses halfway toward the tip of the volcano.

On the main street of polangui, which reminded me of a set in an old american Western
movie—almost two-dimensional, chaotic, and crowded—we finally found the bakery of Tita
Ong Samson, our hostess for our brief stay there. I first heard of Tita Samson and her aunt,
Mama Auyan, at Cendrillon, when our good friend Owi Ruivivar suggested that I may be
interested in meeting her mother's relatives in Polangui, a small town about 12 miles northeast of Legazpi.

Mama Auyan arrived in the Philippines from China in 1937 when she was only sixteen
years old and was taught how to cook Fujianese by Tita's mother. Tita and Mama Auyan are
the last of their line in this particular branch that holds so many keys to our understanding
of the Chinese aspect of the Filipino culture. We talked about the cooking session planned
for the next day, which included recipes of old-style Chinese-Filipino cooking preserved by
Mama Auyan.

Tita was born in 1942 of parents who were dubbed as "agaw buhay"—caught in a space
between life and death. The Chinese believe that it is unlucky for a child to be born of sick
parents and so she was immediately given to her grandparents for caring. However, her mother
eventually claimed her back, only to be rewarded with early death. Tita was also born with
a lameness that made it impossible for her to walk straight. She was told that if she were to
get well and walk straight, her father would die in exchange for her good fortune. In 1980,

her physical condition improved and she began to walk upright, and that same year her father died.

It was our Bicol guide Marichi Francisco, knowledgeable of Chinese customs and religious beliefs, who explained to me about Tita's devotion to the Chinese goddess Kwan Yin, whom she called Santa Kwanina. Later research taught me that Kwan Yin, or Guanyin, is also called the Goddess of Mercy, a Hindu male divinity that was reincarnated into a Buddhist goddess.

Tita's life is ruled by the advice of Santa Kwanina, a Hispanicized and Christianized version of the Buddhist deity. In fact, she confessed that when Ninya, Owi's mom, first called her to ask if we could visit and interview her about their Chinese cooking, she prayed to the Santa and luckily, the Santa told her to go ahead because we were "good people."

That night was an excruciating one for me. I was still nursing my wounds from my fall and the strangeness of my surroundings overwhelmed me. To complicate matters, the bathroom was a long trudge from our second-floor quarters—if one wanted to take a shower in a bathroom where the door refused to stay shut, one had to walk out of the house onto a wide open veranda whose only protection was from twisted barbed wire on the far side.

Morning finally came and we set out early for the market. And our luck finally panned out. Rows and rows of the tiny flower-like mushrooms were laid out on a side street outside the market, carefully arranged on fresh taro leaves that are used to wrap them when sold. There were dried ones and fresh ones, and in our excitement we bought a lot of both.

Neal learned about the kurakding from his close friend José Maria "Peng" Olaguera, whose parents come from the neighboring towns of Ligao and Guinobatan. Peng says that the mushrooms appear only in very specific weather conditions: consistent rainfall then sunshine—too much rain would rot them and too much sunshine would dry and disintegrate them. To cook kurakding, Peng soaks them, if dried, stems them, then sautés garlic, onion or shallot, ginger, and tinapa before adding coconut milk, alamang, the kurakding, chiles, and vegetables such as malunggay leaves or longbeans. Unripe santol may be added as a souring agent, and pork if it is preferred to the more traditional tinapa. The kurakding, even with all the richness of the coconut milk and the other ingredients, retained its woody and earthy flavors.

As we packed up for our next trip, to Irosin, Sorsogon, we said our good-byes to Tita and Mama Auyan. I thought of this strong and generous family unit thriving in this far-off place of Polangui. I went to Polangui because I thought I would unearth secrets of Chinese cooking, but the secret I uncovered was how intact our ties were between Chinese and Filipino. It was fitting that the hunt for the kurakding ended in Polangui.

The Vendor of Naga

I was introduced to Mariano "Obi" Obias, by Marichi Francisco, our tour guide for the Bicol trip. Obi worked for Caltex and was stationed in Asia, Africa, and the United States and has written eloquently about the food of his childhood growing up in Naga just before, during, and immediately after the Japanese occupation of the Philippines in the 1940s. He gives this account (with traditional Bicolano spelling retained):

Like many of his customers, we would lay in wait, hailing the cook/vendor as he passed by our house on the way to market. He carried pinangat, chopped lucadon, and small shrimp wrapped in natong [taro] leaves and cooked in coconut milk in the coron [lidded, round-bottomed clay pot]. This was balanced on top of his head, atop a flattened, ring-shaped turban, which stabilized the pot and protected his head. He carried a flattened roll of banana leaf sheets, which he had previously heated over linubluban [fire] to make them more flexible, to wrap individual purchases. He also had a big spoon crafted from coconut shell, bamboo, and cuhit [rattan], which he used to dispense individual purchases without directly touching the food. His final destination in the marketplace was the carihan [local public eating place]. Since he could not serve full meals, he also counted the vendors operating the eating stalls as his customers.

This same man sometimes made tinumtuman, a soup dish of coconut milk "guta" with bamboo shoots and "bibi" (not the Tagalog duck but the Bicolano's river clams) and proper condiments. Those who wanted them a bit hot would add sili [hot pepper] to the preparation. We bought them by the bowl, usually still steaming hot. While he used the same type of clay pot, he carried the product to market in a different manner. The pot was hung on one end of a sturdy bamboo stick sitting on his shoulder, and counterbalanced with a galvanized pail of water on the other end. The pot sat on a rounded rattan ring hung on three strands of GI wire. The pail of water had soup bowls and spoons immersed in it. Sidewalk patrons would sip their timumtuman from these bowls on the spot. My brothers still ask our old cook to make homemade timumtuman on special occasions.

The vendor also sold pork dinuguan, which was thicker than his timumtuman, but still fluid in consistency. This he made from fatty pork meat, chopped small intestines, pork blood kept liquid in vinegar, a leaf flavoring called "tanglad," and appropriate condiments. On other occasions, he would make hinuloghulog, a sweet merienda item of little starch balls swimming in a hot salabat-[sweetened ginger] type brew. Or he would make "guinatan" from chunks of camote [sweet potato], saba [ripe banana], linza [taro roots], camoteng cahoy [cassava], lángca [ripe jackfruit] strips, sago pellets, sángcaca [panocha], and coconut milk.

The Pili of Bicol

It was such a pleasure to read Obi's food memories that I could not resist asking him to write about the pili nut of Bicol. Pili nuts, endemic to Bicol, are consumed as fruit, nut-in-shell, or shelled, fresh, roasted, or candied. The ripe, deep purple fruits, shaped like a zeppelin, are just over an inch long. The pili meat comes from the edible husk of the fruit. The thin purple skin is peeled from the blanched husk enclosing the hard nut shell. The cooked meat has a very unique, rich flavor called *natoc*. The fruit can be eaten as is, right off the nut shell, or the softened meat can be separated from the nut and mashed, either in thick coconut milk, to which patis and spring onions may be added, or with sugar.

Pili nuts are often roasted and salted. Halved roasted nuts may also be prepared like pralines, blanched, stirred with sugar, water, and vanilla in a wok until the sugar has crystallized, then buttered or oiled to keep the nuts from sticking together. The Bicolanos collectively call the candied forms dulce pili. Among these, suspiros resemble nut brittle, the roasted nuts embedded in stretched, hardened sugar. A lot of stirring is involved in its preparation, along with a unique thumping movement of the whole pan held by the two handles in the settling stage. At the right time, before the mixture thoroughly hardens, a skillfully handled knife is used to make slices. Suspiros are eaten in their crunchy rectangular form as a dessert or melted in glasses of water to make a sweet drink.

From top to bottom: tilmok, sinanglay na tilapia, and suman from Catanduanes.

Holy Week in Catanduanes

Teddy Arcilla grew up in Catanduanes, an island off the eastern coast of Bicol. It is an island of mixed blessings filled with rivers, streams, and waterfalls. I flew over the island once to see an amazing sight of streams within lakes within rivers — water and land blending together to make a reluctant island. It is also located in the typhoon corridor, making it hostile territory during the months of June through October. Teddy described Holy Week (usually in April or May) to me as the best time to go to Catanduanes, when the community stages a weeklong celebration of the Crucifixion and Resurrection of Christ.

During this week, meatless Catanduanes food is prepared and eaten. It is only on Sunday that meat is eaten: chicken soup with sotanghon [mung bean noodles]. The high point of the breakfast on Easter Sunday is the pinoronan, an octagon-shaped sweet made of ground rice flour and mashed sweet potatoes wrapped in coconut leaf.

Nelia Bagadiong and Fe Caspe, both of Catanduanes, came to the Milky Way kitchen in Makati to show me how to make the pinoronan and other dishes traditionally cooked during Holy Week in Catanduanes.

Pinoronan: The basis of this native dessert is the camote [sweet potato] of Catanduanes, which is allowed to mature in the ground for six months before harvesting. There are three types of camote that can be used for pinoronan: white, yellow, and violet. The camote is boiled and mashed with coconut milk, sugar, water, fine rice flour (preferably from a special milagrosa rice called *sinanduming*), and salt to form a dry dough. The dough is wrapped in a coconut leaf to form a flat octagon. They are stacked in a pot of water and boiled until the rice flour is fully cooked.

Tilmok: Reserved for Good Friday, this Bicol version of tamales uses grated coconut in place of rice or corn. The main flavor is from freshwater shrimp called *ulang* [*buyod* in Bicol], which are fermented for a day or two before the heads and shells are pounded to extract the juice. The meat of the shrimp is chopped and mixed with a distinctive, large-leaf variety of oregano and herba buena, a local version of mint. The shrimp and herbs are mixed with grated coconut, minced garlic, chopped chiles, and salt and the mixture is then wrapped in calabaza [squash] leaves, tied in pairs, and boiled.

Sinanglay na tilapia: This is a dish of tilapia (dalag or mudfish can be substituted) that is salted, stuffed with chopped tomatoes, onions, and garlic, then wrapped in pechay [bok choy]. These packages of fish are layered in a pot with vinegar, coconut milk, whole garlic cloves, whole chiles, and lemongrass, and simmered, uncovered, until the coconut milk thickens. Just before the fish is ready, coconut cream is added.

Parallel Memories of Irosin

Listening to my husband Romy's stories of his childhood in Irosin is never dull. His world was so different from what I knew as a child in Manila that he might as well have come from Pluto. Growing up in an agricultural town, he told me that classes ended early in the public school he attended, so that the kids could work in the garden cutting grass with their bolos [small machetes]. Children with small machetes? I look back at my grade school afternoons playing tame patintero games of tag with schoolmates in a huge, fully cemented, enclosed playground. The story I savor most is of the day Romy got so furious with a schoolmate that he chased the ruffian all over, crashing through the stalls in the market, bolo in hand, scandalizing the whole town. That night was the first time his father lost his temper enough to exact corporal punishment.

Food is a major part of Romy's memories. He remembers their Chinese cook Sinco, the most ill-tempered man he has ever met, who would allow no one to observe what he did in the kitchen. Their food at home was basically a mixture of Chinese and the traditional Bicolano food cooked with coconut milk and chiles. After Sinco left, the food was never as good.

I traveled down to the southernmost tip of Bicol to Irosin, Sorsogon, in search of Romy's lost food memories. It was Romy's idea to hold a picnic at Masacrot Springs, to showcase Irosin food. Masacrot Springs, a local resort built around a cold spring that flows from the foot of Mt. Bulusan, was a favorite picnic spot of the Dorotan family. What transpired was a miracle. We had asked his brother Eddie Dorotan, a medical doctor and former mayor of Irosin, to help us with this task, and he in turn called on sixteen barangay captains to help produce the event. They were asked to seek out classic Irosin dishes and reproduce them using traditional methods. Eddie and his wife, Oyen, assumed that these barangay captains would rely on their parents or grandparents to cook the food. No such thing. These men cooked the dishes themselves! It was a project that fired up such unprecedented excitement and energy among the men and their families that they spent many sleepless nights preparing for the event.

Dressed in T-shirts and rubber flip-flops, these community leaders, old and young, filled the picnic area at Masacrot Springs with the tangibles of their past. Some dishes were difficult to make because ingredients were disappearing and some dishes could no longer be made. For a special dish like the kinagang, a tamale-type delicacy made of grated young coconut (page 164) flavored with the meat and fat of the talangka [small crab], the men had to go farther into the provincial interior to search for the elusive crabs. Unfortunately, Romy's most favorite dessert, kuping—thin, fragile wafers made of pounded rice or cassava—could no longer be

Linusak [mashed boiled bananas].

made. The skill and knowledge needed to make such delicate crisps have simply passed away with the previous generation.

But there were two desserts that I was eager to see and taste: the linusak and the sinapot. From the day I met Romy, he has always talked about these two favorites. The sinapot—layers of sliced saba [plantains] coated in rice flour batter arranged on a cacao leaf—was his inspiration in creating the Cendrillon ukoy (page 210). Once the saba slices were arranged on the leaf, they could be slowly lowered into the hot fat for frying. The leaf is crucial for keeping the bananas from dispersing in the oil. The linusak (also called nilupak) was brought out toward the end of the picnic, a fitting highlight to end the feast. A boiling cauldron was started on a wood fire to cook the unpeeled saba and sweet potato (taro or cassava can also be used). The saba bananas were peeled while steaming hot, then pounded with sweet potatoes, grated buko, sugar, and butter in a wooden mortar. Once fully incorporated, the linusak has to be eaten immediately before it gets cold.

In addition to the local Irosin food, the Sorsogon City contingent led by Pilar Yrastorza Leocadio, chief of staff for the governor of Sorsogon, Irma Guhit, and Jing Hayag, who owns a small diner at the Sorsogon City market, brought their own homemade kakanin: ibous, suman sa ligia, cuchinta, sapin-sapin, puto with cheese, cassava pudding, and bachang, a Chinese-style suman filled with adobo, chorizo, and peanuts. If one wants to experience what a power breakfast is like in Sorsogon, visit Jing's place, where you will run into the governor of Sorsogon and other local personalities like Irma Guhit, a local broadcaster.

The food that was served at the Masacrot Springs picnic gave me insight into the heights that good Filipino food could reach. The dishes were simple, unadulterated, and unforgettable. There was none of the heavy hand or strident flavors that plague much of what is bad in Philippine cooking today. One of my favorites was pinakro, slices of unripe saba slowly cooked in thick coconut milk and salt. This was served for breakfast and I loved it so much that I shamelessly ate a whole bowlful of it.

As I thanked and said good-bye to the townspeople of Irosin, I had to control a strong impulse to bring them with me to Manila to share my precious discovery. People who live a few hundred miles away have no clue such delicacies exist. The pride and pleasure that these men showed was enough to reduce me to tears at the end of the day as I called New York to tell Romy about my incredible experience.

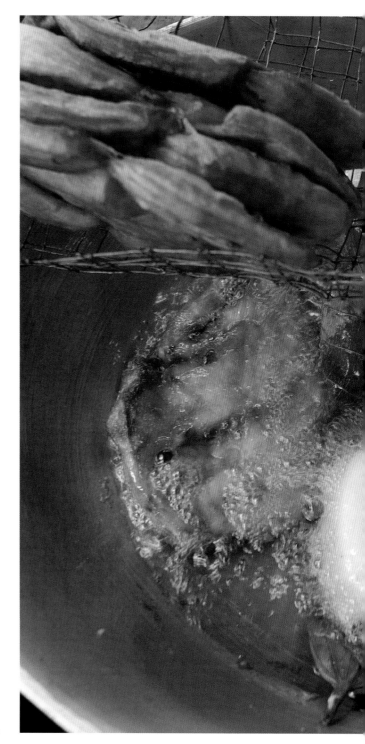

Sinapot.

Here are some of the dishes the barangay captains prepared for the picnic. Others included kinunot na pagi [stingray in coconut milk] and different types of suman: kalabasa [squash], malagkit [glutinous rice], and ibous (in coconut leaf wrapping).

Leni Maravilla's cassava puto

Leni is a local vendor of puto in Irosin. This was the most amazing discovery in Irosin. The puto is cooked similarly to the puto bumbong, steamed in plastic funnels whose stems are inserted into a huge cylindrical steamer. These breast-shaped spongy and delicious cakes are filled with bukayo [lukadon cooked in panocha].

Kapitan Felipo Martinez's hinagom:

This method of toasting unhusked glutinous rice [palay], then milling, grinding, and cooking it, is a harvest-time tradition that corresponds with a courtship ritual between young men and women. The men did the bayuhan [pounding the unhusked rice in a wooden mortar] and the women boiled the hinagom with coconut cream, brown sugar, ground toasted malagkit, and buko.

Kapitan Islaw Santos's kinagang:

This version of kinagang is made by mashing together grated lukadon, the meat and fat of talangka [small crabs], chopped scallions, minced garlic, salt, and the native mint, which they call herba buena, to form a uniform mass. The mixture is wrapped in a native leaf called bamban or hagikhik, which imparts a clean flavor and does not disintegrate when steamed.

Haile Artile and Galopa's tinutungan na manok:

Burnt coconut (page 145) gives this chicken dish a wonderful barbecued flavor. To achieve this, grated coconut meat is singed and used to make a smoky tasting coconut milk. Chicken is marinated in vinegar, ginger, and salt, sautéed with garlic and onion, then braised in its marinade until almost dry. Burnt coconut cream and siling labuyo [tiny, slim chiles] are added and simmered to marry the flavors.

KINAGANG

This is an easier version of the Irosin kinagang, which we serve as an appetizer special at the restaurant. We combine buko, crabmeat, sliced scallions, and lemongrass, wrap the mixture in banana leaf, and steam it. As a variation, you could add shrimp or scallops to the crabmeat for a more full seafood flavor.

MAKES 8 KINAGANG

One 1-pound package banana leaves
½ cup lime juice
1 or 2 chopped red or green chiles
2 cups (1 pound) lump crabmeat
Four 1-pound packages shredded unsweetened buko, drained and coarsely chopped
2 shallots, thinly sliced
4 scallions, white and green parts, thinly sliced
1 teaspoon salt
½ teaspoon freshly ground black pepper
2 lemongrass stalks, cut into 2-inch pieces and cut in half lengthwise

1. Cut out eight 10-by-12-inch pieces from the banana leaves. Cut off the tough rib at the top of the banana leaves. Cut out ¼-inch wide strips of banana leaves to use for tying the kinagang—you'll need to tie two or three of them together to make them long enough to fit around the kinagang. (Alternatively you can use kitchen string.) Clean the banana leaf sections by wiping them on both sides with a damp paper towel. Pass them over a medium flame on both sides to soften and make them more pliable.

2. Combine the lime juice and the chiles in a small serving bowl and set aside.

3. In a large bowl, combine the crabmeat, buko, shallots, scallions, salt, and pepper. Place 1 cup of the crabmeat mixture in the center of each banana leaf section. Flatten to create a square shape about 4 inches square. Place two lemongrass sections over the mixture.

4. Firmly wrap the kinagang in the banana leaves by folding over the sides, first lengthwise, then widthwise. Place seam side down and tie together on either side with the banana leaf strips.

5. Place the kinagang in a steamer basket placed over simmering water. Cover and steam for about 5 minutes, just to heat through. Unwrap the kinagang and serve with the lime-chile mixture.

CHICKEN TINOLA

This is one of the easiest and most delicious chicken soups to make. Just like the mythical chicken soups of other cultures, this soup is good for restoring one's health. By the time we got to Irosin, our photographer, Neal, was very sick and debilitated. I asked the kitchen staff to make a chicken tinola with lots of ginger, green papaya, chile, and malunggay leaves; within a few hours Neal was back on his feet.

SERVES 4 TO 6

2   tablespoons canola oil
1/3   cup chopped onion
One 1-inch piece fresh ginger, peeled and julienned
4   garlic cloves, crushed
1   stewing chicken, cut into pieces
2   tablespoons fish sauce, plus more to taste
1   small green papaya, peeled, seeded,
      and sliced 1/2-inch thick
1   cup fresh or frozen sili [chile] leaves (available in
      Asian markets), or substitute watercress or water
      spinach
1/2   cup malunggay leaves (optional)

1. In a large saucepan over medium heat, warm the oil. Add the onions, ginger, and garlic and sauté until softened, about 5 minutes.

2. Add the chicken pieces and fish sauce and cook, stirring, until the chicken is well coated with oil, 1 to 2 minutes. Add 8 cups of water, raise the heat, and bring to boil. Reduce the heat and simmer, uncovered, adding the papaya when the chicken is almost tender, 30 to 40 minutes total. Stir in the sili and malunggay leaves, if using. Cook until heated through and wilted if fresh. Season with fish sauce, to taste.

Malunggay leaves.

The Childhood Delights of Irosin

Bicolanos, like most Filipinos, are prodigious consumers of native desserts. These snacks are creative variations of basic ingredients: starch (rice, banana, or cassava), sugar (white, brown, muscovado, or panocha), and coconut (buko meat or milk from mature coconuts). In my interviews with many Filipinos, food memories always recall desserts. These local sweets and

kakanin are not easily replicated and invariably have to be enjoyed in their locality. Furthermore, it is now more difficult to find people who have the skills to keep these traditions alive. In Romy's large family (Romy is the eighth of thirteen children), the age gap between the older group of siblings and the younger ones is so wide that they represent different generations of food memories. By the time the youngest, José (Ping), was born, children were eating different treats than his older siblings had.

At home in New York, I sat down with Romy's sister Adelfa, brother Danny, niece Beya, and several other homesick Irosinians to reminisce about the childhood treats they recall.

Balikucha: A taffy or nougat similar to the Tagalog tira-tira. Romy calls this "tooth-decay treat" because the taffy is so tough that it sticks to one's teeth.

Binut-ong: Sticky rice, coconut cream, anise flavoring, and salt that is wrapped in several layers of young banana leaves, gathered like a pouch, then cooked in coconut water or plain water for about two hours.

Bunguran: Used as an ingredient in guinataan. Grated saba or regular unripe banana is pounded in a mortar, rolled into balls, and cooked in boiling coconut milk and sugar along with the rest of the guinataan. Grated cassava can also be used.

Ginamos: Like the Tagalog maruya, overripe saba is mashed, mixed with rice flour and sugar, formed into small patties, and deep-fried. (Bicolano ginamos should not be confused with the Cebuano guinamos, which is fermented fish or shrimp paste.)

Guinataan: Traditionally eaten for merienda, this is made by boiling coconut milk and sugar and then dropping in pieces of gabi [taro], cassava [yucca], camote [sweet potato], saba [plantain], bunguran, jackfruit, and young coconut.

Kinalingking: Sweet potato or camote that are cut like french fries, mixed with rice flour, water, and sugar, and fried on cacao leaves.

Kuping: Finely grated cassava (or rice) rolled into very thin sheets, dried under the sun, then deep fried. This is similar to kiping from Lucban, Quezon, which are painted in different colors and made into shapes such as leaves.

Pinakrö: Unripe saba sliced into several long pieces and cooked in coconut milk, then seasoned with salt to taste. Coconut cream is added just before the bananas are done.

Tabog-tabog: Grated cassava that are rolled into a ball with salt and scallions and deep-fried.

Top: guinataan. Above: kinalingking. Opposite: binut-ong.

Visayas
The Freshest Seafood in the Philippines

A New York sugba: pompano in banana leaf, octopus, and red snapper on the grill. Opposite: barbecued pork skewers.

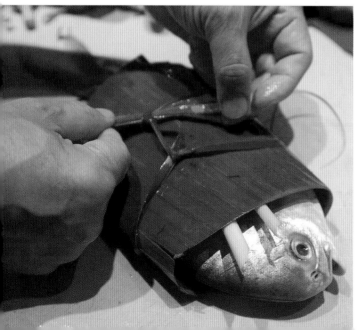

I always look forward to a trip to the Visayas, where the seafood is pristine and the people speak with a sweet lilt to their Cebuano or Ilonggo. We traveled to Cebu, to be hosted by the Escaño, Unchuan, and Moraza families. Then it was off to Iloilo City, Iloilo where Lourdes "Bopeep" Ladrido took us to places and people that represent Ilonggo food. There can never be any Visayan trip for me without visiting my cousin Lyn Besa-Gamboa, who lives in Silay, a short drive from Bacolod. In Silay, Maget Gaston Locsin showed us how to make bunuelos and pancit Molo. We also had the good luck to meet up with Charlie Co and his wife, Ann Legazpi, whose aunts make the famous piaya of Silay, and another aunt, Emma Lacson, who is famous for her empanadas and lumpia ubod.

There is a row of eateries in Cebu that feature the Visayan traditional way of eating called *sutokil*. Intentionally mispronounced for "foreigners" like us as "shoot to kill," sutokil is an acronym for sugba [grill], tola, towa, or tinola [boiled] and kilaw or kinilaw [ceviche] (page 48). These are all very simple methods of cooking relying on the freshness of Visayan seafood.

Tinola, or tola, is the Visayan version of sinigang, lightly soured by tomato or a batuan [a small, round green fruit found in the south]. (Note that Tagalog tinola, page 165, is something else entirely.) My friend Ding Pajaron, who comes from Davao City in Mindanao, told me that she grew up eating tinolang isda [fish]. Mindanao was resettled by Visayans, so many of these cooking methods are in Mindanao, too. Tinola is what any Visayan craves after eating rich dishes. It cleanses the system, refreshes the spirit, and rejuvenates the diner. It's made with a broth of water, ginger, onions, scallions, and tomatoes, to which vegetables such as malunggay or horseradish leaves are added. Once the broth and vegetables are ready, fish, preferably swordfish, is gently poached in it.

Sugba dishes are grilled seafood, and the best sugba is usually found along the wharf. Like kinilaw, sugba is about participating in the catching, cleaning, and preparing of the dish, which is why this cooking method is not easily translated farther from the source.

Back in New York, we wanted to re-create the experience and taste of a sugba. We gathered the freshest seafood available: snapper, pompano, catfish, squid, shrimp, and baby octopus; then skewered and placed them on the grill, after seasoning with a sprinkling of sea salt and lightly brushed with oil. The pompano was wrapped in banana leaf to protect its delicate skin.

BARBECUED CHICKEN SKEWERS

Barbecued skewers of chicken are perfect appetizers and always popular at cocktail parties. The key is to keep the meat moist and tender. Do not overmarinate the chicken, as this will draw a lot of the moisture from the meat. Basting the skewers continuously while they're on the grill causes the sugar in the marinade to caramelize.

SERVES 4

Marinade:

3   garlic cloves, chopped

One ½-inch piece fresh ginger, peeled and chopped

2   sticks lemongrass, trimmed and chopped

1   cup rice wine

1   tablespoon salt

2   teaspoons sugar

¼   cup canola oil

2 whole boneless skinless chicken breasts, cut into
      1-inch cubes

Twelve 8-inch wooden skewers, soaked in water for 1 hour

1. Combine the garlic, ginger, and lemongrass in a food processor and process until a rough paste is formed. Place in a large nonreactive bowl and stir in the wine, salt, and sugar. Add the chicken, toss well, cover with plastic, and marinate for 2 to 3 hours in the refrigerator, turning a couple of times.

2. Preheat the broiler or fire up the grill. Take the chicken from the marinade and place it in a clean bowl. Reserve the marinade for basting. Add the oil to the chicken and stir to coat. Thread about 6 pieces of chicken onto each skewer and place on a foil-lined broiler pan or on a lightly oiled grill rack and broil or grill for 5 to 7 minutes on each side, basting with marinade a couple of times, until the chicken is cooked through and nicely browned.

3. Serve with Peanut Sauce (recipe follows).

PEANUT SAUCE

We love the Indonesian peanut sauce for the satays, and so we developed our own. This can be used for both the chicken and pork skewers.

MAKES ABOUT 1¼ CUPS

1   cup roasted unsalted
      peanuts

1   tablespoon peanut oil

2   shallots, peeled and
      chopped

2   garlic cloves, chopped

1   stalk lemongrass,
      white part only, chopped

½   fresh red chile, seeded
      and chopped

1¼   cups coconut milk

1   tablespoon lime juice

1   teaspoon soy sauce

1   teaspoon fish sauce

1. Combine the peanuts, oil, shallots, garlic, lemongrass, and chile in a food processor and process to a smooth paste. Transfer to a small saucepan and place over low heat. Add the coconut milk, lime juice, soy sauce, and fish sauce and stir until smooth. Cook until the sauce is warmed through, about 2 minutes.

2. Taste and add more soy sauce, fish sauce, or lime juice if needed. If the sauce is too thick, add coconut milk or water to thin it out.

BARBECUED PORK SKEWERS

Barbecued pork skewers always bring back memories of New Year's Eve celebrations with my Besa cousins, children of Gaudencio (Tatay Ocho) and Pacencia (Tita Pat) Besa. No feast was complete unless it had Tita Pat's caramelized pork barbecue and her chicken macaroni salad to go with it.

SERVES 4 TO 6 (MAKES ABOUT 15 SKEWERS)

2   garlic cloves, peeled and chopped

1   shallot, peeled and chopped

⅔   cup soy sauce

2   tablespoons rice wine

2   teaspoons sugar

1½   pounds pork butt, cut into ¾-inch cubes

2   tablespoons canola oil

1. Combine the garlic and shallot in a food processor and process until a paste forms. Place in a large bowl, add the soy sauce, rice wine, and sugar and stir to combine. Add the pork, cover, and marinate in the refrigerator for 6 hours or overnight.

2. Preheat the broiler or fire up the grill. Take the pork from the marinade and place it in a clean bowl. Reserve the marinade. Add the oil to the pork, stir, then thread the pork onto skewers, 5 or 6 pieces per skewer. Grill or broil for about 5 minutes on each side, basting with the marinade, until the pork pieces carmelize.

3. Serve with Peanut Sauce (see left).

Samar: Glenda's Sinacugan

Whenever the Philippines needs a food ambassador to send abroad, Glenda Rosales-Barretto is called. Glenda has decades of food production experience, organizing presidential state dinners at Malacanang Palace, supervising provincial celebrations for thousands, and running her restaurants in Makati. When I first returned to the Philippines after a long absence, my brother Tristan knew where to bring me for my first authentic Filipino merienda: Via Mare, Glenda's flagship restaurant specializing in Filipino food. There I had my first taste of charcoal-broiled bibingka and freshly steamed puto bumbong after twenty years of dreaming about them.

Since then, I've gotten to know Glenda personally. In a country where people are generous and kind to a fault, Glenda wholeheartedly and sincerely redefines the meaning of both. Glenda's mission in life is to fulfill food cravings and fantasies, so during my last trip home, I asked Glenda to give me a glimpse of her own personal comfort foods. Glenda comes from Samar, the most northern of all the Visayan islands, just below the boundary of the Bicol peninsula, and she told me about sinacugan, served during fiestas only in Samar and some parts of Leyte. When she returns home for a visit, this is what she looks forward to eating.

Sinacugan is a special rice dish, which is served with hot chocolate and is eaten with humba, escabeche, and daing. For dessert, Glenda's comfort meal would close with pinaklob and conserva. Glenda cooked this sinacugan meal for us in the kitchen of her newest restaurant, the Oyster Bar, located in the Greenbelt area of Makati.

Sinacugan: A combination of black rice (pirurutong or tapol), regular rice, and glutinous rice cooked in coconut milk.

Hot chocolate: A drink made from native chocolate tablets (called *tablea*) boiled with water, whisked until all the chocolate is dissolved, then simmered with breakfast cocoa, sugar, and evaporated milk, served in a batidor, and whipped.

Daing: Brined fish such as mackerel or hasa-hasa that is air- or sun-dried and fried crisp.

Escabeche: Sweet and sour fish (page 103).

Above, from left to right: daing, humba, pinaklob.

Humba: A dish traditionally made from pig's knuckles or trotters, but Glenda uses pork belly for a spectacular presentation, parboiling it, reserving the broth, scoring each piece, and marinating it overnight in vinegar, soy sauce, garlic, peanuts, black beans, mashed tajure [salted bean curd], bay leaves, and brown sugar, then braising it until fork tender (for a similar preparation, see Mrs. Relova's Pata Estofado, page 137).

Pinaklob: Sweet stuffed taro, similar to the Irosin kakanin called kinalû-kô, that is halved horizontally, the taro scraped out, combined with coconut milk and panocha [brown sugar], cooked until thick, then restuffed into the taro, which is wrapped in banana leaves and cooked in coconut milk.

Conserva: Called irait na conserva in Samar, this suman is made with grated cassava and stuffed with bukayo [a mixture of grated young coconut, panocha, and a pinch of anise cooked in coconut milk until thick].

SINACUGAN

I was first introduced to the concept of eating native chocolate poured over rice and viand in the early 1990s when I traveled to Taal, Batangas, with my friend Becky Villegas. I was surprised to see this combination again in the Sinacugan of Samar. If you are not ready to eat chocolate with your pork and fish dishes, just try this rice dish, which is truly a comfort food and delicious with hot chocolate (page 200).

SERVES 4 TO 6

1	cup short-grain rice
½	cup short-grain sticky rice
½	cup black rice
2	cups coconut milk
1	teaspoon salt

Rinse all the rice, drain, and combine in a large saucepan with the coconut milk, 1 ½ cups water, and salt. Bring to a boil over high heat, then reduce the heat and simmer, covered, until the rice is tender, about 40 minutes. Stir to incorporate any coconut milk that has risen to the top, then replace the cover and let sit for 5 to 10 minutes before serving.

Iloilo Markets and Food

In Jaro, Iloilo, Thursday is market day. Called *Huebesan* (*Jueves* is Thursday in Spanish),
it is a very old tradition of selling finished goods without a middleman. Vendors from all over
the island go from one market to another for a day at a time. All kinds of products are sold:
food, rope, tobacco, farming implements, knives of all shapes and sizes, clay pots, and woven
mats. Even the people who dabble in superstition and mysticism get their raw materials
here. At one table, Rosario Tuam presides over herbals and exotic items called *anting-anting*,
amulets to ward off evil or bring good luck to the wearer. Tiny bottles filled with red seeds,
dried strands of bark or root are an antidote for desperate people, "para sa mga sawi," who
believe that someone has put a hex on them. In larger dark bottles is a tonic she calls Vino
Agoso, "para sa nerbiyos" (for the nerves) made from cocoa, banana bark, and sugar. There
are the vegetable trademarks of classic Ilonggo cooking: the tambo [bamboo shoot] and ubad
[pith of the banana bark], which some vendors recommend cooking with grated native corn,
coconut milk, tugabang, saluyot, and takway [all local leaves]. There are baby mangrove
crabs (on their way to extinction) and dried fish made with local fish like gumaa for daing
[butterflied, dried fish] and the tabagak for tuyo.

The town is known for la paz batchoy [pork broth with noodles], grilled fresh seafood
[sugba], grilled chicken [inasal], and baked products. A quick tour of Iloilo's well-known
attractions, organized by Lourdes "Bopeep" Ladrido, brought us to the famous seafood
restaurant Breakthrough, at Villa Beach. The restaurant is filled with giant aerated water
tanks filled with live pitik-pitik [slipper lobster], mangrove crabs, several kinds of clams,
and fish. Then it was off to Tatoy's Manokan. Tatoy's rags-to-riches story is a staple of Iloilo
lore. His sprawling eatery started with one small grill that he would bring to the beach to
sell chicken barbecue.

What is Ilonggo Food?

I asked Corona Villanueva-de Leon, owner of Mama's Kitchen, Chef Kevin Piamonte of Villa Sagrado, and Aling Cheling Montelibano, a local food producer, what they considered to be true Ilonggo food. Here's what they told me:

Corona Villanueva-de Leon bakes different flavors of cookies based on local native ingredients: cacao beans, cashew, pinipig, peanuts, and mango. From Corona, I learned that Ilonggos love to cook with achuete. Corona cooks adobo by boiling the meat in achuete water, garlic, onion, and bay leaves until tender. Then she adds the vinegar and lets it cook until the adobo is dry. Oil is added to the meat to fry the adobo until crisp; the rice is fried in it, too.

Kevin Piamonte said that the classic Ilonggo dish is the combination of kadios [soft peas], baboy [pork], and langka [unripe jackfruit]. But his childhood favorite recipe is amorgoso [bitter melon]. He says that the best way to cook amorgoso is to squeeze it in salt. "I discovered that the best way to cook it is to cook it very fast. The longer you cook it, the more bitter it gets." His favorite bitter melon recipe is to sauté garlic, onions, and shrimp and then add the sliced amorgoso. You scramble eggs separately and then add them to the amorgoso — a very Ilonggo touch.

Aling Cheling Montelibano makes and sells many products from her home, such as masa podrida [a local version of shortbread cookie], ensaimada, sans rival, malacanang rolls [sponge cake with chocolate filling and boiled icing], beef flakes, and binoro, salted and fermented bilong bilong [moonfish]. Aling Cheling is proud of her technique of salting the fish without touching it. She salts the fish using two saucers, rubbing continuously until the fish wilts. When the moisture comes out, the fish are put in a container with ground ginger and salt for three days, then the fish are fried, one by one. The juice that comes out of the fish during fermentation is seasoned with ginger, garlic, sugar, vinegar, and spirits [alcohol].

From left to right: unripe jackfruit, masa podrida, patane [lima beans]. Opposite, far left: nga-nga [beetle nut and leaves]; top: banana trunk.

Batchoy

Batchoy, or batsoy, is derived from the Chinese *ba chui*, meaning "meat water." The batchoy of La Paz Market, Iloilo's signature dish, is a rich pork and beef-based broth filled with yellow noodles and topped with cut-up roast pork, chicharron, fried garlic, and scallions. Reynaldo Guillergan owns the original batchoy stand at the La Paz Market in Iloilo City. He inherited the recipe and business from his father, who worked for and later bought the original noodle stand from its Chinese owners who started it fifty years ago.

The La Paz batchoy begins with a basic batchoy stock made with a mix of pork bones, intestines, liver, and beef bone marrow simmered in a stockpot with water seasoned with salt, sugar, and guinamos [Visayan fermented fish paste] for hours. The next day, the stock is skimmed and he adds two separately prepared stocks: sautéed red onions (called *Bombay* in Iloilo) simmered in water, and guinamos boiled in water and strained. Sahog is the pre-cooked and cut-up meat that is added to the soup. The meat from the stock ingredients is added, including the pork liver. Before serving, the marrow from the beef bones is added, along with pieces from a lechon snipped with scissors. The soup is garnished with fried garlic, chopped scallions, and pieces of crispy chicharron [pork skin cracklings made especially crisp by boiling until tender, then sun-drying for three days before frying]. The steaming batchoy is ladled into a bowl, and pieces of freshly made yellow noodles from a huge pile on the side are cut straight into the hot soup. The batchoy is traditionally served with white puto.

CHICKEN INASAL

This is the Cendrillon version of Chicken Inasal, one of my favorite meals at the end of a long night at the restaurant. This is better grilled, but it can also be roasted in an oven.

SERVES 4

Marinade:

¼	cup achuete oil (page 17)
3	garlic cloves, finely chopped
1	stalk lemongrass, trimmed and finely chopped
3	tablespoons freshly squeezed Kalamansi or regular lime juice
2	tablespoons red wine vinegar or coconut vinegar
1	tablespoon sugar
2	teaspoons salt
1	teaspoon finely chopped fresh ginger
¼	teaspoon freshly ground black pepper

One 3½-pound chicken, quartered

1. In a large nonreactive bowl, combine all the marinade ingredients. Add the chicken pieces, cover tightly with plastic wrap, and refrigerate for at least 2 hours or overnight.

2. Preheat the oven to 375° F. Transfer the chicken to a foil-lined baking sheet, reserving the marinade.

3. Roast the chicken, basting occasionally with the reserved marinade, until the chicken is cooked through, about 45 minutes.

Molo! Molo!

Pancit Molo is a soup of pork dumplings in chicken broth. It is named after one of the oldest sections of Iloilo on the island of Panay in the Visayas. Molo was originally the Parian, the Chinese quarters in Iloilo established in the eighteenth century by the Spanish to segregate the growing Chinese population

in the islands. Melanie Padilla, a historian based at the University of the Philippines in Iloilo City, told me that the name Molo, according to local legend, came about when the Chinese called out a warning against approaching Moros [Filipinos from Mindanao] in their vintas who were notorious for raiding coastal villages at the time. The Chinese could not pronounce the *r* and cried out, "Molo! Molo!"

The pancit Molo is a Visayan staple that has traveled from the Parian of Iloilo to the elegant homes of the wealthy elite in both Cebu and Bacolod. From the simple "caldo" – the chicken broth – there are richer and more flavorful versions that I encountered in homes and in stories. Bing Escano-Garrido told me that her mother was famous in Cebu for her pancit molo and that her secret was a small amount of tahure [fermented soybean paste] in the broth. In Bacolod, Maget Gaston Locsin cooked a molo for us with a rich broth packed with ham and chicken. It was quite an experience to go to the source. At the Panaderia de Molo, where most of these things reputedly originated, we had our pancit Molo, a very simple and plain chicken broth served with delicate pork dumplings topped with chopped chives.

PANCIT MOLO

This is our basic pancit Molo recipe as we do it at Cendrillon, and it is more closely akin to that offered at the Panaderia de Molo. I loved the way Maget Gaston Locsin shaped her dumplings like nuns' hats, reminiscent of the original nuns in the Molo district, and I've adopted that technique. (Once you get going, it makes sense to make a lot of dumplings – it's pretty quick work, and they freeze well.) A third of the recipe, in 12 cups of chicken stock, will feed six, so you can keep two more batches (of dumplings) in the freezer.

MAKES ABOUT 80 DUMPLINGS

Dumplings:
1 pound ground pork
8 large shrimp, peeled, deveined, and minced
1/4 cup diced jicama or fresh water chestnuts
1 small carrot, minced
1/2 leek, white parts only, minced
1 large egg
1 1/2 teaspoons cornstarch
1 teaspoon salt
1 teaspoon freshly ground black pepper

Assembly:
About 80 square wonton wrappers
Egg whites for brushing the wrappers
12 cups homemade chicken stock
2 leeks, white parts only, thinly sliced
2 tablespoons salt
2 teaspoons ground white pepper
Fish sauce (optional)

1. Place all the dumpling ingredients in a large bowl, and use clean hands to mix until well combined. To roll the dumplings like a nun's hat, place a wonton wrapper on a work surface or on your hand so one corner is facing you. Place 1 teaspoon of the filling on the lower corner. Fold the

corner over the mixture and roll the filled part up and over a little past the center. Press on both sides of the filling to enclose it. Brush egg white over the side points and fold the points into the center, one side overlapping the other. Repeat. You should have about 80 dumplings.

2. Place the stock in a large saucepan and add the leeks, salt, pepper, and fish sauce to taste, if using. Bring to a simmer and gently add 24 of the dumplings until cooked, about 2 minutes. Place 4 dumplings in each of 6 serving bowls and cover each with 2 cups of the broth.

3. Freeze the remaining dumplings on cookie sheets until solid, then transfer to an airtight container, where they'll keep for a month.

Panaderia de Molo

The 130-year old Panaderia de Molo is the oldest bakery in Iloilo. Built beside the Molo cathedral in the old Parian district of Iloilo, the bakery was started by Luisa Jason Sanson when nuns from a nearby convent donated surplus egg yolks to

her and her sisters. In the 1800s, egg whites were used as a binding agent in building the walls of the cathedral and other churches. To this day, most of the Panaderia classics use egg yolks, including the galletas, hojaldres, barquillos, bañadas, broas, kinamuncil, and rosquetes. Chicken and pork dumplings for the classic Ilonggo soup, pancit Molo, are also produced and retailed there. The bakery still uses the original concrete, custom-built, wood-fired ovens, according to Georgina Gaona and Heather Maloto, two of Luisa's grandchildren. The Panaderia products, sold in the distinctive large round tins with the green and white label, have always been the official Iloilo pasalubong [gift from one's travel] of several generations of Filipinos for friends and family.

Bacolod, the Land of the Sweet

Bacolod and Silay were once the domain of powerful sugar barons. The sugar industry was the brainchild of the former British Vice Consul Nicholas Loney in the 1850s. Initially he set up the plantations and the mechanical infrastructure in Iloilo. Eventually the industry leapfrogged over to the western part of Negros, where the land was found to be more suitable for this crop. Scions of the Iloilo aristocracy were sent over to Negros to start and manage the plantations, and workers were brought in from neighboring Visayan islands. By the next decade, Negros was the leading producer of sugar in the Philippines.

The Ilonggo spoken in Iloilo is the same as the Ilonggo in Bacolod. Peque Gallaga, a director for film and theater, claims that many of the wealthy Ilonggo families bought sugar plantations in Negros and sent the black sheep of their families to Bacolod to tend to the plantations. This, he says, is why the Negrosanons have an inherent maverick culture, while Iloilo is "sophisticated, cultured, traditional, and sometimes boring." How else, he asks, "does one account for family eccentricities such as a very wealthy aunt who wears cauliflower in her hair and diamonds on her shoes?"

From 1900 to 1945, the Philippine sugar industry benefited from favorable U.S. tariff laws and a quota system that guaranteed a protected market for Philippine sugar in the United States. Then, in the 1960s, the United States developed competitive sources of sugar. For the past three decades, the sun has been slowly setting on the Negros sugar aristocracy. Negros is not unlike the American South, with its old graceful cotton plantations and a bygone culture that its northern industrial counterpart never quite aspired to.

My personal connection to this part of the world came via my cousin Lyn Besa, who married Nil Gamboa, the son of a sugar planter, and became part of a family steeped in culture and history. As soon as Lyn settled in Silay, she actively worked to preserve old historic mansions and stately homes that had been abandoned and neglected by families who fled to Manila or abroad.

I was a young child when Lyn moved to Silay. Besa family reunions were always more promising whenever Lyn was in town. She brought lumpia ubod (page 181), homemade carabao milk ice cream with pinipig [toasted young rice] made from a hand-cranked, old-style garapiniera, and the bihud, fermented fish eggs that we sautéed in garlic, onions, and tomatoes and ate with steaming white rice. What could not be transported had to be eaten in situ: chicken inasal at Manokan Country and the fresh seafood at the daily bagsakan. Unfortunately, the Bacolod specialty, the diwal [angel wing clams], is threatened with extinction.

Bacolod, Visayas

During my last few days in Manila, when time was getting short, I met with Fernando "Fern" Aracama, chef and owner of Uva, in the Greenbelt section of Makati. Fern, a Visayan, is one of the most respected young chefs in the Philippines today and his restaurant is a functioning culinary vision of the promise that Philippine food can offer. The best way to capture the spark of this gifted chef is in his voice, recalling what he ate as a child in Bacolod. Here are excerpts of our memorable conversation that late afternoon in Uva:

I am from Bacolod. Mama is a Cavitena (from Luzon) and Papa is from Escalante, Negros Occidental. Both my parents cooked, and at home we ate a combination of Visayan and Tagalog food. We ate Tagalog dishes like paksiw [meat or fish poached in vinegar] and kare kare and Papa's cooking, which we called "tropical Spanish." He used a lot of garlic and pimenton [smoked paprika], brought directly from Spain by a relative. He loved to make salads. He would grow a lot of peppers in the backyard and grill them with olive oil. Mama would mash up avocados with evaporated milk to make little ice cube avocados, like popsicle treats, for the kids.

Above: making pakaskas in a vat; below: pakaskas.

We always had muscovado sugar. We could run out of salt in the house first, but never sugar. When muscovado catches moisture in the jar, it turns into little rocks of sugar. I spent many afternoons opening the jar and eating these little sugar balls. And I loved everything that Mama did with muscovado. She would make a syrup and drop freshly grated buko in it and let it melt.

It was not a conscious effort on our part that food had to be very special. But food was given respect. Papa did not allow us to eat in our T-shirts. We had to wear sleeves and regardless of what was on the table, we always had a napkin and flatware, even if we were just having tuyo [dried fish] with suka [vinegar] and guinamos [Visayan fermented fish paste].

We ate simple adobo with long green bananas called *buungan*, which are very aromatic. To make the adobo, in a kawali [a small wok] you combine pork, garlic, peppercorn, bay leaf, soy sauce, vinegar (more vinegar than soy sauce), and water to cover the meat, then cook until the pork is tender, the liquid evaporates, the oil comes out, and the meat browns in its own fat. Each one of us would get our own banana, mash it, and shape it into a small volcano. We put the oil from the adobo in the middle, sprinkled salt around the banana, covered it with rice, and mixed it all up. Then we ate the adobo with the rice and the banana. I have never seen anyone else do that.

Sources of Sugar

The Philippines derives most of its sugar from sugar-cane. Raw, unrefined sugar is called muscovado in the Visayas and panocha in the Tagalog region. It comes either in granulated form or as cakes that are grated and served with native desserts such as puto bumbong [violet rice cakes steamed in bamboo tubes].

However, in areas such as Isla Verde, Batangas, south of Manila, where the buri palm, or sugar palm trees, grow in abundance, the sweet sap of the palm tree is boiled and turned into molded palm sugar cakes, called pakaskas (see photos). The pakaskas is the equivalent to the jaggery or gur of South Asia or the gula java of Indonesia.

CHICKEN BINAKOL

Remedios "Aling Reming" Sugon, a successful caterer and restaurant owner in Bacolod, generously spent an entire morning demonstrating this dish to us in a makeshift kitchen under the atrium of the Negros Museum. Aling Reming learned to cook the original chicken binakol from her mother, using a bamboo tube as a cooking vessel for chicken, young coconut, and herbs. The tube was sealed with lemongrass, covered with a banana leaf, and tied securely with string. A hole would be dug in the ground just big enough to fit the bamboo. Live coal would be put at the bottom and the bamboo fitted into the hole. It was then regularly rotated and banged against a hard surface to prevent the chicken from sticking to the sides.

It is possible to replicate the results in a regular stewing pot with a few pieces of fresh bamboo thrown in to capture that authentic binakol flavor. Serve this chunky soup over steamed white rice.

Libas [batuan leaf].

SERVES 4 TO 6

One 3½-pound chicken, cut into pieces

4   medium potatoes, peeled and quartered

1   medium tomato, quartered

1   large onion, quartered

4   scallions, cut into 2-inch lengths

2   cups buko meat sliced from about 4 coconuts
     (page 144), or use frozen shredded buko,
     thawed and drained, juice reserved

4   cups buko juice (from about 4 coconuts, or drained
     from the frozen buko)

2   stalks lemongrass, smashed and quartered
     lengthwise

One 1-inch piece fresh ginger, peeled and julienned

1   stalk rhubarb, cut into 4 pieces
     (or substitute ¼ cup lemon juice)

1   teaspoon each salt and freshly ground black pepper,
     plus additional to taste

2   sticks fresh bamboo (about 4 inches long,
     1 inch thick), (optional)

Combine all the ingredients in a Dutch oven and bring to a boil. Reduce the heat and simmer, uncovered, until the chicken is tender, 30 to 40 minutes. Taste and add more salt and pepper if needed.

LUMPIA UBOD

There are several versions of the ubod filling; this is the simplest. In place of Baby Lacson's paper-thin lumpia wrapper, we recommend using Tita Ding's delicate recipe.

MAKES ABOUT 12 LUMPIA

1	tablespoon canola oil
1	small onion, finely chopped
2	garlic cloves, minced
½	pound pork butt, cut into ¼-inch cubes
1	pound fresh ubod (hearts of palm), preferably coconut ubod, julienned and soaked in water until ready to use
1	teaspoon sugar
2	tablespoons fish sauce, or to taste
½	pound shrimp, peeled, deveined, and finely chopped
6	scallions, trimmed and cut in half, or 6 lettuce leaves

½	recipe Tita Ding's Fresh Lumpia Wrappers (recipe follows)
½	recipe Lumpia Escaño Sauce (page 187)

1. In a large saucepan over medium-high heat, warm the oil. Add the onion and garlic and sauté until softened, about 3 minutes. Add the pork and cook until it turns white, about 5 minutes. Add 1 cup water and bring to a simmer. Add the ubod, sugar, and fish sauce and cook until the ubod is tender, about 5 minutes. Add the shrimp and cook for another minute. Taste and add more fish sauce if needed. Set aside to cool.

2. To assemble, place a wrapper on a flat work surface. Spread about 2 tablespoons of the sauce over the wrapper. Top with about ¼ cup of the filling and place a scallion half over the filling, extending past the outer edge of the wrapper. Fold the bottom of the wrapper up over the mixture. Fold in the sides so they overlap. Serve at room temperature.

TITA DING'S FRESH LUMPIA WRAPPERS

Tita Ding is my mother's youngest sister, Isabel Camara-Garcia. Tita Ding and her family are very much a part of my memories of Nanay and Iba, Zambales. I found this recipe in my mother's notebook of treasured recipes. We find that it is delicate, easy to make, and reliable for our fresh lumpia.

MAKES ABOUT 24 WRAPPERS

¾   cup cornstarch
½   cup all-purpose flour
Pinch of salt
5   large eggs

1. Place the cornstarch, flour, and salt in a large bowl and whisk to combine. Add 1½ cups water, whisking. The batter should be fairly wet. Add the eggs, one at a time, whisking to combine.

2. Cover and refrigerate for 30 minutes.

3. Warm an 8-inch nonstick skillet over medium heat. Add 2 tablespoons batter (using a 1-ounce ladle is the easiest way of getting all the batter into the pan quickly) to the pan and quickly rotate, spreading a thin layer over the pan. Cook until set and the edges begin to curl, about 30 seconds. Flip and cook on the other side until cooked through, about 10 seconds. Stack, overlapping, on a large plate, keeping the wrappers covered with a slightly damp towel to prevent drying.

BUNUELOS DE VIENTO

Translated as wind puffs, bunuelos are Maget Gaston Locsin's specialty, recalling a time when old Negrosanon families would serve a festive meal ending in these treats. They are deep-fried little pieces of dough that are coated with syrup—the skill for making these must come easily to people from sugar country.

You want to make sure you fry the bunuelos well: Fry and test the first one to be sure it is cooked through, before frying the rest. If the batter is not completely cooked inside, fry the bunuelos a little longer, lowering the heat a little if they're browning too fast.

MAKES ABOUT 2 DOZEN

Syrup:

½   cup sugar

Bunuelos:

4   tablespoons unsalted butter, cut into pieces

1   tablespoon sugar

¼   teaspoon salt

1   cup all-purpose flour

4   large eggs

Canola oil, for frying

1. For the syrup, in a medium saucepan over medium-low heat, combine the sugar with 1 cup of water, stirring gently with a wooden spoon to dissolve the sugar. Heat the mixture until it reads 225° F on a candy thermometer. Simmer for 5 minutes without stirring.

2. For the bunuelos, in a large saucepan over medium heat, combine the butter, sugar, and salt with 1 cup of water and bring to a boil, stirring to melt the butter and dissolve the sugar. Take the pan off the heat and add the flour all at once, beating continuously with a wooden spoon until the mixture leaves the sides of the pan and forms a ball. Transfer to an electric mixer bowl and let cool slightly. With a paddle attachment, beat in the eggs, one at a time, until smooth. Cool completely.

3. While the batter is cooling, fill a large saucepan with about 4 inches of oil. Place over medium-high heat and heat until the temperature reads 360° F on a candy thermometer.

4. Drop the batter by the tablespoon into the oil, making about 6 at a time, adjusting the heat to keep the oil at a constant 360° F. Fry the bunuelos, turning to cook evenly on all sides, until they have risen to the top and are nicely browned and puffed, 6 to 7 minutes. Use a spider or slotted spoon to transfer the bunuelos to paper towels.

5. Reheat the syrup and pour it over the bunuelos or pass in a pitcher alongside.

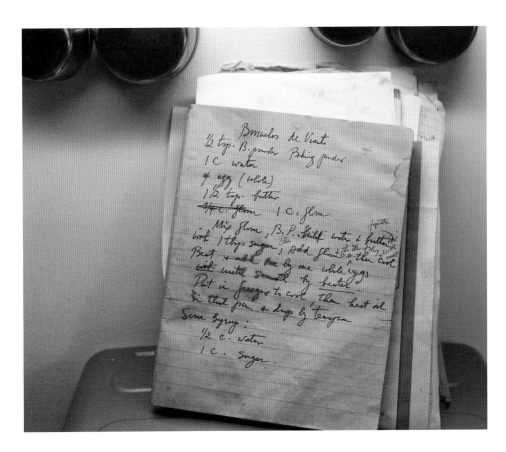

The Manuglibod

The vision of the manuglibod, the ambulant vendors of Bacolod and Silay, traditionally dressed and balancing a woven basket of native delicacies on his or her head, will probably soon pass into the world of memories. The manuglibod collected the best native treats from famous local kakanin makers and brought them directly to people's homes. Unfortunately, the native Visayan kakanin, known as *kalan-unon*, are slowly being replaced by spaghetti and ham and cheese sandwiches. Even the art of wrapping with banana and coconut leaves is giving way to Styrofoam and plastic wrap. We met with a manuglibod, Amalia Sabobo, one early morning in Lyn's Silay home, where she gave us this taste of the kalan-unon:

Kalamayhati: Coconut milk and panocha or muscovado sugar cooked in a vat until thick, then cut into strips and wrapped in banana leaves. **Bicho-bicho:** A rice flour-based dough rolled, looped, fried, and glazed in muscovado syrup. This is similar to the Tagalog pilipit. **Puto taktak:** A steamed cassava cake. **Ibos:** Suman wrapped in a tube of coconut leaves. **But-ong:** Triangle-shaped suman, similar to ibos, which takes on a green hue from the banana leaf. **Buchi:** Boiled camote [sweet potato], mashed with milk, flour, and sugar and fried. **Bae-bae:** Glutinous rice or pinipig, brown sugar, and young coconut pounded in a mortar until properly mixed, then cooked in banana leaves. **Inday-Inday:** Flattened balls of glutinous rice flour dough boiled in water and rolled in sugar, grated coconut, and toasted sesame seeds. **Suman latik:** Suman with coconut syrup, the by-product of coconut milk that has been cooked (the other by-product is coconut oil). **Biko:** Bibingka made with whole-grain glutinous rice. **Puto tikoy:** Tikoy comes from the Chinese term for sticky cake, and is made from glutinous rice flour [malagkit], dyed with purple food coloring. **Puto lansong:** Violet colored steamed rice cake that was originally made with pirurutong [purple rice]. Pirurutong is nearly extinct in the Philippines, so this is made with food coloring now. **Butung-butong:** Coconut milk slowly cooked with muscovado sugar to a candy consistency. The soft dough is rolled in sesame seeds, cut into small pieces, and wrapped like candy. **Piaya:** Flaky dough with muscovado sugar filling, these round biscuits are baked on a griddle heated with charcoal. The flaky dough is similar to the dough of the Chinese cake specialty called hopia. **Puto Manapla:** A soft, spongy rice cake from the town of Manapla, steamed in banana leaves. **Ukoy:** Rice flour fritter with a whole shrimp on top. **Dulce gatas:** Carabao milk slowly cooked with sugar until it caramelizes.

My Memories of Ambulant Vendors

The manuglibod of Bacolod and Silay brought back memories of the joys of growing up with the strange and wondrous food of the ambulant vendors of Manila. From my room on the second floor of our house in Malate, I heard the regular call of the slim, wiry men intoning "ba-luuut" [fertilized duck eggs] and "taho" [soybean custard in caramel sauce]. Balancing a long, elastic bamboo pole on one shoulder, bobbing with the weight of the covered metal containers hung on each end, these vendors tirelessly served neighborhoods like mine to share goods we otherwise would never have tasted. The taho man would open the lid of the container and we would get a whiff of freshly made, hot, steaming soybean custard. He had a ritual. With a flattened scoop, he would skim the custard and discard extra water that had risen to the top before deftly spooning thin horizontal slices of the taho into a bowl and pouring the arnibal (caramel) on it.

Other memorable foods were only vended in specific places. At the Luneta grounds near the Jose Rizal statue, we used to buy chicharron with sukang paombong spiked with labuyo chiles. As a college student at the University of the Philippines on the Diliman campus, no merienda was complete without the banana cue [caramelized saba bananas] sold on the steps of the library. And I must be among many of my generation who wistfully recall, now and again, the familiar bell rung by vendors of the homemade (no brand) ice cream that was known fondly as "dirty ice cream" because it was made in people's homes.

The Games of Bacolod and Silay

Life in Bacolod and Silay cannot be told in its entirety without the passion and humor that come with the stories of panggingge and mahjong. Panggingge, a game using tarot cards, introduced by the Spanish in the Philippines in the late 1800s, is no longer played. What people can remember is how it affected their forebears. Historian Roque Hofilena reminisced that he was born in the middle of a panggingge game that his mother refused to abandon.

Mahjong, introduced sometime in the 1960s, took over where panggingge left off and is firmly entrenched in Philippine society today. Although other forms of gambling such as monte, poker, blackjack, and baccarat took hold after the war, mahjong is still the game of choice for many Filipinos. Beneath its simple-sounding rules lies a daunting world of mind games. A master mahjongera or mahjongero can smell fear and can detect the slightest hesitation, wobble, indecision, or for that matter, any sense of satisfaction with one's cards.

My friend Lilia V. Villanueva wrote, "I enjoy mahjong more for the social interaction rather than the gambling aspect. The game is different when played with family instead of strangers. Small talk and gossip are passed along as revelations. No matter what happens to the rest of the world—such as news about a husband's infidelity or a neighbor's out-of-wedlock pregnancy—the game must go on."

Cecile Locsin-Nava, a Bacolod-based linguist and cultural historian, told me that the most notorious gamblers in Bacolod history were men who had great wealth and social influence. When local officials tried to criminalize gambling, people resorted to building private gambling dens in their attics and basements.

I was asked to do research on these old houses on Cinco de Noviembre Street. Two of my former students brought me to this house with a secret room on the second floor where people could hide and play panggingge. Apparently it was high stakes gambling and periodically the mayor would go through the motions and run after these people, since these activities were illegal.

The famous gamblers were men. They gambled with their chekero [an assistant holding their checkbooks] beside them, but they also bet their jewelry and properties. They would gamble 48 hours straight. They could not be bothered to stand up and take their food, especially when they were on a winning streak. The manuglibod would come and bring their food, and while they were gambling they would eat.

The Escaño Recipe Collection of Cebu

Cebu is the first and the oldest city in the Philippines. The Portuguese navigator and explorer Ferdinand Magellan, as a result of navigational errors in his search for the Moluccas [Spice Islands], sailed into Cebu harbor on April 17, 1521. One of my nieces likens modern Cebu to Manila fifty years ago, before it became a traffic-clogged, overpopulated metropolis. This vibrant and pleasant city in the heart of Visayan country is the envy of many Manileños today. My second visit to Cebu, in 2003, proved to be one of my most memorable and enjoyable trips back home. I was hosted by members of three old Cebuano families, the Escaño, Unchuan, and Moraza families, all of which have contributed to the financial and manufacturing lifeblood of this historic city.

The Recipe Collection from the Kitchen of Lolo Mamerto and Lola Mena Escaño is a rare glimpse of Spanish-Cebuano lifestyle in the early 1900s. The typewritten recipes, mostly in Spanish with a few in English and one in Cebuano, have been copied and hardbound by the Escaño grandchildren, to preserve the memory of their grandmother's kitchen. Leafing through the copy our friend and customer Nieves "Bing" Escano-Garrido (granddaughter of Lolo Mamerto and Lola Mena) lent me, I wished my grandmother had left such records.

The Escaños are descended from an old Spanish line. The branch that settled in Cebu prospered through the shipping industry. Mamerto Escaño and Mena Fortich were married on May 11, 1909 at the Bishop's Palace in Cebu. They had eight children. After going through the cookbook, one can imagine the busy life of Lola Mena, besieged by children and grandchildren for her cakes, cookies, and fiesta fare. Her repertoire included native Filipino desserts (bibingkas, puto pinalutaw), Spanish classics (relleno de pavo, morcillas, relleno de huevos con espinacas), noodle recipes (pancit à la Vicenta Rodriguez), and American classics (angel food, devil's food, sponge cakes, bread pudding). She had recipes for ensaimada, tocino del cielo, pan de sal, and several ice cream flavors (pineapple, tutti frutti, chocolate, and Klim powdered milk).

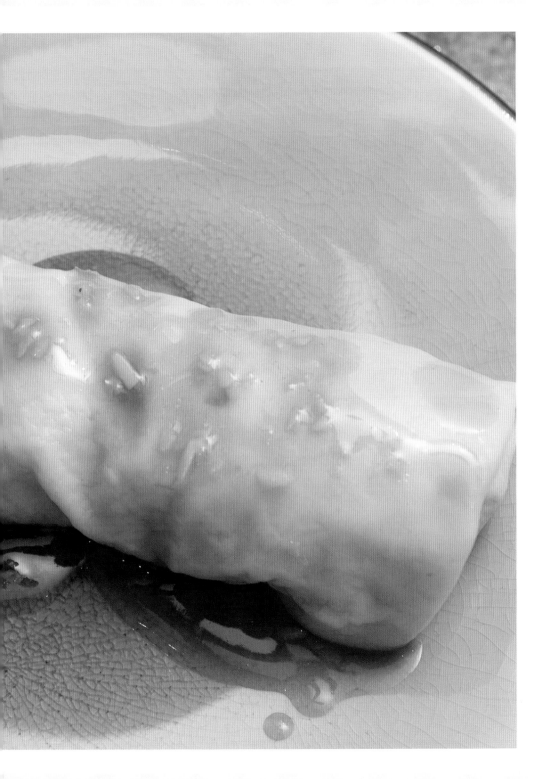

FRESH LUMPIA ESCAÑO

Fresh lumpia, or lumpia sariwa, is the lumpia that is served for any fiesta or meal showcasing the most traditional and representative dishes of the Philippines. Although there are many variations, the dish is unmistakable, with a fresh lettuce leaf peeking out of a neatly wrapped filling of sautéed vegetables, pork, and shrimp. A sweet-salty sauce is spooned over the roll and garnished with chopped peanuts and fried garlic. This version from the Escaños of Cebu adds ubod [hearts of the coconut tree] to the filling and minced garlic to the sauce.

MAKES 20 TO 24 LUMPIA

Filling:

$1/2$	pound large shrimp, with heads and shells
Half a chicken, cut into pieces	
1	large onion, quartered
1	pound pork butt, cut into $1/4$-inch cubes
1	medium russet potato, peeled and julienned
3	tablespoons achuete oil (page 17)
1	small onion, finely chopped
6	garlic cloves, minced
$1/2$	pound fresh ubod, preferably coconut ubod, julienned and soaked in water until ready to use
$1/2$	small head green cabbage, thinly sliced
$1/2$	cup cooked (or canned and drained) garbanzo beans
3	tablespoons fish sauce, or to taste
$1/2$	cup chicken stock, or as needed

Sauce:

3	cups chicken stock
3	tablespoons soy sauce
2	tablespoons cornstarch
$3/4$	cup sugar
2	tablespoons minced garlic
1	recipe Tita Ding's Fresh Lumpia Wrappers (page 181)
Fried garlic slices (page 79), for garnish (optional)	

1. Cut the heads off the shrimp and peel off the shells. Place the heads and shells in a food processor with ½ cup water. Process until the heads and shells have broken down. Strain through a fine-mesh strainer, pressing down on the solids to remove all the juice. Cover and refrigerate the juice until ready to use. Devein and julienne the shrimp bodies and set aside.

2. To prepare the filling, place the chicken and quartered onion in a large saucepan with water to cover. Bring to a boil, then lower the heat and simmer, uncovered, until the chicken is tender, about 40 minutes. Strain, reserving the broth. When the chicken is cool enough to handle, remove the meat from the bones and cut it into ¼-inch pieces. Set aside.

3. While the chicken is cooking, prepare the pork. Place the pork in a medium saucepan with water to cover. Bring to a boil, then lower the heat and simmer, uncovered, until the pork is tender, about 10 minutes. Strain the pork and discard the cooking liquid. Set aside to cool.

4. While the chicken and pork are cooking, fill a medium saucepan with water, bring to a boil over high heat, and add the julienned potatoes. Reduce the heat and simmer until tender, about 5 minutes. Drain and set aside to cool.

5. In a large skillet or wok over medium heat, warm the achuete oil. Add the onions and garlic and sauté until softened, about 3 minutes. Add the shrimp juice, bring the mixture to a boil, then add the pork, shrimp, and ubod and cook until the shrimp begin to turn pink, about 3 minutes. Add the cabbage, potatoes, and garbanzo beans and cook until the cabbage is softened, about 3 minutes. Add the chicken and fish sauce and cook for 2 minutes, or until the chicken is warmed through. Taste and add more fish sauce if needed. The filling should be moist but not wet. If it is too dry, add a little of the reserved chicken broth. Keep the filling warm while you make the sauce.

6. To make the sauce, combine 1 cup of the chicken stock with the soy sauce and cornstarch in a small bowl. Whisk to dissolve the cornstarch.

7. Place the sugar in a small, heavy saucepan. Drizzle 2 tablespoons water over the top. Cook over medium-high heat, gently swirling the pan but not stirring, until the sugar has melted into a deep amber-colored syrup. Slowly add the remaining 2 cups chicken broth and stir to dissolve the sugar. Add the stock-cornstarch mixture and simmer, stirring, until the sauce has thickened, about 3 minutes. Add the garlic.

8. To wrap the lumpia, lay a wrapper on a flat surface and spread about ¼ cup of the filling over it. Roll into a thick cylinder, seam side down. Continue rolling until you've used up all the filling. Spoon the sauce over the lumpia and serve sprinkled with fried garlic slices, if using.

Ubod [hearts of coconut].

BUTIFARRAS ESCAÑO

The Escaño recipe for butifarras stands out as a classic. Presiding over the kitchen of her son and daughter-in-law in Cebu, Tina Escaño-Unchuan demonstrated how to stuff, boil, then fry the sausages to a beautiful crisp brown. When they were ready, her son Jovie Unchuan sat down, reverently surveyed the sausages, then cut them with great care and anticipation.

The Escaños serve this for breakfast or as appetizers for cocktail parties. If you don't want to use sausage casing, the filling can be fried as patties – it will be equally delicious.

MAKES ABOUT 1 DOZEN 6-INCH LINKS

2	pounds pork butt, coarsely chopped
1	pound pork fatback, coarsely chopped
1 ½	teaspoons freshly ground white pepper
1 ½	teaspoons freshly ground black pepper
1 ½	tablespoons salt
5	egg yolks
Pork casing	
2	tablespoons vegetable oil, for frying

1. Combine all the ingredients except the pork casing in a large bowl. Mix very well, using your clean hands to incorporate the eggs. Cover and refrigerate for at least 2 hours, or overnight.

2. Soak the sausage casing in a bowl filled with warm water for 30 minutes, then put one end of the casing over the end of your kitchen faucet and wash the inside with warm water. Change the water in the bowl and soak for another 30 minutes.

3. To make the sausage, use a food grinder with a sausage stuffer attachment. Pull the entire length of casing over the tip of the sausage horn and tie a knot at the end. Fill the feed tube of the grinder with the meat mixture and crank the meat through the grinder to fill the casing until you have used all the meat. Remove the casing from the horn and tie the sausage every 6 inches with kitchen twine. Prick the sausages with a pin to remove any air bubbles. Cut the sausages into individual links.

4. Place the sausage links in a large skillet and add water to come halfway up the sides of the links. Place over medium-high heat and cook, turning the sausages, until the water is evaporated, about 5 minutes. Add 2 tablespoons oil and continue frying until nicely browned, about 3 minutes on each side.

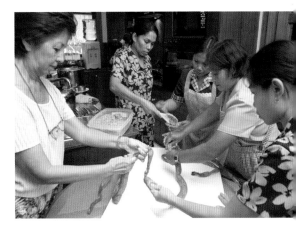

Overleaf, clockwise from top left corner: kalamay [sticky rice cake colored with food coloring], sinapot, guinamos [Visayan fermented shrimp], imbao [mangrove clams], kaimito [star apple], kinilaw ingredients at market, sinamak, nga-nga, kurakding, clams, making chicken inasal, and currachas [Zamboanga crabs].

Christmas season in the Philippines lasts for six weeks, starting with four Sundays of Advent before Christmas Day until the Epiphany or Three Kings Day, celebrated on January 6. One tradition is the *Misa de Gallo* (called Mass of the Rooster because the mass is held at daybreak when the cock crows), held nine days before Christmas. *Noche Buena* is the most special Christmas feast. After midnight mass on Christmas Eve, the hungry mass-goers (people normally fast before going to mass) are greeted by hordes of street vendors outside the church selling puto bumbong, bibingka, and hot salabat.

At home, the *Noche Buena* meal includes ensaimadas and queso de bola [Edam cheese sealed in round tin cans] with hot chocolate. Main courses are glazed ham, roast stuffed turkey [pavo embuchado], or chicken [galantina or chicken relleno]. These dishes are Spanish in origin—stuffed with forced meat, chorizos, pimenton [paprika], and olives. Historical notes on the galleons that used to dock in Cavite describe great excitement from the locals upon the arrival of the galleon, because it carried the goods for Christmas: the olives, olive oils, queso de bola, and turrones de alicante [hard nougats with almonds].

Food is the most popular Christmas gift item. Local bakeries and kakanin makers do sell-out business for their ensaimadas, sans rival, yemas, brazos Mercedes, puto (pandan and ube), cassava bibingka, and suman sa ligia.

The Chinese in the Philippines have also contributed to the flavors of Christmas with their holiday gift baskets filled with Chinese ham, queso de bola, tikoy [a hard cake made with sticky rice flour that could be steamed or fried], boxes of Jacob's cream crackers, biscuits, and other candies, all made by Chinese manufacturers in the Philippines.

Spain brought Christmas to the Philippines and America brought the extra trimmings, but it is fully anchored on Philippine values of family and community. Christmas is a Filipino tradition, infusing the love of food and the embrace of other cultures into the spirit of giving, hospitality, and generosity. It is a time when everyone brings to the table whatever traditions, customs, and food they love—wherever it comes from.

Above: chestnuts.
Opposite: parol [Christmas lanterns from Pampanga].

From left to right: making babingka, heirloom rice from the terraces, dalandan, and chocolate tablets from Cebu. Opposite: a typical Filipino Christmas feast.

A Season to Celebrate the Harvest

The Christmas season coincides with harvest in the Philippines. Freshly harvested rice is transformed into countless varieties of bibingka, puto, and suman. In November, Sta. Rita, Pampanga, celebrates the harvest of its precious duman, the immature rice grains of the Milagrosa species. The annual yield for these delicate, light-green grains of rice is small and pre-sold to a few families who can afford to buy it before it reaches the market. Poured into a hot steaming cup of chocolate and carabao milk, the grains melt to a puddinglike consistency at the bottom of the cup. This is also the season of the dalandan, or dalanghita, the native orange of the Philippines. Once underappreciated by Filipinos, its freshly squeezed juice is now served by many restaurants as a drink or a frozen shake. When shopping for dalandan, one looks for the tell-tale white streaks on its green rind. Called *kalawang* (Tagalog for rust), it indicates that the orange is quite sweet.

CHRISTMAS HAM

I remember one Christmas when my mother decided to cook the Chinese ham for Christmas Day. The ham was soaked for a couple of days in several changes of water, then it was simmered in pineapple juice and brown sugar. When it was cooked, the skin was peeled off and the fat sprinkled with sugar. An iron spatula called a plancha was heated in the fire, then pressed firmly on the sugared fat to caramelize the ham. This was an old-fashioned method developed in rural areas where there were no large ovens in people's homes to finish the ham. If you are serving this at a Christmas party, the ham will be a dramatic centerpiece and will be delicious and moist straight from the oven when the glaze is fresh. Leftover ham was what I always looked forward to. I would fry the ham slices in butter, sprinkle some sugar, and squeeze some orange juice on it and let it caramelize.

SERVES 12 TO 15

One 17- to 20-pound fresh, ready-to-eat, bone-in
    smoked ham
Six 46-ounce cans unsweetened pineapple juice
½   liter dark rum
One 1-pound box dark-brown sugar
About 1 cup granulated sugar, for glazing the ham
Pickled Pineapple (recipe follows), for serving

1. In a stockpot large enough to hold the ham and the juice, combine 5 cans of the pineapple juice with the rum and brown sugar and place over high heat. Bring to a boil, stirring to dissolve the sugar. Add the ham. If the pineapple-juice mixture doesn't cover the ham, add more pineapple juice or water to cover. Bring back to a boil, then reduce the heat to medium-high and simmer until you can peel off the skin, about 1½ hours. Leave the ham in the stockpot for another hour to let the flavors settle.

2. Take the ham out of the pot and set on a wire rack in a large roasting pan lined with foil. Let the ham cool slightly, about 30 minutes.

3. Preheat the oven to 425° F. Using a small, sharp paring knife, take the skin off the ham, keeping as much of the fat as possible.

4. Score the fat in a crisscross fashion with the point of a sharp knife and sprinkle generously with granulated sugar. Bake the ham until the fat and the sugar caramelize, about 20 minutes, watching carefully that the sugar doesn't burn.

PICKLED PINEAPPLE

I found this recipe in the *Philippine Sunday Tribune Magazine*, published August 16, 1936. It is a perfect condiment for the Christmas ham cooked in pineapple juice.

MAKES ABOUT 1 QUART

One large (4- to 5-pound)
    pineapple
1   teaspoon whole cloves
½   teaspoon whole black
    peppercorns
1   cinnamon stick,
    broken into pieces
5   cups rice vinegar
4   cups sugar

1. Peel and core the pineapple. Slice the pineapple into ½-inch pieces, then cut the slices into quarters. Tie the cloves, peppercorns, and cinnamon in cheesecloth.

2. Combine the vinegar, sugar, and spices in a large nonreactive saucepan and place over medium-high heat. Bring to a boil, then reduce the heat and simmer, stirring to dissolve the sugar, for 20 minutes.

3. Add the pineapple, bring the liquid back to a simmer, and cook until the pineapple is tender, about 1 hour. Using a slotted spoon, transfer the fruit to a heatproof container. Raise the heat and boil the liquid until it has a syrupy consistency, about 30 minutes. Pour the syrup over the pineapple, let cool, and refrigerate.

CHICKEN RELLENO

In our recipe for chicken relleno [roast stuffed chicken], we have done away with any canned sausages and sweet pickles and returned the olive to its rightful place as a wonderful counterpoint to the ground pork-chorizo filling.

SERVES 4 TO 6

2	tablespoons canola oil
1	garlic clove, minced
1	medium onion, diced
1	medium carrot, diced
¼	pound chanterelle or shiitake mushroom caps, diced
1	pound ground pork
1	small chorizo, diced
1	roasted red bell pepper, diced
6	green olives, pitted and diced
⅓	cup raisins soaked in ½ cup brandy for 30 minutes, then drained

Salt

Freshly ground black pepper

1	tablespoon cornstarch or sweet potato starch
1	large egg
One	4-pound de-boned chicken (have your butcher do this for you)
2	hard-boiled eggs, shelled
1	large carrot, cut in half and sliced lengthwise
2	tablespoons unsalted butter, softened

1. In a large skillet over medium heat, warm the oil. Add the garlic, onions, and carrots and sauté until softened, about 3 minutes. Add the mushrooms and sauté until they release their juices, about 3 minutes. Transfer the mixture to a large bowl and set aside to cool completely.

2. Add the pork, chorizo, bell pepper, olives, raisins, 2 teaspoons salt, ½ teaspoon black pepper, cornstarch, and egg to the cooled vegetable mixture. Using clean hands, mix well until well combined.

3. Preheat the oven to 425° F. Season the chicken with salt and pepper inside and out and place on a work surface breast side up. Stuff the chicken with the filling through the neck cavity, nestling the eggs in the middle. Using a large needle and sturdy thread, starting with the neck opening, sew the chicken around all the skin openings to seal it. Tuck the wings under the chicken and truss the chicken with kitchen twine by tying the legs together and then tying again around the length and width of the chicken.

4. Line a roasting pan with foil. Line the foil with the carrot slices and place the chicken on top. Brush the chicken with the butter and sprinkle with salt. Roast, basting occasionally, until the internal temperature of a thigh reads 180° F and the temperature of the stuffing reads 165° F, about 1 hour and 15 minutes. Discard the trussing strings and let stand for 5 to 10 minutes before carving.

The Galantina and Chicken Relleno

I asked Rachel Laudan, a culinary historian presently living in Mexico, to enlighten me about the difference between chicken relleno and galantina. She tells me that rellenos are alive and well there, while she has not encountered galantinas, which she considers nineteenth-century cuisine. Filipinos, on the other hand, have sometimes used the terms interchangeably, assuming that the chicken relleno is a Filipino version of Spanish galantina using ground pork, canned sausages, sweet pickles, and a boiled egg to stuff the chicken. A Philippine archival recipe I encountered for galantina used canned "Oxford sausages" and "lengua de carnero" (referring either to its literal translation of sheep's tongue or to a Spanish herb) to stuff the deboned chicken. The chicken was sewn up, wrapped in cheesecloth, and steamed until cooked. It was allowed to cool, then pressed to flatten it slightly before slicing and serving.

ENSAIMADA

We consulted several sources, including Marc Medina, to find the best brioche recipe. This is a version we feel people can do at home.

MAKES 12

Dough:

2	envelopes active dry yeast
¾	cup milk, warmed
3	cups all-purpose flour
2	cups bread flour
5	tablespoons sugar
4	teaspoons salt
3	whole eggs, at room temperature
9	egg yolks, at room temperature
3	sticks unsalted butter, softened, plus additional for the tart pans
3	cups grated Gouda, Edam, or manchego cheese

Topping:

2	egg yolks beaten with 2 tablespoons milk, for brushing
4	tablespoons unsalted butter, softened, for brushing
4	tablespoons sugar, for sprinkling
6	tablespoons grated Gouda, Edam, or manchego cheese, for sprinkling

1. Dissolve yeast in warm milk and let stand until foamy, 3 to 5 minutes.

2. In a large bowl, sift together the all-purpose flour, bread flour, sugar, and salt. Transfer to a stand mixer fitted with a paddle attachment. Add the yeast mixture and beat for 2 to 3 minutes. In a separate bowl, lightly beat the eggs and the eggs yolks. Add to the dough and beat for 3 to 5 minutes. Add the softened butter 2 tablespoons at a time until fully blended.

3. Exchanging the paddle for the hook attachment, knead the dough for 7 minutes at medium speed.

4. Transfer the dough to a clean bowl, cover with plastic, and let rise until doubled, about 1 hour. Punch the dough down, cover with plastic wrap, and refrigerate overnight.

5. The next day, pinch off twenty-four 2-ounce pieces of dough and roll them into balls (about 2 inches). Place on a baking sheet, cover with plastic, and let rise for 1 hour.

6. Liberally butter twelve 4- or 5-inch tart rings (without the bottoms) and arrange them on baking sheets. On a lightly floured work surface, roll out a dough ball with a rolling pin into a 12-by-4-inch rectangle. Spread 2 tablespoons of the cheese over the dough, leaving a little room at the edges. Roll the dough lengthwise, encircling the cheese into a snug rope shape about 14 inches long and ½ inch thick. Repeat with the rest of the dough—you will have 24 ropes.

7. Take two of the ropes and twist them around each other. Hold one end down, then wind the rest of the rope around it to form a spiral shape, and tuck in the ends. Repeat with the rest of the rest of the ropes. Place each spiral in the middle of a tart ring and place on the baking sheets. The spiral should come almost to the edge of the tart ring. Cover with plastic and set aside to rise for about 1 hour, or until the dough reaches the sides of the ring.

8. During the final rise, preheat the oven to 400° F. Brush with the egg wash and bake, turning the pan halfway through baking, until lightly browned on top, 10 to 12 minutes. Let cool slightly, then brush with the softened butter, and sprinkle with the sugar and cheese. The ensaimada can be wrapped in plastic wrap and frozen.

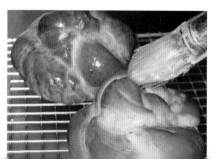

The Historical Significance of Ensaimada

The Philippine ensaimada is a coiled brioche sweet roll that traces its origins to Mallorca in the Balearic Islands of Spain. Alan Davidson, in his *Oxford Companion to Food*, writes that ensaimada came from the Mallorquinese word *saim*, which means pork lard. How this sweet bread came to Mallorca is a bit muddled, but some sources point to either a Jewish or Arab bread called *gulema* that was shaped like a turban and whose dough was made with olive oil.

In the late 1300s and early 1400s, the Spanish Inquisition forced Jews to either leave Spain or convert to Christianity (Conversos) if they wanted to stay. In order to ferret out baptized Jews and their descendants who were suspected of secretly practicing their Jewish rituals and religiously pre-scribed diets (Marranos), the Catholic Church mandated the use of pork and pork products. This explains the predominance of pork lard in breads and dishes of Spain following this period. To this day, the official recipe of Mallorca ensaimada requires the use of pork lard as its main ingredient. Families in the Philippines who take pride in their ensaimada recipes now use butter instead of lard, unaware of this bit of historical significance to their beloved sweet roll.

1 pound fresh ginger, cut into large chunks
2 oranges, peeled and sliced
2 apples, peeled, cored, and sliced
Honey, for serving

Place the ginger and orange and apple slices in a large saucepan. Add 10 cups water, bring to a boil, then reduce the heat and simmer for about 10 minutes, or until the brew has developed a nice flavor. Strain through a very fine sieve into a large teapot or two small teapots. Serve with honey.

BRAZO DE MERCEDES

This recipe, which my mother was able to get from Gilda Cordero-Fernando's mother, uses an old-fashioned, labor-intensive method of cooking the egg yolks and sugar to a syrupy texture, to which melted butter is added. Mrs. Cordero's brazos were huge and fluffy. Although it takes some patience and skill to master, I have never found a recipe better than this one.

SERVES 8 TO 10

Meringue:
12 large egg whites, at room temperature
½ teaspoon cream of tartar
Pinch of salt
1 cup superfine sugar
Egg Yolk Pastry:
12 large egg yolks
½ cup sugar
8 tablespoons unsalted butter, cut into pieces

1. Preheat the oven to 325° F. Line a 12-by-16-inch baking pan with parchment paper, cutting slits in each corner of the paper to allow the parchment to fit snugly into and up the sides of the pan. *(continued)*

HOT SALABAT

At Cendrillon we serve salabat to customers who request it and offer it to people who come in suffering from sore throats or colds. It is a soothing and healing brew that can compete with Mom's chicken soup anytime.

The most straightforward way to make the salabat is to boil pieces of ginger until you get a beverage that has some bite to it. Romy adds a couple of other ingredients to the brew to soften the ginger's edge: oranges, apples, or better yet, during the fall, quince. The aroma of brewing ginger and quince will fill your kitchen and home and lighten your heart. This is also the best time to bring out that special honey that you have been keeping in your cupboard to serve alongside.

A Gypsy's Arm

The "arm of Mercedes," as it is literally translated, was an adaptation of the Spanish "Brazo de Gitano," or "arm of a Gypsy." How an arm of a gypsy with a sponge cake base became Mercedes's lightweight meringue wrap enveloping egg yolk, butter, and syrup filling becomes moot once you taste this favorite Filipino dessert.

2. To make the meringue, in the bowl of an electric mixer fitted with the whisk attachment, beat the egg whites with a pinch of salt on medium speed until foamy. Add the cream of tartar and beat until just before soft peaks form. Gradually beat in the sugar on high speed until soft peaks form. Using a rubber spatula, evenly spread the meringue over the pan. Smooth the top with an offset spatula.

3. Bake until the meringue is set and very lightly browned, about 30 minutes. Transfer the meringue to a wire rack and let cool in the pan.

4. To make the egg yolk pastry, set a fine-mesh strainer over a bowl and have it ready near the stove. Combine the yolks, sugar, and butter in the top of a double boiler or in a metal bowl set over, not in, simmering water. Do not let the water come to a boil. Whisk constantly until the butter has melted, then switch to a heatproof rubber spatula and continue to cook, stirring constantly and scraping the sides, until the mixture is thickened, about 15 minutes. Adjust the heat as necessary while cooking to ensure that the water doesn't simmer too actively (this can cause the eggs to curdle). Strain the mixture immediately.

5. With a paring knife, loosen the sides of the meringue from the pan. Put a buttered parchment paper on top of the meringue, invert, and remove bottom parchment paper. Using a rubber spatula, carefully spread the egg yolk pastry thinly over the cooled meringue, leaving about an inch of the meringue on all sides without egg pastry. With the short end of the cake facing you, gently pull the cake from the parchment and roll it away from you, like a jellyroll. Using a serrated knife, cut the roll crosswise into slices and serve.

HOT CHOCOLATE

The Pampanga hot chocolate is made from native cacao mixed with a small amount of ground peanuts. The cacao comes in balls or tablets (called tableas), which are melted in hot carabao milk and brought to the guest in a batidor, a tall, narrow pitcher with a wooden beater and a handle that is rotated in swift motions by the palms of both hands to create a frothy top.

For this version, we have omitted the ground peanuts. We do a combination of native chocolate (which can be found in some Asian stores) and other brands of chocolate to soften the edge of the native variety. Mexican chocolate can be used as a substitute for the Philippine cacao.

MAKES EIGHT 4-OUNCE SERVINGS

1	cup heavy cream
2	cups milk
5	ounces Philippine chocolates, chopped
10	ounces bittersweet chocolate, chopped
½	cup muscovado or other brown sugar

Whipped cream, for serving

In a large saucepan over medium heat, combine the cream and milk and heat until the liquid just comes to a boil, about 5 minutes. Whisk in the chocolates and sugar until dissolved. Serve topped with whipped cream.

Serving Salabat and Chocolate

Salabat, along with hot chocolate, are the two most traditional beverages served during Christmas. Salabat is native and therefore served with kakanin [native desserts] such as suman or bibingka, while hot chocolate is foreign (from Spain and Mexico) and served with ensaimada or other sweet fried doughs such as gollorias or churros [deep-fried fritters for breakfast or merienda].

Christmas in Tarlac, Tarlac

Nanay, my maternal grandmother, died when I was ten, and the family ties that had brought us to Iba, Zambales, on a regular basis began to fade. The bucolic picnics floating down the Bangkal river on rafts and riding water buffaloes on the black beaches of Masinloc gave way to the more urban setting of Tarlac, Tarlac, a few hours drive north of Manila in Central Luzon. I distinctly remember this shift from one side of the family to the other.

My father's oldest brother, Tomas Besa, was the undisputed patriarch of the huge Besa clan, having raised his younger siblings, who were orphaned early in their lives. Tom Daddy, as we all called him, had built a huge, exquisitely intricate home along the main street of Tarlac. The ground floor alone was a warren of corridors leading from my uncle's office (in a country that likes to convey titular respect, he was referred to as Attorney) to the kitchen opening up to a grand living room with an elevated dining room on the side lined with wide planks of polished hardwood. There were French doors everywhere opening up to gardens and a wide expanse of grassy area where the cousins played softball with room to spare.

This house was the setting for the most memorable Besa family Christmas reunions. We were five families, with more than thirty cousins. On Christmas Eve, the whole clan would dress up in their best and head to church for midnight mass. Midnight mass in an old Filipino church, underneath vaulted ceilings, stays with you forever because of the distinct smell of burning votive candles, incense, old wooden pews, and stone walls amid the scent of people's perfumes. When the mass had ended in exultant singing, the family would head back to the house for *Noche Buena*, gift giving and serious socializing.

As soon as the *Noche Buena* meal was cleared away and the adults had repaired to the living room for cigars and political discussions, the twenty-foot-long table in the dining room was transformed into a big blackjack table for the cousins. This is where one's true mettle was tested, for the humor would get personal. Kanchawan (a friendly form of teasing or taunting) is a national pastime and one can easily fall into the trap of being pikon [a sore loser]. My mother abhorred gambling and I remember her anxious glances our way as we eagerly pulled out our peso bills for the "bank." Since I was barely in my teens then and financially dependent on my parents, there was not much that I could lose anyway. But this was our annual rite of passage, and if one survived the personal taunts with grace and good humor, one was assured a permanent place in that esteemed state of "cousinhood."

Our household received a steady stream of gifts, mostly food, during this time. Because my father was a doctor who performed free operations on a weekly basis at the National Orthopedic Hospital, his grateful patients thanked him for his kindness at Christmas.

Overleaf, clockwise from top left: vendor in Silay, agar agar, candied pili nuts, eggplants, chestnuts, pili nuts in shell, heirloom rice, sago, carabao milk.

chapter 6

A problem facing any immigrant is that he now craves the food that he left behind. For Filipinos, the challenges are to replicate the sourness derived from tropical fruits in our food (what is the substitute for the kamias, fresh unripe tamarind, kalamansi and the Visayan batuan?) and how to cook with bagoong and patis in a small apartment without incurring the wrath of neighbors? It is surprising how the taste for bitterness has survived. Some Filipino customers still ask wistfully for bitter melon in their pinakbet.

When it comes to satisfying food cravings, Filipinos cannot be deterred. They have figured out how to do lechon in their backyard. In Hawaii, the Ilocanos grow their green exotica: saluyot, malunggay, and katuday. In many communities, skilled hands do their special kakanin and market them through the local stores. Philippine-based bakeries have branches in the United States to do pan de sal, ensaimada, sans rival, brazo de Mercedes, and mango tarts.

New landscapes in the United States also offer opportunities in culinary creativity. How can we use the abundant produce, fruits, and condiments from every culture imaginable that are available in our local markets? Mexican immigrants have established successful food businesses everywhere they settle, and I am intrigued by the new convergence of our cultures, echoing a process that started four hundred years ago.

Among the major cultural ties developed throughout Philippine history, it is that of the Chinese that is profoundly enduring. Next to home cooking, Filipinos instinctively seek out Chinese food. In New York's Chinatown, several store signs advertise that they carry Philippine products. In one local sio pao [steamed filled bun] shop, the Chinese men behind the counter talk to their legions of loyal Filipino customers in Tagalog. And what about our ties to American food? Fortunately, American food sensibilities have found a counterbalance to processed food in the organic movement borne by the new American cuisine that gained momentum in the 1970s.

At Cendrillon, a decade of re-creating dishes that recall our childhood has given us much satisfaction as we reinterpret foods of the past. The fresh lumpia, black rice paella, coffee-roasted fish, and ube pan de sal with adobo flakes on our menu all stem from foods that held something, in their original concept, that we wanted to emphasize or improve on.

FRESH LUMPIA

Fresh lumpia was one of the first dishes we tackled. We wanted a lumpia wrapper that was different, so we made it with purple yam. The traditional sauce for a fresh lumpia is a sweet and salty sauce thickened with cornstarch and garnished with ground peanuts and raw minced garlic. We decided instead to incorporate the peanuts into our sauce and created a peanut-lemongrass-garlic flavored sauce.

MAKES ABOUT 30 LUMPIA

Wrappers:

1   cup all-purpose flour
1   cup rice flour (not glutinous)
⅓   cup ube (purple yam) flour
½   teaspoon salt
2   large eggs, beaten
1   cup coconut milk

Filling:

3   tablespoons vegetable oil
2   cloves garlic, minced
2   leeks, white parts only, trimmed, cleaned, and thinly sliced
½   Napa cabbage, thinly sliced
2   cups bean sprouts
1   large carrot, cut into matchstick pieces
1   small jicama, peeled and cut into matchstick pieces
12   snowpeas, trimmed and thinly sliced on the diagonal
12   shiitake mushrooms, stemmed, cleaned, and thinly sliced
4   teaspoons fish sauce, or to taste
½   teaspoon freshly ground black pepper, or to taste

Peanut Sauce:

1   tablespoon vegetable or peanut oil
1   stalk lemongrass, white part only, minced
1   garlic clove, minced
1   shallot, minced
One 2-inch piece fresh ginger, peeled and minced
1½   cup roasted peanuts, finely ground in a food processor
1   cup coconut milk
1–2 small fresh birdseye chiles, minced (optional)
2   tablespoons rice vinegar
1   tablespoon soy sauce
2   teaspoons fish sauce, or to taste
¼   teaspoon freshly ground black pepper, or to taste

Fried garlic slices, for serving (page 79)
½   cup roasted peanuts, coarsely chopped (optional)

1. To make the wrappers, sift together the flours and salt into a large bowl. In a separate bowl, whisk the eggs with the coconut milk and 1½ cups water and add to the flour mixture. Whisk until blended and smooth, adding more water if the batter is too thick. (It should have the consistency of heavy cream.)

2. Warm an 8-inch nonstick skillet over medium-low heat. Add about 2 tablespoons batter (using a 1-ounce ladle is the easiest way of getting all the batter into the pan quickly) to the pan and quickly rotate, spreading over a thin layer, like a thick crêpe. Cook until the wrapper is set and the edges begin to curl, about 2 minutes. (The underside should stay purple—if it starts to brown, turn the heat down a little.) Flip and cook on the other side for 30 seconds longer, until cooked through. Stack, overlapping, on a large plate. You'll have about 30 wrappers that measure about 6 inches in circumference. Keep covered with a very slightly damp towel to prevent drying.

3. For the filling, in a large skillet or wok, warm the oil. Add the garlic and stir over medium-high heat until fragrant, about 1 minute. Add the leeks, and sauté until slightly softened, about 2 minutes. Add the cabbage, bean sprouts, carrots, jicama, snowpeas, and mushrooms. Cook, stirring often, until the vegetables are tender but still crunchy, about 5 minutes. Season with the fish sauce and black pepper to taste.

4. To make the peanut sauce, heat the oil in a small saucepan over medium-high heat. Add the lemongrass, garlic, shallots, and ginger. Cook, stirring often, until lightly browned, 2 to 3 minutes. Add the peanuts and the coconut milk. Reduce the heat to medium and simmer, uncovered, stirring often, until thickened, about 5 minutes. If the sauce is too thick, stir in a little water. Add the chiles, vinegar, soy sauce, fish sauce and black pepper to taste and cook for another minute. The sauce can be made several days in advance.

5. To assemble, lay a wrapper on a plate. Spread with ¼ cup of the filling, and roll into a thick cylinder, seam side up. Top the finished rolls with peanut sauce, fried garlic slices and the coarsely ground peanuts, if desired.

BLACK RICE PAELLA

We first encountered black rice, in all places, at Sun Valley, Idaho, in the late 1980s. While vacationing there one summer, we walked into a small gourmet store selling heirloom beans and different varieties of rice. We bought a lot of the black rice and brought it back to New York for Romy to experiment with. We later found that the rice is available in Chinatown in New York.

In the Philippines, black rice is called pirurutong and is the major ingredient of puto bumbong (page 67). Filipinos use it primarily for dessert, cooking it in coconut milk and sugar, never for a main course. Romy then created this paella using coconut milk, and flavored with lemongrass and pandan leaves. In place of chicken or chorizo, Romy used seafood—clams, shrimp, scallops, and crab, and the dish is cooked in two clay pots (available in Asian markets) instead of the typical paella pan.

SERVES 8

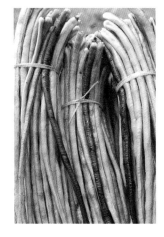

Sitao [longbeans]

2   cups black rice

6   tablespoons vegetable oil

1   small onion, finely chopped

1   small carrot, cut into ¼-inch dice

2   pandan leaves (optional)

1   stalk lemongrass, trimmed, bruised with the back of a knife or with a rolling pin, and cut into 4-inch lengths

1   teaspoon salt

3   garlic cloves, finely chopped

2   small shallots, minced

2   leeks, white parts only, trimmed, cleaned, and thinly sliced

1   fresh green chile, cored, seeded, and finely chopped

One 1-inch piece fresh ginger, peeled and finely chopped

¼   pound fresh shiitake mushrooms caps, trimmed, cleaned, and sliced

1½   cups coconut milk

2   teaspoons fish sauce, or to taste

2   teaspoons lemon juice, or to taste

2   medium plum tomatoes, quartered

2   Chinese eggplants, quartered lengthwise and cut into 2-inch pieces

5   Chinese longbeans, cut into 2-inch pieces

1   pound sea scallops, trimmed and rinsed

1½   dozen Manila clams, scrubbed

4   large live blue crabs, cleaned (see Note)

1   pound whole unpeeled large shrimp, preferably with heads on, shells slit through the back and deveined

1. Rinse the rice in cold water and drain. In a large saucepan (for which you have a cover) over medium-high heat, warm half of the vegetable oil. Add the onions and carrots and cook, stirring often, until softened, 3 to 5 minutes. Stir in the rice and pour in 4 cups cold water. Increase the heat to high and bring to a boil. Add the pandan leaves, if using, and the lemongrass and salt. Reduce the heat to low, cover, and simmer until the water is absorbed and the rice is tender but still al dente, about 40 minutes. Take the pan off the heat, discard the pandan leaves and lemongrass, and keep warm.

2. In a large skillet or wok over medium heat, warm the remaining oil. Add the garlic, shallots, and leeks and cook for 3 minutes, until slightly softened. Add the chile, ginger, and mushrooms and cook until the mushrooms start to release their liquid, about 5 minutes. Add 1 cup of the coconut milk and bring to a simmer, then add the fish sauce and lemon juice and cook for about 3 minutes so the flavors meld.

3. Arrange the rice over the bottom of two large clay pots. Arrange the tomatoes, eggplant, and longbeans on top. Pour the coconut milk mixture on top, reserving ½ cup. Place half the scallops, half the clams, and 2 of the crabs on top of the rice in each pot. Cover the pots and cook over medium-high heat until the clams start to open and the crab shells turn red, 5 to 8 minutes. Mix the shrimp and the remaining scallops with the reserved ½ cup coconut milk and add half to each pot, cover, and cook for another 5 minutes, or until all the seafood and vegetables are cooked through.

Note: To clean live blue crabs, chill in the refrigerator or put in ice water for five minutes for easy handling. Pull off the apron (belly flap) and then the top shell. Remove the gills and rinse the crab and the top shell with water. Cut the crabs in half. Put the crab halves together and replace the top shell.

COFFEE-ROASTED POMPANO

Roasting a fish calls for flavorful and aromatic oil, and Romy found it in coffee beans mixed with cacao beans, lemongrass, and spices. After roasting the fish, he scrapes the beans and spices along with the fish drippings from the pan into a saucepan and simmers it with coconut milk. The sauce is then strained and poured onto the fish. The touch of mocha spice in the sauce gives added richness to the sweetness of the fresh fish. Red snapper can also work well in this dish.

SERVES 4

2   large pieces banana leaf, wiped clean with
     a damp cloth
Two whole pompanos or red snapper
     (1½ to 2 pounds each), cleaned
Salt, to taste
6   tablespoons canola oil
6   whole shallots
12   garlic cloves
1   stalk lemongrass, trimmed, bruised, and cut
     into 2-inch diagonal pieces
5   bay leaves
4   whole fresh red chiles
2   cinnamon sticks
4   cardamom pods
1   tablespoon black peppercorns
1   tablespoon coriander seeds
1   cup whole coffee beans
¼   cup cacao beans (optional)
1½   cups coconut milk
1   tablespoon fish sauce, or to taste
Freshly squeezed juice of 1 lime, or to taste
½   tablespoon ground coffee beans (optional)

1. Line a baking sheet with the banana leaves and preheat the oven to 400° F. Cut 2 widthwise slits across both sides of each fish. Liberally coat both sides with salt. Warm 3 tablespoons of the oil in each of two large skillets over medium-high heat. Sear the fish until the skin is lightly browned and crisp, about 2 minutes on each side. Tip one fish, along with the oil it was cooked in, into the other pan.

2. In the empty pan, combine the shallots, garlic, lemongrass, bay leaves, chiles, cinnamon, cardamom, peppercorns, coriander seeds, and coffee beans. Stir over medium-high heat until the shallots and garlic are lightly browned and the mixture is aromatic, about 3 minutes.

3. Spread the spice mixture over the banana leaves on the baking pan and lay the fish on top. Roast, turning the pan halfway through cooking, until the fish is cooked through and soft to the touch, about 25 minutes. Transfer the fish to a serving plate and tent with foil while you make the sauce.

4. To make the sauce, transfer the coffee bean and spice mixture from the baking sheet to a large saucepan and place over medium-high heat. Add the coconut milk and simmer for 3 minutes. Turn off the heat. Add the fish sauce, lime juice, and ground coffee, if using, and let steep for a minute. Taste and add more fish sauce or lime juice, if needed. Strain and serve over the fish. Garnish with a few of the shallots, garlic cloves, and coffee beans.

UKOY

The ukoy is the most popular item on our menu. Rice flour gives the added crunch to these shrimp and vegetable fritters. As with many fried foods, some achara (page 17) goes well here.

MAKES ABOUT 12 FRITTERS

½   banana leaf, thawed if frozen

Batter:

¾   cup rice flour

⅓   cup all-purpose flour

½   teaspoon baking powder

¼   teaspoon salt

1   large egg

Filling:

1   cup julienned Napa cabbage

1   cup julienned carrots

1   cup julienned snowpeas

1   cup julienned leeks (white parts only)

1½   cups bean sprouts

1   cup chopped peeled and deveined shrimp

2   teaspoons fish sauce

¼   teaspoon freshly ground black pepper

1-2   tablespoons all-purpose flour

Canola oil, for frying

Rice vinegar with sliced garlic and chopped chiles to taste, for serving

1. Using a damp towel, wipe the banana leaf clean on both sides. Cut out 4-by-4-inch squares from the banana leaf. Set aside on a baking sheet. Brush one side lightly with oil.

2. To make the batter, sift the rice flour, all-purpose flour, baking powder, and salt in a large bowl. In a medium bowl, beat the egg with ¾ cup water, then stir this into the dry ingredients, to form a thick but smooth batter. Refrigerate the batter for 30 minutes to 1 hour.

3. Fill a deep saucepan or wok with 3 inches canola oil and warm over medium heat until the temperature is between 350° F and 365° F.

4. While the oil is heating, prepare the filling: Combine the Napa cabbage, carrots, snowpeas, leeks, bean sprouts, shrimp, fish sauce, and black pepper in a large bowl. Stir the batter and pour just enought into the filling to coat the ingredients. Sprinkle 1 to 2 tablespoons over the mixture and toss to firm it up if necessary (it should not be too wet).

5. Put about ⅓ cup of the filling on the oiled side of each banana leaf square. Place a square on a spider and lower it into the oil. Fry until the fritter is set (about 1 minute), lift from the oil, and remove the banana leaf. Continue frying for another minute until the fritter is lightly browned. Flip and brown the other side until crisp, 1½ to 2 minutes. Life out of the oil with the pider and place on a paper towel–lined baking sheet to drain. Repeat until all the filling is fried. Serve hot with the vinegar dipping sauce.

PINEAPPLE BREAD PUDDING

Romy stews fresh pineapple in white wine and red pepper flakes to give this dessert an unexpected burst of heat.

SERVES 6 TO 8

½	cup raisins
½	cup dark rum
1	fresh ripe pineapple
1	cup dry white wine
1½	cups sugar
1	teaspoon dried red pepper flakes
3	cinnamon sticks
4	whole cardamom seeds
4	whole cloves
2	vanilla beans, split lengthwise
5	cups artisanal bread, cut into 1-inch cubes
4	tablespoons unsalted butter
2	cups milk
1	cup heavy cream
3	whole eggs
3	egg yolks

1. Soak the raisins in the rum overnight and drain just before using.

2. Butter a 2-quart casserole or gratin dish and preheat the oven to 350° F. Peel the pineapple and remove the eyes. Slice lengthwise into quarters and cut away the core. Thinly slice two of the quarters and reserve to use on top of the pudding. Cut the other two quarters into ¼-inch cubes.

3. Combine the wine, 1 cup of the sugar, the pepper flakes, 2 of the cinnamon sticks, the cardamom seeds, cloves, and 1 of the vanilla beans in a small saucepan. Bring to a boil over high heat, stirring until the sugar has dissolved. Reduce the heat to medium-low, add the cubed pineapple, and simmer for 10 minutes. Drain and reserve the syrup and the pineapple cubes. (Remove and discard the spices from the pineapple.) Return the syrup to the

pan and simmer over medium-low heat until thick, about 5 minutes.

4. Melt the butter in a large skillet. Add the bread cubes and cook over medium-high heat, stirring often, until lightly browned, about 5 minutes. Cool slightly.

5. Combine the milk, cream, and remaining ½ cup sugar in a small saucepan. Add the remaining cinnamon stick and vanilla bean. Bring almost to a simmer over medium heat. Remove from heat and let steep for 5 minutes. Discard the cinnamon stick and vanilla bean. Beat the eggs and yolks together in a large heatproof bowl. Pour the milk and cream mixture into the eggs, stirring constantly. (Discard the cinnamon stick and vanilla bean.) Gently stir in the bread cubes and set aside until the bread has absorbed some of the liquid, about 10 minutes. Mix in the raisins and pineapple cubes, stir well, and pour into the casserole.

6. Arrange the sliced pineapple decoratively over the top of the pudding, overlapping. Brush with a small amount of the syrup. Bake until the pudding is set in the center and lightly browned on top, about 45 minutes. Serve warm with any remaining syrup on the side.

KALAMANSI MERINGUE PIE

When I was in the Philippines I always dreamt of tasting the best American lemon meringue pie, but when I arrived in the United States I could never find a good one. Our version uses kalamansi lime curd instead.

MAKES ONE 9-INCH TART

For the crust:

All-purpose flour, for dusting

½   recipe Basic Pie Pastry (page 107)

For the kalamansi curd:

¾   cup granulated sugar

⅓   cup kalamansi lime juice

8   egg yolks, lightly beaten

3   tablespoons unsalted butter, cut into small pieces

For the meringue:

4   egg whites, at room temperature

¼   teaspoon cream of tartar

½   cup superfine sugar

1. On a lightly floured work surface with a lightly floured rolling pin, roll the dough into a 14-inch circle about ⅛-inch thick. Transfer to a 10-inch tart pan with a removable bottom, pressing the dough into the pan. Trim away excess dough from the edges of the pan. Cover the tart with plastic wrap and refrigerate for at least 1 hour or overnight.

2. While the dough is chilling, make the filling: In a metal bowl (or the top of a double boiler) set over, not in, simmering water, whisk together the sugar and kalamansi juice. Do not let the water come to a boil. Whisk until the sugar completely dissolves, about 3 minutes. Take the bowl off the heat and keep the pot of water at a steady simmer.

3. In a separate, heatproof bowl, whisk the egg yolks. Whisking constantly, slowly pour a small amount of the hot lime juice mixture into the yolks, gradually adding more juice until all of it has been incorporated.

4. Using a rubber spatula, scrape the tempered egg-lime mixture back into the metal bowl, and set the bowl over the simmering water. Add the butter and whisk constantly until thickened, about 10 minutes. (The mixture should read 130° F.) Take the bowl off the heat.

5. Strain the curd through a fine-mesh strainer into a bowl. Let cool slightly, then place a piece of plastic wrap directly onto the surface of the filling, and refrigerate until ready to use. The curd can be made up to 1 day in advance.

6. To bake the crust, preheat the oven to 350° F. Remove the plastic wrap from the tart shell and prick the bottom of the pastry all over with a fork. Line the tart shell with enough parchment paper to cover the bottom and come up the sides. Fill the bottom of the pan with pie weights or dried beans so the dough doesn't puff during baking.

7. Transfer the tart shell to the oven and bake until set and lightly browned around the edges, about 15 minutes, removing the parchment paper and weights about 3 minutes before the pastry is finished baking to ensure that the pastry is evenly browned. Transfer the shell to a wire rack to cool completely. Increase the oven temperature to 400° F.

8. Make the meringue: In the clean bowl of an electric mixer fitted with the whisk attachment, beat the egg whites on medium speed until foamy. Add the cream of tartar and beat until soft peaks form. Gradually add the superfine sugar and beat on high speed until glossy and stiff, but not dry, peaks are formed.

9. To assemble the pie, spread the kalamansi curd evenly over the bottom of the cooked pie shell. Cover with the meringue, smoothing it with a rubber spatula and making sure the meringue touches the edges of the tart shell. Transfer the tart to a baking sheet and bake until the meringue is golden brown on top, 10 minutes. Transfer to a wire rack to cool. Refrigerate for 20 minutes to allow the curd to set before serving.

BANANA CRÊPES

This is a dessert that we can never take off the menu. A few years ago we removed it and received many messages from customers threatening never to return unless we put it back, so it now holds permanent residence. The crêpes contain pandan extract, which is available in Asian markets. It makes the batter aromatic and gives it a light green color. At the restaurant, we serve the warm crêpes with a scoop of banana-rum ice cream on the side, but any compatible ice cream flavor will do.

SERVES 8

Crêpes:

½   cup all-purpose flour

¼   cup rice flour

½   teaspoon sugar

Pinch of salt

¼   cup coconut milk

2   large eggs

2   tiny drops pandan extract

Melted unsalted butter, for brushing the pan

Sauce:

2   cups coconut milk

½   cup packed brown sugar

1   vanilla bean, split

4-6 ripe but firm bananas

Vanilla or other flavor ice cream, for serving

1. For the crêpe batter, whisk together the flours, sugar, and salt. In a separate bowl, whisk the coconut milk, eggs, and pandan extract with 1 cup of water. Add the dry ingredients to the wet, whisking until smooth, and adding more water if necessary to make a fairly thin batter. Cover and refrigerate for at least 30 minutes, or overnight.

2. While the batter is resting, make the sauce: In a medium saucepan over medium heat, whisk together the coconut milk, brown sugar, and vanilla bean. Bring to a simmer, stirring occasionally, until slightly thickened but still pourable, about 25 minutes. Keep warm over low heat while you make the crêpes, or reheat just before serving.

3. Heat an 8-inch nonstick skillet over medium-low heat until hot. Whisk the crêpe batter and add a little water to the batter if needed to make it pourable. Pour about 3 tablespoons batter into the pan and tilt to coat the bottom. Cook until the crêpe is just set and the edges are starting to curl, about 1 minute. Flip the crêpe with a spatula and cook until just cooked through, about 20 seconds more. Transfer the crêpe to a plate. Make crêpes with the remaining batter, stacking them on the plate as you go.

4. Just before serving, reheat the sauce. Thinly slice the bananas and add them to the sauce. Cook over medium heat for 2 to 3 minutes, to soften the bananas a little and warm them through.

5. To serve, place one crêpe on each serving plate. Spread a generous amount of the bananas and sauce over the lower half of each crêpe and fold over. Serve with a scoop of ice cream on the side.

UBE ICE CREAM

The ube, or purple yam, is uniquely Filipino. It is technically a yam and not to be confused with taro or any purple potato or tuber. We use the purple yam ice cream as a topping for our halo-halo.

MAKES ABOUT 1 QUART

Haleyang Ube or Purple Yam Jam:

½ cup heavy cream
½ cup whole milk
1 cup coconut milk
¾ cup sugar
½ cup purple yam flour
½ pound (2 cups) frozen grated purple yam, defrosted

Ice Cream Base:

1½ cups heavy cream
1½ cups whole milk
¾ cup sugar

1. For the purple yam pastry cream, in a medium saucepan over medium heat, whisk together the cream, milk, coconut milk, and sugar. Bring to a simmer. Whisk in the purple yam flour, then the grated purple yam. Lower the heat and cook, stirring with awooden spoon, until the mixture holds together and starts to pull away from the pan, about 5-8 minutes. Set aside.

2. For the ice cream base, in a clean medium saucepan over medium heat, whisk together the cream, milk, and sugar. Simmer for 1-2 minutes. Whisk in the purple yam jam until fully blended. Place the mixture in a blender and blend until smooth, then transfer to a clean bowl and refrigerate until cold, at least 3 hours.

3. Blend the chilled custard again and strain through a fine-mesh strainer. Freeze in an electric ice cream maker following the manufacturer's instructions. Transfer to an airtight container and freeze until firm.

Ube [purple yam].
Bottom: mangoes.

MANGO ICE CREAM

Mangoes always make Filipinos homesick because nothing can take the place of Philippine mangoes. When sweet mangoes reach the markets in New York City, we make our popular mango tart and serve this ice cream with it.

MAKES ABOUT 1 QUART

2 medium-sized ripe mangoes, peeled and pitted
2 cups heavy cream
1 cup whole milk
⅔ cup sugar
4 egg yolks

1. Place 1 mango in a blender or bowl of a food processor and puree until smooth. Finely chop the remaining mango. Transfer the puree and the diced mango to separate bowls (you should have about ⅓ cup of each).

2. Have ready a fine-mesh strainer set over a bowl by the stove. In a medium saucepan over medium-low heat, combine the cream, milk, and ⅓ cup of the sugar. Bring the mixture to a simmer. Whisk the remaining ⅓ cup sugar with the egg yolks in a large, heatproof bowl until light and lemon-colored.

3. Whisking constantly, slowly pour abouta quarter of the hot cream mixture into the eggs to temper. Continuing to whisk, slowly pour in the remaining cream mixture, then transfer the custard back to the saucepan and place over low heat. Cook, stirring constantly, over low heat, until the custard is thick enough to coat the back of a spoon, about 10 minutes. Do not let it boil or the custard will curdle. Strain and let cool, stirring occasionally. Cover and refrigerate until cold, at least 3 hours.

4. Whisk the mango puree into the chilled custard and freeze in an electric ice cream maker following the manufacturers' instructions. Fold in the chopped mangoes, transfer to an airtight container and freeze until firm.

JACKFRUIT ICE CREAM

Romy discovered how to make this when we held a dinner at the restaurant featuring Maya Kaimal's Keralan cuisine. We use it in our parfait dessert along with avocado ice cream, watermelon ice, and fresh fruits, which our dear friend Cris Tabora insists on calling "frozen halo-halo."

MAKES ABOUT 1 QUART

1½ cups whole milk
1 cup heavy cream
¾ cup sugar
4 egg yolks
20-ounce can jackfruit in syrup, drained
½ cup diced drained jackfruit in syrup

1. Have ready a fine-mesh strainer set over a bowl by the stove. In a medium saucepan over medium low heat, combine the milk, cream, and 6 tablespoons of the sugar. Bring the mixture to a simmer, then whisk the remaining 6 tablespoons sugar with the egg yolks in a large, heat-proof bowl until light and lemon-colored.

2. Whisking constantly, slowly pour about a quarter of the hot cream mixture into the eggs to temper. Continuing to whisk, slowly pour in the remaining cream mixture, then transfer the custard back to the saucepan and place over low heat.

3. Cook, stirring constantly, until the custard is thick enough to coat the back of a spoon, about 10 minutes. Do not let it boil or the custard will curdle. Strain and let cool, stirring occasionally. Cover and refrigerate until cold, at least 3 hours.

4. Place the 2 cups jackfruit in a blender and puree until smooth. Stir into the custard mixture. Freeze in an electric ice cream maker following the manufacturers' instructions, adding the diced jackfruit halfway through churning. Transfer to an airtight container and freeze until firm.

AVOCADO ICE CREAM

Filipinos have been eating homemade avocado ice cream forever. At home we would scoop out and mash the avocado in a bowl with sugar and evaporated milk, then drop in a few ice cubes, and that would be our chilled dessert.

MAKES ABOUT 1 QUART

1½ cups whole milk
1 cup heavy cream
¾ cup sugar
4 egg yolks
1 ripe Hass avocado

1. Have ready a fine-mesh strainer set over a bowl by the stove. In a medium saucepan over medium low heat, combine the milk, cream, and 6 tablespoons of the sugar. Bring the mixture to a simmer, then whisk the remaining 6 tablespoons sugar with the egg yolks in a large, heat-proof bowl until light and lemon-colored.

2. Whisking constantly, slowly pour about a quarter of the hot cream mixture into the eggs to temper. Continuing to whisk, slowly pour in the remaining cream mixture, then transfer the custard back to the saucepan and place over low heat.

3. Cook, stirring constantly, until the custard is thick enough to coat the back of a spoon, about 10 minutes. Do not let it boil or the custard will curdle. Strain and let cool, stirring occasionally. Cover and refrigerate until cold, at least 3 hours.

4. Halve the avocado and remove the pit. Use a small spoon to scoop out the flesh and discard the peel. Combine the avocado with half of the custard in a blender and blend until smooth. Stir the avocado mixture into the remaining half of the custard and freeze in an electric ice cream maker following the manufacturers' instructions. Transfer to an airtight container and freeze until firm.

Overleaf, clockwise from top left corner: puso [cooked rice in heart-shaped woven leaves], Philippine rice terraces, farmers planting rice, vintage postcard of fishing boat, Batanes Beach, fishermen off Batangas coast, Mercer Street in SoHo, Flora de Filipinas by Fr. Manuel Blanco: coconut tree, kalamansi lime, patola [squash], patani [lima beans], Ambrose Chiu, kesong puti [cheese made from carabao milk] and pan de sel, piaya, Little Quiapo [restaurant serving comfort foods], Aristocrat restaurant, Philippine native hut (archival), televised cooking demonstration (archival).

Where Do We Go from Here?

When Romy and I opened Cendrillon eleven years ago, we not only wanted to produce good Filipino food—we wanted to show how good it could be. The first years at the restaurant were spent applying the concepts and philosophies of the new American cuisine movement to Filipino traditional dishes. This was the philosophy of freshness, using local and organic produce. But it brought us forward only so much, and at some point we realized that we could no longer do what we wanted to do unless we went back to search for our roots, our history and our past.

Some of the recipes in this book look difficult to make at first glance, which is why I set them aside when they were first given to us. But as we were finalizing the book's recipe list, we took a second look and were exhilarated when we were able to reproduce them. We tested Marc Medina's bringhe (page 126), and it came out just the way it looked in the photo Neal took that day in Arayat. It was a moment of great triumph and pleasure. The best part of the dish was the tutong [crust] that formed at the bottom, and we fought over it just like we did when we were kids. When we told Marc that the bringhe was successful, he was so excited that he sent us some more recipes to be tested here in the United States. He was eager to see how the recipes that his family had been cooking for several generations would travel the geographical and cultural divide.

Working on this book has certainly pushed us forward in a way that we never expected. We never realized how difficult and complicated some of the Philippine dishes could be. So many were labor intensive—like the lumpia recipes that require prepping a dozen ingredients, including shrimp juice, achuete water, and garnishes like fried garlic and chopped scallions. I can make bibingka and suman, but I gave up on puto, which came out like a brick every time we tried to experiment with it. But I know that one day we will come up with a good puto. We just have to keep trying while keeping alive the memory of the best puto I ever ate, in Digos, a town outside Davao, Mindanao.

That's what memories are for. *Kumain na tayo!* [Come, let's eat!]

Afterword

BARBARA KIRSHENBLATT-GIMBLETT

If the Philippines is an archipelago, Cendrillon is one of its outlying islands. Enter the doors and the generous hospitality for which Filipinos are justly famed will envelop you. My favorite spot is a booth facing the open kitchen at full sizzle. With its interior of exposed brick and bamboo lanterns and its burble of conviviality, Cendrillon is an outpost of the Philippines and an oasis of calm in bustling SoHo. We have come here to remember the great Filipino food scholar Doreen Fernandez, after she passed away, to launch a new cookbook, to showcase Asian chefs and poets, and to raise funds to preserve heritage foods in the Philippines. This is where we come to celebrate or just to feel at home, no matter where we are from.

Home is a central theme of *Memories of Philippine Kitchens* and it is home cooking that this book celebrates. Home is somewhere in particular, and the Philippines is very particular about place. A country that loves food and loves to talk about food understands itself as a culinary landscape. *Memories of Philippine Kitchens* offers the reader an edible map: you know where you are by how the place tastes and it tastes best on the spot, whether on a boat with the fresh catch eaten raw with seasoned vinegar or lime or near a coconut grove to take advantage of the distinctive qualities of the coconut at each precise stage of its development.

Home is the Filipino memory palace par excellence and home cooking is a perfect medium for capturing and retrieving memories of home because nothing else so firmly sediments experience in the body. In paying homage to a vanishing generation of home cooks, *Memories of Philippine Kitchens* celebrates culinary skills that are based on sense memory, on feel, taste, and texture, and remembers those who cook this way with a sensory fullness that only food can offer: Grandmother giving Amy an egg with a soft shell, the quest for the kurakding mushroom in a local market, the intricate preparation of pork belly in the kitchen, the conviviality of a shared meal around a big table.

This cooking has depth not only of flavor, but also of meaning, for the entire history of the Philippines is remembered in its food: its indigenous roots (kinilaw), colonial relations with Spain through Mexico (tomatoes, olives, saffron) and later the United States (evaporated milk, chiffon cake), migration histories linking it to other parts of Southeast Asia (Malaysia, Indonesia, China), which brought noodles, and to other parts of the world, as well as to wars and occupations, exile and emigration.

Nowhere is this history more fully displayed than during the six-week Christmas season. Brought to the Philippines by Spain, along with Catholicism, Christmas is the most elaborated culinary occasion in the Philippine calendar and a time for family reunions: Amy remembers five families with more than thirty cousins on her paternal side gathering for Christmas. While the dinner after midnight mass on Christmas Eve features glazed ham and turkey or chicken stuffed with chorizos and olives, the legacy of an elite Spanish presence, crackers, biscuits, and candies made by local Chinese manufacturers are included in gift baskets, street vendors outside the church sell steamed rice cakes, bibingka, and hot salabat, and local bakeries make sweets out of cassava, pandan, and ube.

All cuisines evolve through a symbiotic relationship with other culinary traditions. How they do so makes them what they are. In the case of the Philippines, there is a long history of indigenizing the culinary resources at hand, whether that means adding purple yam flour to white bread dough for Ube Pan de Sal or keeping the components separate so that specialties from an elite Spanish repertoire are reserved for the most festive occasions, or whether that means, as it does at Cendrillon, creatively reinterpreting the tradition by roasting whole pompano on a layer of coffee beans and spices.

What distinguishes Filipino cuisine is the uncanny ability to experience the fusion, while maintaining an awareness of the sources. The culinary language is one reminder: panciteria, which refers to a noodle eatery, is a Hispanized version (-eria) of a Filipino word (pancit) for a Chinese dish (noodles). Culinary culture—the ingredients, names of dishes, methods of preparation, distinctive palate (the varieties of sour and bitter), and ways of eating together —carries deep within itself the memory of where the food came from and how it got that way, which makes Filipino food a powerful metaphor for those who create and eat it, indeed, for the Philippines itself.

Barbara Kirshenblatt-Gimblett is University Professor and Professor of Performance Studies at New York University, where she served on the academic advisory committee for the Department of Nutrition and Food Studies. She writes on the history of Jewish food and serves on the editorial board of Gastronomica. *Her books include* Destination Culture: Tourism, Museums, and Heritage *and* Painted Memories: A Jewish Childhood in Poland Before the Holocaust, *in collaboration with her father.*

Glossary

Achara: pickled vegetables or fruits in brine or with vinegar

Achuete: annatto seeds; used as red food coloring

Adobo: a dish of meat, seafood, or vegetable cooked in vinegar garlic, salt, or soy sauce

Alamang: tiny shrimp for salting and making bagoong

Alimango: freshwater crab

Alimasag: saltwater crab, blue crab

Almondiga (Span.)**:** meatball

Alokon: vegetable belonging to the sitao (longbean) family

Alugbati: Malabar spinach

Amorgozo; amorgoso: variety of ampalaya

Ampalaya: Momordica cylindrical, bitter melon; amargoso

Anahaw: a type of palm with beautiful leaves that are used for decoration

Aratiles: a small cherry-like fruit

Arnibal: caramel

Baboy: pork

Bae-bae: glutinous rice, coconut milk, and grated coconut, cooked in banana leaves

Bagnet (Ilocano)**:** deep-fried pork belly with crispy skin

Bagoong: fermented shrimp or fish paste. Central Luzon provinces use tiny shrimp frye called alamang, while the Ilocanos of northern Luzon use fish called monamon. In the Visayas, fermented shrimp or fish paste is called guinamos

Balut: boiled fertilized duck egg

Bangus: milkfish

Barako coffee: only coffee bean indigenous to the Philippines

Barangay: the smallest political unit in the Philippines

Batuan: a small sour green fruit used for souring tinola (Visayan sinigang)

Bicho-bicho: a rice flour-based dough that is fried and glazed in syrup

Bihon: Philippine rice noodle

Biko: a type of bibingka where whole-grain glutinous rice is cooked first with coconut before baking with a topping

Binoro; binuro (Ilonggo)**:** fish salted in layers; buro (kapampan-gan) is teh process of fermenting shrimp, fish, or pork in cooked rice and salt

Birdseye chiles: some sources describe these as Capsicum frutescens, which would make it equivalent to the siling labuyo, the hottest pepper in the Philippines

Biscocho: dried bread, which is usually ground up to use as breadcrumbs

Buchi: boiled sweet potato mashed with milk and sugar, then fried

Budbud; bodbod (Cebuano)**:** glutinous rice cooked with coconut milk and wrapped in banana leaf; budbud kabog, another Cebuano specialty, is made with millet

Bukayo: a sweet made from mature coconut

Buko: young coconut prized for its juice and tender meat; used for making pies and salads

But-ong: triangle-shaped suman, similar to Ibos

Butong-butong: coconut milk slowly cooked to a candy consistency

Camote: sweet potato

Canela: Mexican cinnamon

Capiz: windowpane oyster

Carinderia/Karinderia: small restaurant serving pre-cooked food, usually found in markets or along roadsides

Chicharron: crispy deep-fried pork rind; crackling

Cuchinta: same as kutsinta

Dahon ng sili: chile leaves

Dayap: type of lime similar to the green limes of the U.S.

Dorade: sea bream

Duhat: Java plum

Dungon: prehistoric fruit used for kinilaw

Gabi: taro root

Galangal: member of the ginger family

Galapong: rice soaked overnight and then ground to the consis-tency of cornmeal

Gata: coconut milk extracted from grated mature coconut; the first extraction has the consistency of heavy cream and is called kakang gata

Guinamos: Visayan fermented shrimp or fish paste

Halabos: steamed shrimps or prawns

Hibe: small shrimps, peeled and dried

Hipon: regular-size shrimp

Ibus: suman wrapped in a tube of coconut leaves

Inday-inday: balls of glutinous rice, rolled in sugar, coconut, and toasted sesame seeds

Itik: native duck of the Philippines

Jackfruit: langka, nangka

Kadyos/Kadios: pigeon pea

Kakanin: snacks, light cakes, usually made of rice

Kalabasa: pumpkin

Kalabaw (mangang): variety of mango that is unusually sweet and not as fibrous as those grown in Mexico

Kalamansi: Philippine lime

Kalamay: cake made from malagkit rice and coconut milk

Kamias: a small sour fruit akin to starfruit used as a souring agent for sinigang and kinilaw

Kangkong: swamp cabbage, water spinach

Katuray/Katuday: West Indian pea, flower or blossom of the Hummingbird or Corkwood tree used in pinakbet (vegetable stews) and salads in the Ilocos retion

Kinchay: Chinese celery

Kropec: Deep-fried, shrimp-flavored flour crackers

Kurakding: a wild mushroom that grows on rotting barks of trees found at the foot of volcanoes and mountains

Kutchay: chives

Kutsinta: a little cake made of a steamed mixture of sugar, rice, and lye

Labanos: radish

Labong: edible tender shoot of bamboo

Langka; nangka: jackfruit; fruit generally eaten raw; ripe fruit made into sweets and can-dies. Starchy seeds may be roasted or boiled.

Lasona: small purple onions

Latik; latek: by-product of coconut milk or meat after extracting oil

Latundan; saging: sweet variety of banana

Libas or batuan leaf: a leaf only available in the Visayas

Liempo: pork belly

Ligia; lihia: lye, an alkaline substance used in cooking to improve texture and color

Linubak: same as linusak, which is a Bicol dessert using pounded boiled saba, young coconut, buko, and brown sugar

Longaniza: Filipino chorizo or pork sausage

Lugao; lugaw: rice porridge or gruel

Lukadon: term for a coconut in the middle stage between the young (buko) and mature

Lumpia: generic term for vegetable, meat, or fish filling in a wrapper; can be either deep fried (spring rolls) or not (fresh lumpia or lumpia sariwa)

Luya: ginger

Macopa: Curaçao apple tree cultivated for its fleshy, juicy, pear-shaped edible fruit

Malagkit: a rice variety that is glutinous or sticky

Malunggay: horseradish tree whose flowers, leaves, and young pods are eaten as vegetables

Mami: a dish of noodles, chicken or beef, and broth

Mangga: mango

Marautong: the young fruit of the malunggay (horseradish) tree

Merienda: Filipino tradition of mid-morning or mid-afternoon meal

Miki: noodles made of wheat and eggs

Milagrosa: an aromatic and semi-sticky variety of rice

Mirin: sweet Japanese rice wine

Misua; miswa; misoa: very fine and tender Chinese noodles resembling vermicelli and made from non-alkaline wheat dough

Muscovado sugar: brown or unrefined sugar from sugar-cane; the term comes from the Spanish *mas acabado*, meanitn "more refined."

Nangka (Cebuano): see Langka

Nata; nata de coco: a sweet made by growing a culture on coconut water

Nipa; Nipa fruticans; sasa: source of tuba, a native beverage

Pagui: stingray

Pako: edible fern

Palabok: sauce made from shrimp juice, achuete water, and cornstarch; used for pancit luglug or pancit malabon

Palay: unhusked rice grains

Palayok: round-bottomed clay pot

Paminta: black peppercorns, pamienta

Pancit; pansit: general term for any dish of noodles and shrimp, fish, meat, or vegetables

Pandan: screw pine leaf; widely used for flavoring native desserts, juices, and tap water

Panocha: dark, solid cake made from sugarcane juice and molded in a half coconut shell

Papaya: when green, made into pickles or cooked as a vegetable

Pasotes: epazote leaves; found in the Ilocos region

Patane; patani: lima beans

Pating: shark

Patis: liquid that rises to the top when fish are layered in salt and fermented in earthen jars to make bagoong. In Cebu, the word patis actually means soy sauce; fish sauce is referred to by its most famous brand, Rufina

Pechay; petsay: bok choy, pak choy

Piaya: flaky dough with muscovado sugar as filling

Pili nut: a hard nut endemic to the Bicol region of the Philippines

Pinangat: taro purses filled with alamang, ulang, and shredded taro leaves cooked in coconut milk (Bicol); fish cooked in vinegar, ginger, and salt (Tagalog)

Pirurutong: purple rice that is now almost extinct in the Philippines; basic ingredient of the puto bumbong; closest variety is called tapol in the Visayas

Pitik-pitik: slipper lobster

Pla-pla: Nile Tilapia

Puso ng saging: banana blossom; banana heart

Puto: steamed rice cake

Puto Manapla: a soft, spongy cake from the town of Manapla, steamed in banana leaves

Puto taktak: a steamed cake made of pure cassava

Rosangis: pinhead-size clams

Saba; saging na: a cooking variety of banana similar to plantains

Sahog: pre-cooked and cut-up meat, chicken, or shrimps used to flavor noodle dishes

Saluyot: Jews' mallow, a native leaf

Sangkaka: from the Spanish chancaca, brown cake of molasses

Sili: general term for all chiles. In the Philippines, there are generally two types of chiles: siling labuyo (tiny, slim and fiery peppers akin to the Thai birds-eye chiles used for spiking vinegar dips and condiments) and siling haba (a long pepper that is used to flavor dinuguan and coconut-based dishes)

Siling haba: Louisiana long pepper, used in pickles and for seasoning

Siling labuyo: cayenne or chile

Siniguelas: Spanish plum

Sitao; sitaw: longbeans

Sotanghon: mung bean noodles

Spider: Chinese strainer used for fishing ingredients from boiling water or hot oil

Suahe or suaje: small shrimp

Sukang Paombong: vinegar from the sap of the nipa palm from Paombong, a town in the province of Bulacan; one of the most common native vinegars in the Philippines today.

Sugpo: prawns

Suman: a grain or root cake (rice is the most common ingredient) wrapped in banana or coconut leaves and boiled

Suman sa latek: boiled rice cake with coconut caramel sauce

Tabagwang: river snails

Tabon-tabon: fruit whose juice is used for kinilaw

Taclobo: giant clam

Taho: Chinese soybean custard in caramel sauce

Takway: a native leaf of Iloilo (Visayas)

Talangka: crablets that are fermented and their fat extracted

Tamban: a variety of fish of the sardine family

Tambo: bamboo shoot (Visayan)

Tanglad: lemongrass

Tanigue: Spanish mackerel

Tapayan: earthen water jar

Tapuy: Igorot rice wine

Taro: a starchy tuber

Taure: fermented soybean paste

Tausi; tawsi: Chinese soybeans preserved in dehydrated salt sauce

Tikoy: comes from the Chinese term for sticky cake, made with glutinous rice flour

Tinapa: Smoked fish

Tocino: cured pork

Toyo: soy sauce

Tugabang: a native leaf of Iloilo (Visayas)

Tuyo: salted and air-dried fish

Ubad: Pith of saba banana plant

Ube; ubi: purple yam, used for jams, ice cream, and sweets

Ubod: heart, core, or pith of the coconut tree; in the U.S., the closest equivalent is the heart of palm, the pith of the sabal Palmetto

Ulang: fresh water shrimp or prawn characterized by a much larger head, similar to that of craw- or crayfish

Wansoy: coriander leaf; cilantro

Yemas: egg yolk–based candy

Further Reading

Books

Achaya, K. T.
Indian Food: A Historical Companion.
Oxford India Paperbacks, 1998.

Agdan, Nieves. *Farm Cooking ni Manang Nieves.* Institute of Women's Studies, St. Scholastica's College.
Manila: Raintree Publishing, 2001

Aklat ng Pagluluto. Edited and compiled by Rosendo Ignacio. J. Martinez, Intramuros, 1919.

Alegre, Edilberto N. *Inumang Pinoy.*
Manila: Anvil Publishing, 1992.

Alford, Jeffrey, and Naomi Duguid.
Flatbreads and Flavors: A Baker's Atlas.
New York: William Morrow, 1995.

Duguid, Naomi & Jeffrey Alford.
Home Baking. New York: Artisan, 2003.

Duguid, Naomi & Jeffrey Alford.
Hot Sour Salty Sweet: A Culinary Journey Through Southeast Asia.
New York: Artisan, 2000.

Anderson, E.N. *The Food of China.*
New Haven and London:
Yale University Press, 1988.

Besa, Solita F. Camara. *Up Close with Me: Memoirs of Solita F. Camara-Besa, M.D.*
Quezon City, Philippines: The University of the Philippines Press, 2004.

Barretto, Glenda Rosales. *Flavors of the Philippines: A Culinary Guide to the Best of the Islands.* Manila: Via Mare Catering Services, 1997.

Cebu: More Than An Island. Edited by Resil B. Mojares and Susan F. Quimpo. Manila: Cebuano Studies Center, University of San Carlos, and Ayala Foundation, 1997.

Centro Escolar University.
Filipino Cuisine. Manila: Centro Escolar University Publishing, 1998.

Clark, Samuel and Samantha.
Moro: The Cookbook.
London: Ebury Press, 2001.

Clayton, Bernard.
Complete Book of Small Breads.
New York: Simon & Schuster, 1998.

Cordero-Fernando, Gilda. *Philippine Food and Life.* Manila: Anvil Publishing, 1992.

Corn, Charles. *The Scents of Eden: A History of the Spice Trade.* New York: Kodansha America, 1997

David-Perez, Enriqueta. *Recipes of the Philippines.* Manila: Zone Printing, 1973.

Davidson, Alan.
The Oxford Companion to Food.
New York: Oxford University Press, 1999.

Daza, Nora. *Let's Cook with Nora.*
Asia Book Corporation of America: 1975.

De Jesus, Pascuala. *Rice: Its Nutritive Values and Culinary Uses with 101 Tested Recipes.* Quezon City, Philippines: Carla Publications, 1960

Fenix, Michaela. *Philippine Cuisine: A Country's Heritage.* Monterey Farms Corporation, 1995.

Fernandez, Doreen G. Tikim:
Essays on Philippine Food and Culture.
Manila: Anvil Publishing, 1994.

Fernandez, Doreen G.
Fruits of the Philippines. Makati City, Philippines: Bookmark, 1997.

Fernandez, Doreen G.
Palayok: Philippine Food Through Time on Site, in the Pot. Makati City, Philippines: Bookmark, 2000.

Fernandez, Doreen G. "Food and War," from *Vestiges of War: The Philippine-American War and the Aftermath of an Imperial Dream, 1899-1999.* Edited by Angel Shaw and Luis H. Francia. Asian/Pacific/American Studies Program and Institute. New York: New York University Press, 2002.

Fernandez, Doreen G., and Edilberto N. Alegre. *Kinilaw: A Philippine Cuisine of Freshness.* Makati City, Philippines: Bookmark, 1991

Fernandez, Doreen G., and Edilberto N. Alegre. *Sarap: Essays on Philippine Food.* Manila: Mr. & Ms. Publishing, 1988.

Gerona, Danilo Madrid.
Naga: The Birth and Rebirth of a City.
Naga, Philippines: City of Naga, 2003.

Gonzalez, Gene R. Cocina Sulipena:
Culinary Gems from Old Pampanga.
Makati City, Philippines: Bookmark, 1993.

Gitlitz, David M., and Linda Kay Davidson.
A Drizzle of Honey: The Lives and Recipes of Spain's Secret Jews.
New York: St. Martin's Press, 1999.

Hahn, Emily, and the Editors of Time-Life Books. *The Cooking of China.* Foods of the World Series. New York: Time Inc., 1968.

Henson, Mariano A. *The Tastes and Ways of a Pampango.* N.p., 1960.

Joaquin, Nick, *Manila, My Manila,*
Bookmark, Inc., 1999.

Kasaysayan: The Story of the Filipino People. Vol. 2. Asia Publishing Company, 1998.

Kasaysayan: Life in the Colony. Vol. 4. Asia Publishing Company, 1998.

Kennedy, Diana.
My Mexico: A Culinary Odyssey.
New York: Clarkson Potter, 1998.

Laudan, Rachel. *The Food of Paradise: Exploring Hawaii's Culinary Heritage.* Honolulu: University of Hawaii Press, 1996.

Malgieri, Nick. *Nick Malgieri's Perfect Pastry.* New York: MacMillan, 1989

Manila Chronicle Recipe Book. Vol. 3. Manila: The Manila Chronicle, 1960.

Mintz, Sidney W. *Tasting Food, Tasting Freedom: Excursions into Eating, Culture and the Past.* Boston: Beacon Press, 1996.

Mong, Lee Siow. *Spectrum of Chinese Culture.* Malaysia: Pelanduk Publications, 1995.

Musni, Lord Francis D. *Saniculas: A Rich Pampango Cultural Heritage.* Thesis, Pontifical and Royal University of Santo Tomas, Manila, 2003.

National Centennial Commission and Adarna Book Services. *100 Events That Shaped the Philippines.* Manila: National Centennial Commission, 1999.

One Hundred Plus One Banana Recipes. Banana Export Industry Foundation. Quezon City, Philippines: New Day Publishers, 1976 and 2001.

Our Favorite Recipes. Produced and sold for the benefit of the British War Relief Association of the Philippines; all recipes were contributed by residents of the Philippines in Cebu and throughout the islands. Cebu, Philippines: October 4, 1941.

Quintana, Patricia. *A Taste of Mexico.* New York: Stewart, Tabori & Chang, 1993.

Ramos, Celia S., and Carmen S. Reyes.
Gayuma, The Prevailing Charm of Filipino Cookery.
Manila: Rex Bookstore, 1981.

Roden, Claudia. *The Book of Jewish Food: An Odyssey from Samarkand to New York.* New York: Knopf, 1996.

Rogers, Ruth, and Rose Gray. *Rogers Gray Italian Country Cook Book: The River Café*. New York: Random House, 1995.

Rootcrops, Your Cookmate. Project of the Development Academy of the Philippines, Quezon City, Philippines: New Day Publishers, 1981.

Sokolov, Raymond. W*hy We Eat What We Eat: How the Encounter Between the New World and the Old Changed the Way Everyone on the Planet Eats*. New York: Summit, 1991.

Treasures of Pila. Brochure prepared by the Pila Historical Society Foundation.

Trutter, Marion. *Culinaria Spain*. Cologne: Könemann, 1998.

Wright, Clifford. *A Mediterranean Feast*. New York: William Morrow, 1999.

Ybanez-Noval, Gertrudes. *The Harvest Cook Book*. Gertrudes Enterprises, 1977.

Magazines

The Sunday Tribune Magazine, August 16, 1936.

Internet Sources

On the Katuday (katuray), Eleanor Nakama-Mitsunaga, StarBulletin.com, Oct 23, 2002.

Bibingka:
Egullet.com

Spekkoek (Lapis Legit)
www.iias.nl/iiasn/iiasn4/ascul/tropen.txt
www.indochef.com/page39.html

Suman
www.philrice.gov.ph/prorice/food/suman.htm

Palitao
www.recipegoldmine.com/worldphil/phil25.html

Spanish Influence
http://en.wikipedia.org/wiki/Andalusia

www.milligazette.com/Archives/15102001/04.htm. Habeeb Salloum, "Muslim Influence in Spain Still Felt in Daily Life Until Today," The Milli Gazette (Indian Muslim newspaper).

Sources

Adriana's Caravan
Toll-free: 1-800 316-0820
www.AdrianasCaravan.com
Spices, food, and tableware from around the world.

Earthy Delights, Inc.
1161 E. Clark Road, Suite 260
DeWitt, Michigan 48820
Toll-free: 1 800 367-4709
www.earthy.com
High-quality specialty food supplier.

Ethnic Grocer
1090 Industrial Drive, Suite 5
Bensenville, Illinois 60106
630 860-1733
www.ethnicgrocer.com
A premier online provider of authentic ethnic products.

Kalustyans
123 Lexington Avenue
New York, New York 10016
212 685-3451
www.kalustyans.com
This specialty food store carries a wide array of spices and specialty food products from around the world.

Melissa's/World Variety
Produce, Inc.
P.O. Box 21127
Los Angeles, California 90021
Toll free: 800 588-0151
www.melissas.com
The largest distributor of specialty produce in the U.S.

Pacific Rim Gourmet
7825 Highlands Village Place, Suite 446
San Diego, California 92129
www.pacificrim-gourmet.com
Online purveyor of ingredients, food, and cooking equipment

Index

Acknowledgments

Food would never have tasted so good were it not for my grandmother's cooking. Food would not be so exciting to talk about were it not for Doreen Fernandez who gave Filipinos of my generation the intellectual foundation and the vocabulary to articulate our culture of food. And it was Stephen Jay Gould, along with his wife, Rhonda Roland Shearer, who first encouraged us to put all of these words and thoughts about our food into a cookbook.

We thank Marisa Bulzone and Stewart, Tabori and Chang for giving us the opportunity to collect, document and share stories and recipes of our generation. We thank Cristina Tabora who connected us to Marisa and whose steadfast confidence in us to do this book was our light at the end of the tunnel.

How does one thank friends who stopped at nothing to make sure the book was the best it could be? Our photographer, Neal Oshima, traveled everywhere with me in good and bad health and functioned as my inner eye and conscience. Our art director Pauline Galiana's light hand put the soul of beauty on Neal's images and our words.

Cendrillon would not be what it is today if it were not for our angels: Peter Kaminsky, Ray Sokolov and Barbara Kirshenblatt-Gimblett whose words had to be an integral part of this book. Thank you for your friendship and the laughter we shared through the years. And thank you to Grace Young who held my hand from day one and whose generous spirit continues to be an inspiration to us.

Thank you to all our dearest friends who generously gave their time to promote a cuisine they love: Reggie Aguinaldo, Stephen Young, Lilia Villanueva, Craig Scharlin and Perry Mamaril. My deepest thanks go to Mike Garrido and Bing Escaño-Garrido who shared her grandmother's collection of recipes with me.

We thank our production team who shepherded this book through a grueling schedule: Production Coordinator John W. Glenn and designer Wendy Palitz.

Special thanks to Leda Scheintaub, our wonderful recipe tester who eventually took over the editing of the manuscript of this book. Thank you to Crispina Reyes, my Philippine-based researcher, for giving me a valuable collection of research material on Philippine food. And thank you, Vicky Garchitorena of the Ayala Foundation, for referring Crispina to me. My love to my special niece, Maya Besa-Roxas (also Doreen Fernandez's niece), who gave the manuscript a careful scrutiny before giving it her blessing.

PHILIPPINES

Manila: I want to thank my mother, Dr. Solita Camara-Besa; my brothers, Vicente, Emmanuel and Tristan; my uncle, Dr. Augusto Camara and my aunt, Isabel Camara-Garcia whose memories of my grandmother, Nanay, augmented and enriched my own.

We thank Clara Lapus, children Joyce and Mark, brother Ramon Reyes and sister Chichi Reyes Tulao of the Aristocrat and Mama Sita family for taking such good care of me and being "my other family" every time I go home to the Philippines to do food research.

We thank this hardcore group of food lovers who live and breathe Filipino food on a daily basis: Lyn Besa-Gamboa, Glenda Rosales-Barretto, Larry Cruz, Claude and Mary Ann Tayag, Marc Medina and Becky Villegas. Thanks to Rosa Laurel-Liamson and her mother, Teresa "Tiks" Laurel of Mama Rosa restaurant for sharing their homemade sauces and exotic vinegars with me. Thanks to the beautiful Mrs. Virginia Gonzales whose memories were fading but lent me boxes of recipes she had developed for her television shows. Thank you to Lourdes "Nani" Labrador of Castillejos Farms, for always being there for me.

There were new friendships formed based on shared memories and good company: Carla M. Pacis, Cora Relova, Marichi Francisco, Lestie Fronteras and brother Emil Puruganan, Lourdes "Bopeep" Ladrido, Peque Gallaga, Fernando "Fern" Aracama, Margarita Fores, Uro del Rosario, Jose "Peng" Olaguera and Butch Perez. They provided many strands of personal, cultural and historical substance that were woven into the stories of this book.

It was a pleasure to establish a connection with Mara Pardo de Tavera, another passionate soul whose legacy lies with the Pardo de Tavera recipes now kept in the archives of the Ateneo de Manila University. I want to thank Stella Chiu-Freund who provided me with archival shots of her father, Ambrose Chiu, bringing back wonderful memories of Manila's panciterias of my youth. I am grateful for all the help given to me by Teresita Ang-See, Trustee of the Kaisa Heritage Center in my research on the Chinese aspect of our food and culture. Thank you to Ellen Palanca of Ateneo de Manila University and Clinton Palanca for historical materials on Chinese Filipinos in the Philippines. Many thanks to Clinton's father, Alfred Palanca, who gave us an insider's tour of Binondo, Aranque market and all the special nooks and crannies of Manila's Chinatown.

LUZON REGION: Ilocos Norte

Laoag: Thanks to Annette Ablan and uncle, Manuel "Nonong" Ablan. Annette not only arranged for her family cook to preprare classic Ilocano dishes for us, but she also drove us to the northernmost tip of the Luzon mainland to see the beautiful beaches of Pagudpud.

Dingras: Thanks to Emil Puruganan and Lestie Fronteras bringing us to Dingras.

Ilocos Sur, Vigan: Thanks to Carla Pacis and cousin, Eddie Quirino, who gave us access to one of the most historic and beautifully preserved mansions of Vigan, the Syquia Mansion. Many thanks to Rusty Ponce, resident cook of the Syquia Mansion, for spending several days with us going to the markets and cooking traditional Ilocano food. We want to thank Jose "Bonito" Singson who brought in his longtime cook, Digna Claudio Mercado, to cook his favorite comfort foods of Vigan. And to Ramon Zarragoza thank you for bringing us to remote barrios of Vigan to see how sukang Iloko (sugarcane vinegar) and the burnay (earthen jars) are made.

Bulacan, Barrio Maronquillo: My special thanks to Hector Fernandez and his relatives who live in this warm and friendly community for giving us a magical day filled with all kinds of kakanin delights.

Pampanga, Sta. Rita: Rosario "Mamang" Guanzon is the grandmother of my nieces, Tricia and Krissy Guanzon Besa. Mamang arranged for a whole day of feasting in the elegant garden of her daughter-in-law Tess Guanzon. I have been a grateful recipient of the Guanzon hospitality for several decades now whenever my former sister-in-law, Linda Guanzon, would give me a gift of duman (fragrant young milagrosa rice grains) from the family reserve. Our gratitude goes to Ramon Ocampo for allowing us to watch and photograph how the Lansang Delicacies bakery make their trademark turrones de casuy and sans rival.

Angeles: Our personal thanks to Claude and Mary Ann Tayag for inviting us to stay in their magnificent house. We will always be grateful to Mary Ann's family cook, Juana Tuazon Miranda, who showed us how to make tamales, bringhe and tibok-tibok. Many thanks to Robby Tantingco, Director of the Center of Kapampangan Studies, Holy Angel University in Angeles, for sharing his insights on Pampango food and providing me with scans of old postcards depicting food and life from another era.

Arayat: We owe Marc Medina, his family and the cooks at Arayat a debt of gratitude for preserving a way of life that is fast disappearing.

Tarlac, Tarlac City: I want to thank my cousins, Betty Ann Besa-Quirino and her sister, Isabel Besa-Morales for making my short visit to my father's hometown an enjoyable one. Isabel set us up with their beloved Auntie Tacing (Anastacia Pineda) whose cooking Betty Ann lovingly remembers as "to die for." We also visited the Tarlac Market where we met up with Beth Buan who showed us how to make tocino (sugar-salt cured pork).

Tiaong, Quezon: To Augusto "Ugo" Bigyan, one of the most talented potters and artists of the Philippines, thank you for your delicious food and telling me all about burnt coconut cream.

Laguna, Pila: Cora Relova brought back special memories of a treasured time of our lives – the 50s and the 60s. Her mother, Loreto Del Mundo-Relova gave us a rare glimpse of the history of the national heritage town of Pila, Laguna. We appreciate Joe Lat's delicious specialties including his leche flan with homemade macapuno.

Bicol, Naga: We thank Gerry Benares and his wife Monica who contacted her mother, Marichi Francisco, who arranged and coordinated our entire Bicol trip. We thank Mayor Jesse M. Robredo for hosting our stay in Naga. We thank Mr, Joe Perez, head of the Visitors Office who took care of our accommodations at the newly renovated Regent.

Many thanks to Lilibeth U. Guysayko, President of the Isarog Garden Cooperative and Chairperson of the Developmental Institute for Bicolano Artists (DIBA) for arranging all of the cooking demonstrations at Clara Verdadero's restaurant, Aling Conching, and at the beautiful Isarog Garden. We thank Tita Aringo who showed us how to make pinangat; City Information Officer Carlos "Itos" Briones who made Bicol Express, and Anita Badong who made caramelized pili nuts.

Thank you to Wong Yee and daughter, Jasmine Wong, owners of New China Restaurant, the oldest Chinese restaurant in Naga, for sharing your interesting personal history with us.

Thank you to Bicol experts: historian Danny Gerona, Honesto General, author of The Coconut Cookery of Bicol; and to Mariano "Obi" Obias who sent me several essays about the food of Naga and his youth.

Polangui: We thank Marc Rakotomalala, Owi Ruivivar and her parents, Rene and Ninya Ruivivar for telling us about this fabled place of Polangui where Ninya's relatives are preserving Chinese food and culture. We thank our Polangui hosts: Tita Ong Samson, her daughter Dina and her fragile aunt, Mama Auyan for their generous help in our search for the kurakding (wild mushroom) and showing me how to cook their Chinese dishes.

Sorsogon City: We thank Pilar Yrastorza Leocadio from the Office of the Mayor and Office of the Governor of Sorsogon; Irma Guhit, local broadcaster; Sonia Lariosa; and Jing Hayag, who owns the most popular gathering place in the Sorsogon City market. We thank Mrs. Petrona Haw in the neighboring town of Juban whose kitchen she graciously allowed us to photograph

Irosin: We thank our family from Irosin who gave us our miracle picnic at Masacrot Springs: Dr. Eddie Dorotan, his wife.Oyen and Danny Dorotan. We give special thanks to the Barangay Captains who cooked classic Irosin dishes and gave us new food memories to cherish. We thank and salute Kap. Miguel Aguilar and wife, Elsa; Haile Artile and Galopa; Kap. Maya Erlano; Kap. Gaspar Espergongate; Kap. Appa Esperanzate; Kap. Alberto Esplano; Kap. Neal Futalan; Mr. Kiko Galicio; Kap. Gaspar Haspela; Kap. Felipo Martinez; Kap. Simplicio Rodriguez; Kap. Wenceslao Santos and Junrick.

Catanduanes: We thank Teddy Arcilla and his cooking retinue, Nelia Bagadiong and Fe Caspe for cooking dishes that many Filipinos still need to discover. Special thanks to Popsie, Luisa and Chef J Gamboa of Milky Way (my favorite childhood restaurant now in Makati), for providing kitchen space for the cooking demonstration.

VISAYAS REGION

Cebu, Cebu City: Our deepest thanks to the family of Nieves "Bing" Escaño-Garrido: Tina Escaño-Unchuan and her son and daughter-in-law, Jovie and Maite for cooking favorite family dishes. We thank Bing's aunt, Rosebud Sala who hosted an elegant merienda for us in her beautiful home. We are grateful to Richie Unchuan, our Master Lechonero, who made his special lechon for us in his Mactan home. Thank you to Raul Arambulo, photographer and raconteur, who took us to the local eateries of Cebu.

Negros Occidental, Bacolod/Silay: Thanks to my cousin, Lyn Besa-Gamboa, Maget Gaston Locsin, Adelma Salado, Remedios Sugon for cooking classic

Bacolod dishes and delicacies for us. We are deeply grateful to our Master Lechonero and Kinilaw Master, Vicente "Enting? Lobaton for our lessons in kinilaw and lechon.

We enjoyed our conversations with linguist and cultural historian, Dr. Cecile Locsin-Nava, historian Roque Hofilefa and Lolita Jardeleza who even sang childhood ditties for us. We were lucky to meet up with Charlie Co and his wife, Ann Legazpi, whose aunts, the three Legazpi sisters, allowed us to photograph their famous piaya. Ann also introduced us to Emma Lacson and her daughter, Nora "Baby" Lacson who gave us a tour of their kitchen where we watched how the famous Silay empanadas and lumpia ubod were made.

Thanks to Lilia Villanueva, her sister, Anabel Villanueva-Salacata and Elena Esparagoza for identifying the kalan-unon in my photographs.

Iloilo, Iloilo City: Lourdes "Bopeep" Ledesma-Ladrido introduced me to the food world of Iloilo. We enjoyed our conversations with historian Melanie Padilla of the University of the Philippines (Visayas); Gerardo "Junjie" Yusay; Cheling Montelibano; restaurateurs Robert Montelibano and Esther Maria Dulce "Doll" Jarancilla; Chef Joey Piamonte of Villa Sagrado; Georgina Gaona and Heather Larraga Maloto of Panaderia de Molo; Cecilia Gison-Villanueva of Sinamay House; Corona Villanueva-de Leon, Mama's Kitchen. From them, we learned much about Iloilo, its history, its families and its food.

Filipino Families in the U.S.

I would like to thank Mona and Carlos Lu and Yaya (Lourdes Ebon) for sharing their recipe of Tata Sing's Bam-i. My special thanks to Marivic and Andy Madrid and family whose initial conversations about the food of their childhood started us on our journey collecting food memories from other friends. Thanks to Mila Manalac and her mother, Clara Grajo-Villanueva, for spending a whole afternoon talking about Bicol delicacies. We met Heny Sison, who runs a cooking school in Manila, at our restaurant. She generously sent me materials about

Bataan and the food that her mother cooks. And thanks to Danny Maclan for his memories of Pancit Malabon. And to our wonderful friend, Jessica Hagedorn, thank you for sharing with me your mother's old cookbooks which proved to be a good source of recipe material for the book.

Photo Shoot credits:

We thank the following owners of galleries, antique and design shops for lending us valuable pieces as props for our photoshoot:

Lilia Villanueva and Craig Scharlin, Tama Gallery: antique tribal wooden boxes and food containers, woven mats and native fabrics

Stephen Hurrell, Notus Gallery: late nineteenth century Brazilian country kitchen table, Imbuia wood, which we used as a mahjong table

Penine Hart, Penine G. Hart: antique cups, saucers, plates and glassware

Federico De Vera, De Vera: antique spoons, metal buckets, wooden bowls and glassware

Jessica Hagedorn: family heirloom Chinese plates

Perry Mamaril: production and design of food shots

Sardi Klein: photographic lighting equipment

Kathy Morano: make-up

Rurungan sa Tubod Foundation (Women Empowered Through Right Livelihood), Palawan, Philippines: piña fabrics (delicate native fabrics woven from pineapple leaves)

Pauline Galiana: design and arrangement of props.

Linda Johnson: prop styling

Published in 2006 by Stewart, Tabori & Chang
An imprint of Harry N. Abrams, Inc.

The authors would like to express their gratitude to the many individual families
who lent personal photographs for use in this book.

Library of Congress Cataloging-in-Publication Data
Besa, Amy.
  Memories of Philippine kitchens : stories and recipes from far and
near / Amy Besa and Romy Dorotan ; photographs by Neal Oshima.
     p. cm.
  Includes index.
  ISBN-13: 978-1-58479-451-6
  ISBN-10: 1-58479-451-8
  1. Cookery, Philippine. 2. Philippines—Social life and customs. I.
Dorotan, Romy. II. Title.

TX724.5.P5B45 2006
641.5'9599—dc22   2006021532

Editor: Marisa Bulzone
Art Director: Pauline Galiana
Designer: Wendy Palitz
Production Manager: Jane Searle

The text of this book was composed in Interstate and ITC Officina Serif

Printed and bound in Thailand
10 9 8 7 6 5 4 3

HNA
harry n. abrams, inc.
a subsidiary of La Martinière Groupe

115 West 18th Street
New York, NY 10011
www.hnabooks.com